REVELATION

REVELATION

A Commentary for Bible Students

RICHARD K. ECKLEY

WESLEYAN BIBLE COMMENTARY SERIES

GENERAL PUBLISHER
Donald D. Cady

EXECUTIVE EDITOR
David W. Holdren, D.D., S.T.D.

EDITORIAL ADVISORY COMMITTEE

Joseph D. Allison, M.Div.
Publishing Manager
Warner Press

Ray E. Barnwell
District Superintendent, Illinois
The Wesleyan Church

Barry L. Callen, M.Div., M.Th., D.Rel.
University Professor of Christian Studies
Anderson University

Ray Easley, M.Div., Ed.D.
Vice President of Academic Affairs
Wesley Biblical Seminary

Dorothy Hitzka
National Consultant for Christian
Education
The Salvation Army

Arthur Kelly
Coordinator of Christian Education
and Congregational Life
Church of God Ministries

Stephen J. Lennox, Ph.D.
Dean of The Chapel and Professor
of Bible
Indiana Wesleyan University

Bonnie J. Perry
Director
Beacon Hill Press of Kansas City

Dan Tipton, D.Min.
General Superintendent
Churches of Christ in Christian Union

John Van Valin
Free Methodist Pastor
Indianapolis, Indiana

EDITORS
Lawrence W. Wilson, M.Div.
Managing Editor

Stephen J. Lennox, Ph.D.
Theological Editor

Darlene Teague, M.Div.
Senior Editor

For my mentor and friend
Dr. Robert W. Lyon (1929–2004)
who desired the world to come
more than this present one.

CONTENTS

EXECUTIVE EDITOR'S PREFACE

Life change. That, we believe, is the goal of God's written revelation. God has given His written Word so that we might know Him and become like Him—holy, as He is holy.

Life change is also the goal of this book, a volume in the Wesleyan Bible Commentary Series. This series has been created with the primary aim of promoting life change in believers by applying God's authoritative truth in relevant, practical ways. This commentary will impact Bible students with fresh insight into God's unchanging Word. Read it with your Bible in hand.

A second purpose of this series is to assist laypersons and pastors in their teaching ministries. Anyone called to assist others in Christian growth and service will appreciate the practical nature of these commentaries. Writers were selected based on their ability to soundly interpret God's Word and apply that unchanging truth in fresh, practical ways. Each biblical book is explained paragraph by paragraph, giving the reader both the big picture and sufficient detail to understand the meaning of significant words and phrases. Their results of scholarly research are presented in enough detail to clarify, for example, the meaning of important Greek or Hebrew words, but not in such a way that readers are overwhelmed. This series will be an invaluable tool for preaching, lesson preparation, and personal or group Bible study.

The third aim of this series is to present a Wesleyan-Arminian interpretation of Scripture in a clear and compelling fashion. Toward that end, the series has been developed with the cooperative effort of scholars, pastors, and church leaders in the Wesleyan, Nazarene, Free Methodist, Salvation Army, Church of God (Anderson), Churches of Christ in Christian Union, Brethren in Christ, and United Methodist denominations. These volumes present reliable interpretation of biblical texts in the tradition of John Wesley, Adam Clarke, and other renowned interpreters.

Throughout the production of this series, authors and editors have approached each Bible passage with this question in mind: How will my life change when I fully understand and apply this scripture?

Let that question be foremost in your mind also, as God speaks again through His Word.

DAVID W. HOLDREN

AUTHOR'S PREFACE

I remember, as a child, a well-known evangelist coming to our small country Pilgrim Holiness church with his charts illustrating the dispensations as specific time periods in which God interacted in certain ways with His creation. For ten long nights he preached through each of the brilliantly-painted panels as we cowered at the Four Horsemen galloping through history, searched our souls to learn if we would condemn ourselves by taking the mark of the beast, and wondered in fear if we would have to endure the Tribulation that was to come.

Those images still haunt me, even after many years of scholarly study of the roots and sources of my spiritual heritage. I am a product of my tradition's clumsy dance with the two partners of a discouraging dispensationalism and a world-affirming Wesleyan view of future events.

For this reason and more, I have found writing a commentary on the book of Revelation to be a very difficult task. Countless well-meaning people have handed me books and pamphlets, all seeking to sway me to a particular view of millennialism or Christ's future thousand-year reign. I had to first deal with the critical questions surrounding the nature of apocalyptic literature such as the prophets and the apostle John.

The basic outline of the book raises chronological and literary issues unlike any in the biblical canon and immediately categorizes the method taken up in the book. All the while I have sought to remain faithful to a Wesleyan reading of the text. Yet, such a reading has not yet taken doctrinal form and could never represent the diverse views of future events within the Wesleyan-Holiness life, past or present. And, of course, there was always in the backdrop of my writing, the explicit textual curse not to "add" or "take away" anything from the prophecy (Rev. 22:18–19).

I was fortunate to have at my disposal many newly published commentaries, technical in differing degrees, but representing a scholarly interest come of age in the book of Revelation. Commentaries by Beale, Mounce (revised), Mulholland, and Reddish are noted examples. I have also been influenced by the many theological expositions, particularly Jacques Ellul and William Stringfellow's classic use of Revelation as a backdrop for a social witness to the gospel. These writers refused to allow the Apocalypse to devolve into simply interesting discussions over "myths and endless genealogies" (1 Tim. 1:4).

I would like to think that my method has sought to blend the two modes of biblical study reflected by these groups of secondary literature: careful investigation of the original meaning of a text in its historical and literary contexts as well as creative theological reflection. It will be the reader who will decide how successful I have been in that goal.

As I did most of the actual writing while on sabbatical in England, I am indebted to Houghton College for the use of an extended period of time and a lovely London flat. I felt the prayer support of the Wesleyan Church of Orchard Park. My wife, Lynn, and my two sons, Benjamin and James, always kept me real even while living with visions. Finally, I must thank my parents, Ed and Beverly Eckley, who first taught me to look for the coming Lord. "Amen, Come, Lord Jesus!"

RICHARD K. ECKLEY

INTRODUCTION TO REVELATION

The book of Revelation, the last book of the Bible, is a fitting closure to God's total message to the world. Yet this fanciful vision's rightful place as an authority for the contemporary Church has either been disregarded because of a perceived strangeness and potential for harm or treated with obsession and fanaticism.

A woeful lack of sound biblical preaching on the social/political—even historical—matters of the faith has been replaced. On one hand, we find worship experiences giving seeking people an anesthesia to their struggles with modern society with no respect for history. On the other hand, we have pious, moral teachings that only address quaint issues of days gone by.

Both approaches have had the same result: Christians are given no large-scale understanding of their place and role in the meaning and end of history. The book of Revelation, like no other canonical text, offers the Christian a cosmic perspective on the implications of the death and resurrection of Jesus Christ.

Most twentieth century interpretations of the book of Revelation have exhibited a deterministic understanding of world history. God is directing all of time and space to a clockwork ending. The Christian is left with no real input into the flow and direction of the powerful river of history. People appear to be swept along by forces unknown to them and outside their control. Christians, as with most of their secular neighbors, have grown cynical of any hope for the human component of political, economic, and even ecclesial reform. This theory of interpretation looks surprisingly like a "conspiracy theory"—even if a divine conspiracy. They have come to believe that someone "out there" is behind all of the isolated events seen on the news each evening.

Many people today enjoy piecing together these many insignificant happenings into a cohesive whole. The assassination of John F. Kennedy, the suicide of Marilyn Monroe, the Bushes belonging to a secret fraternal order of World Trade Organization, and the explosion of a space shuttle are all somehow related to one another. By discovering an undercurrent narrative for and in all things, the seemingly nonsensical events of world history can have meaning.

At the same time, many people are flocking to religious experiences (not just Christian experiences) that lend credence to a hostile view of the world. Worshipers are often encouraged to forget about all the cares of their jobs and families, and enjoy the presence of exhilaration and transcendence. The experiences of alienation and meaninglessness are replaced with a euphoric escape into heavenly, spiritual realms. These people often are encouraged to think of themselves as "aliens," "pilgrims," and "lost children." Life makes sense only when they find a new place to exist, a place far away from the constraints and difficulties of this life.

At the prompting of an early morning telephone call, a pastor made a visit on a woman parishioner. She had been reading the book of Revelation and, with the help of her television Bible commentators, had discovered a "new teaching" which had given her incredible insight into the Christian life. "I'm sure," she said, "you will want to share this with our congregation. It will revolutionize the spiritual life of our church!" The morning droned on, as the woman went from verse to verse, highlighting the Christian's elevation from the cares and concerns of this world in favor of a more heavenly plane of existence. Piles of food-caked dishes were visible in the kitchen; dirty-diapered toddlers called out to their mother for comfort. By the time lunch rolled around, the hungry children could contain themselves no longer and burst into tears. The woman apologized to the pastor and disciplined her children. "Can't you see the pastor and I are talking about things that really matter?"

"No," the pastor responded, "there is nothing more important at this moment than the gifts of these children."

The Gnostic tendency to escape into a world that makes sense—and to reject the material world of flesh and blood—is still very much a part of modern living and the Christian Church.

Surprisingly, an alternative picture of history is just as pervasive. Rather than seeing life as a hostile prison that holds them from true freedom, some people seek to discover the progressive benefits of life through their intelligence and wit. They tend to view history as imminently rational. Everything is figured out through elaborate doctrines, technology, and schemes for living. Marxists expressed a view of history like this as a struggle for the control and distribution of material things. Capitalists, highlighting the worth of the individual, did little better by turning society into a consumer machine, using measurable indicators like the gross national profit to define progress.

Often, though, Christians have developed similar ideologies, sometimes quasi-political, sometimes theological, attempting to control and manipulate the world culture as well. In general, violence and war are outgrowths of making such a close identification of God's plan for the world with human destiny. This eclipsed reading of the book of Revelation has contributed to various malformed views of the world. These distortions can be perilously zealous, as the world saw in the rise of the fascist ideology of Nazi Germany in the middle of the twentieth century.

Whether people seek to escape the world as it is or if they engage in utopian ideologies, these forms of apocalyptic musings must be checked with a proper philosophy of history. The tension that all people must have as they live between mortality and immortality, between this age and the age to come, and between the immanent and the transcendent, are easier to reconcile by falling to one side of the pole or the other. The book of Revelation sees these worlds as converging in the person of Jesus Christ.

Traditional introductory matters associated with studying a biblical text are somewhat extraneous when it comes to the Apocalypse. The book's authorship, dating, audience, and themes are overshadowed by the literature itself. Nonetheless, these items are necessary for helping the reader understand the historic context in which the revelation occurred and the application that it has for our own contemporary setting. Such horizons of meaning are intersected by the drama that unfolds, helping to merge the picture of God's plan for history into our own.

AUTHORSHIP

The book of Revelation begins with the very limited self-identification of the author as **John** (1:1, also 1:4, 9; 22:8). Even though this was a very common name during the era of the primitive Church, this John has often been assumed to be the same author connected with a Gospel and three Epistles found in the New Testament. The audience seems to be well aware of who John is because the seer does not feel compelled to enhance his identity beyond **your brother and companion** (1:9). This is a strong argument against any theory suggesting pseudonymity, that is, that a second-generation writer attempted to use the apostle John's name and reputation to push through his or her own work. Most who sought to gain authority in this way would have gone to great lengths to describe themselves as the apostle they wished to mimic. This author (reminiscent of the "Beloved Disciple" of the gospel of John) takes a near anonymous role in the writing project, viewing himself to be a **servant** (1:1) to the message itself and seeking only to write of the things he **heard and saw** (22:8).

Some have tried to show that the author of this revelation has some of the same theological categories found elsewhere in the Johannine books already mentioned. Along with these inductive evidences, we would note that many early Church leaders gave apostolic identity to this "John." The first to refer to the book is Justin Martyr (a historian who lived in Ephesus during the first part of the second century), who speaks of it as the work of "a certain man, whose name was John, one of the apostles of Christ" (*Dial.* 81.15). Irenaeus of Gaul (A.D. 180), one of the most respected early theologians of the second century and also writing from this very region of Asia, believed this to be the same John associated with the historical Jesus. Since Irenaeus was a student of Polycarp—a disciple of the Apostle John—scholars give gravity to his opinion.[1]

Conversely, some have noted how many words that were so common in the gospel of John and the epistles of John, are not even mentioned in this apocalypse. (An example would be the word "believe," mentioned almost one hundred times in the Gospel and not once in this book.) Foreshadowing modern literary criticism, Dionysius, bishop of

Alexandria (died A.D. 165), noted that the writing style of the gospel of John was obviously very different from that of Revelation. However, this difference in style could be explained by the differing purposes for writing, the time lapse between them, and the differences between the Gospel and apocalyptic genres. In actuality, there are many similarities of ideas and themes, if not vocabulary, between the varieties of writings associated with this apostolic name, John.

The general scholarly consensus on the question of authorship is that the John in question may be someone unknown to us today. This is usually based on the literary character, the ideas and concepts expressed by the author, and the time frame for the writing of the book. Nonetheless, with the general acceptance by the earliest Church authorities that this was the disciple and apostle of Jesus Christ, there is really no reason not to assign the authority of this writing to that John. Despite citing strong internal evidence arguing against a common author for the gospel of John and the Apocalypse, Mounce reminds us that if we recall the same "Sons of Thunder," John (and James) of the synoptic Gospels, who "wanted to call down fire from heaven upon a Samaritan village (Luke 9:54), it does not appear out of character for this same John to be the one who in the Apocalypse describes the plagues that are about to fall upon the enemies of God in the final days."[2]

The long history of the Church's struggle to accept the book of Revelation into the canon probably is more significant a question than the identification of the writer John. Part of the reason that Dionysius cast doubt on the apostolic authorship of the book of Revelation was to stop it from being used by religious fanatics to stir up any one of the myriads of third century chiliastic movements. (The term "chiliasm"—from the Greek word for "thousand"—came to define all those who understood the second coming of Christ to require an anti-worldly outlook and lifestyle.) The Eastern Orthodox Church eventually excluded the book from its canon, even if, liturgically, the apocalyptic worldview provides the backdrop for all of Eastern Christianity. At the time of the Reformation, both Luther and Calvin either figuratively or literally pushed the book to the appendices of their *Sola Scriptura*.

The reasons for these omissions and neglects sometimes were due to doubts over a Johannine or even apostolic origin, but mostly they were pastoral in nature. Because so many sectarian groups used the book to stir up the biblically inept to perverse and heretical practices, many in the Christian Church felt it better left alone. Many pastors today would have the same concerns, particularly as they see Sunday school and Bible study classes swell at the announcement of this topic.

DATE OF WRITING

The attempt to set the date of this work is mostly done through the inductive evidences found in the book that deal with the self-descriptions by the author, the time of persecution, and the social-political history being described by the prophecy itself.

JOHN'S LIFESPAN

It has often been assumed that the apostle John lived longer than any of the other disciples. If this author is thought to be this same John, the date would have to coincide with his lifespan.

WHAT PERSECUTION?

Persecution is the immediate atmosphere of this prophecy. The martyrs in heaven and the suffering on earth are established in a common bond of worship before the throne of God. Identifying the correct period of persecution and the historic context for the details of the Apocalypse would aid in setting the parameters for the date when it was written. Various scholars have attempted to argue for persecutions during the reigns of Nero, Trajan, or Domitian. Following the lead of a number of early patristic supporters, a date at the end of Domitian career is often suggested. Domitian reigned A.D. 81–96 and was placed alongside the life of John by Irenaeus, Eusebius, and many other early witnesses. There is great evidence, supported by Irenaeus (180), Clement of Alexandria (200), Origen (254), and Eusebius (325), that John wrote this message to the churches of Asia somewhere near the end of Domitian's reign, about A.D. 95.

Eusebius, in summing up the tradition of the Church on this subject, assigns John's exile to Patmos, and consequently the composition of the

Apocalypse, to the latter part of the reign of Domitian (A.D. 81–96). Irenaeus (circa A.D. 180) says of the book, "For it [the vision] was seen, not a long time ago, but almost in our own generation, at the end of the reign of Domitian."[3] Clement of Alexandria (who speaks of "the tyrant"), Origen, and later writers confirm this testimony. Epiphanius (fourth century), indeed, puts the exile to Patmos in the reign of Claudius (A.D. 41–54)[4]; but as in the same sentence he speaks of the apostle as ninety years of age, it is plain there is a strange blunder in the name of the emperor. The former date of A.D. 95 answers to the conditions the book describes, that is, time for a decay in the morale of the churches; widespread and severe persecution; and Domitian's preference for this mode of banishment.[5]

PLACE AND AUDIENCE OF WRITING

PLACE

The author is writing from the Isle of Patmos, presumably exiled there because of persecution. The Isle of Patmos, one of several islands off the coast of Asia Minor is located approximately twelve miles from Ephesus. Eusebius, we will recall, recorded that John was banished to this island during the reign of Domitian[6]. John gives the reason for his writing as **because of the Word of God and the testimony of Jesus** (1:9). The interpretation of this phrase is alluded to by both Eusebius and John himself, but it is unclear as to whether John is on the island in order that he might hear the Word of God, and subsequently give witness to it, or if he is there as a punishment for his own preaching of that Word. The latter makes sense if one identifies the period of time of the writing as a time of persecution, even for the author.

ASIA MINOR

The first chapters of the book of Revelation provide the setting and address for John's writing. The book was meant to travel through the trade routes defined in an area of Asia Minor by the seven regional cities and their resident churches. The enumeration is made by **a loud voice**

like a trumpet, which said: "Write on a scroll what you see and send it to the seven churches: to Ephesus, Smyrna, Pergamum, Thyatira, Sardis, Philadelphia and Laodicea" (1:10–11).

IMPERIAL WORSHIP AND GRECO-ROMAN POLITICS

The drama that unfolds in the book of Revelation has the backdrop of the matters of conscience associated with the early Christian confrontation with emperor worship in the Roman Empire. How one understands the level to which this confrontation arose will impact the meaning of the prophecy to some degree. To be sure, the monotheistic religion of the Jews was unable to be reconciled with the religious and political demands of most of the nations that conquered them. The level of homage and loyalty expected by these despotic rulers was a theological impossibility if one were to give exclusive worship to the Lord God of Israel.

At the time of the Roman occupation this demand for imperial worship was not always in such an overt form as in the past, but it is obvious that Jews—and Christians—understood their allegiance to God to be in conflict with the prevailing social expectations. Perhaps modern Christians can identify more closely to this subtle allegiance than to being forced to bow down to idols and dictators as depicted in the Babylonian captivity of Israel.

The first Jewish apocalyptic literature arose out of Israel's captivity by the Greeks around 135 B.C. The book of Daniel, depicting Israel as she faced the consuming powers of Babylon, became an important catechism for the young children of Israel. Stories of powerful rulers seeking worship and allegiance, burning furnaces, and lions' dens are all concluded with the heroes left unconsumed and untainted. This literature helped them withstand the powerful cultural shaping forces that were upon them.

Hellenism was a great temptation to the youth of Israel. Unlike the Babylonian captivity with its coercive use of violent authority to bring Israel into submission, the Greeks won their conquered over willingly, convincing them that they offered them a better way of life than they had experienced before their national defeat. Many in Israel believed this.

They enjoyed the cultural centers, gymnasiums, and philosophical literature of their captors. Israel's children wanted to be Greek, and, as any parent knows, holding them to the old values of their traditional religion and society was very difficult.

Many contemporary scholars have focused their interest again on the Apocalypse because of its setting in the clash between religion and society, between Christ and Satan. "Imperialism" has taken new forms, but it continues to have the same thirst for power and death. The modern reader needs to hear the same message given to the first century hearers of the book of Revelation. It is a shame that our preachers have been sidetracked by the curious elements of the vision while missing the prophetic message that it contains for any who would seek to replace God's worship with the worship of power. John's vision promises all the churches of Asia Minor, and therefore all the Church, rewards for those who "conquer," a word well-attested in the Roman Empire. Now the victorious Christians must not practice idolatry by worshiping imperial power exposed, through the visions, for its impotence and eventual demise.

PURPOSE OF THE REVELATION

John is writing to encourage the faithful Christians to stand firm against the various forms of emperor worship in his day, and all that represents even for our contemporary setting. He couches this concern in a theology of history, believing that a final cosmic battle between God and Satan is imminent. The calm depicted in the throne room of God belies the fact that God is not worried about the final outcome. The victorious Christ through resurrection from the dead has more than personal consequences; it has consequences for the whole cosmos. The persecution that is being experienced undoubtedly

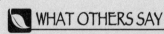

WHAT OTHERS SAY

The Bible deals with the sanctification of the actual history of nations and of human beings in this world as it is while that history is being lived.

—William Stringfellow

will get worse rather than better, but the Church must persevere and become "overcomers" to receive the ultimate reward promised them.

Through the revelation they are encouraged by a peek into the heavens to see that God has already sealed their fate and will protect them from any lasting harm. This temporal encouragement promises a new world where the enemies of Christ's followers are punished, and the people of God are given their rightful place in a world of blessedness and joy.

OUTLINE OF THE BOOK OF REVELATION

As with any commentary, the question of how to structure the exposition of the literature must be addressed at the start. Some are tempted to order their chapters along the lines of the chapter headings of the English Bible. This releases those authors from the difficult task of structuring the prophecy along its inner meaning. There have been many suggestions as to what outline best suits the writer's logic and approach to the book as a whole.[7] Again, it will not be surprising that one's presuppositions about the nature of the prophecy will shape the outcome of that outline. Sometimes it is difficult to discern if Bible students are attempting to "squeeze" their own ideas into an outline that fits the pre-conceived design.

Few today adhere to a theory of multiple authorship or sources that would make the outline of the book indiscernible and incoherent. The tightness of the images and the consistent design of ideas and theological content tie the book together as a unified piece. But, at this point, no consensus for describing that unity has immerged. Generally, commentators will use an outline that derives from an emphasis on the book's form, content, or dramatic action.

FORM

Many commentators, in treating the book as any cohesive literary work, would believe that the author had a structural logic at work from the start. Using the instruction of Christ to John in verse 1:19 to "Write . . . what you have seen, what is now and what will take place later," the structure follows this chronological line of development. The outline usually looks something like:

A. What you have seen (chapter 1)
B. What is now (chapters 2–3)
C. What will take place later (chapters 4–22)[8]

This approach takes for granted that when John records visionary material there is an order by which that vision unfolds and that the sights and sounds of the drama can be placed in a chronological structure like beads on a string. Rather than looking upon an unfolding cinema, this model sees the chapters of the book as determinative to the interpretation. It also makes the bulk of the book (4–22) a futuristic text, revealing what will take place "later."

Another popular approach that seeks to discover the "form" of the book is by unearthing complex literary structures used by Jewish/Christian writers in other biblical books. The chiasm (a literary parallelism that follows the outline of A B C D C' B' A' looking like the Greek letter chi, X) is frequently utilized for this purpose. Elizabeth Fiorenza is a representative of this model. One of her suggestions looks like this:

A. Prologue and Epistolary Greeting (1:1–8)
  B. The Prophetic Messages to the Churches (1:9–3:22)
    C. Christ: The Eschatological Liberator and Regent (4:1–9:21)
      D. The Prophetic Community and Its Oppressors (10:1–15:4)
    C'. The Trial and Sentencing of Babylon/Rome (15:5–19:10)
  B'. Eschatological Judgment and Salvation (19:11–22:9)
A'. Epilogue and Epistolary Frame (22:10–21)[9]

Using chiastic structures to unlock the meaning of the book of Revelation is attractive to those commentators who wish to sidestep issues of chronology, but see a coherent and unified logic to the form of the book. One major theme (or a select few) is highlighted by this structure, arguing that John's vision tends to see a singular vision with many spiraling portrayals of the same thing surrounding it.

CONTENT

Some scholars see the actual ideas and content of the book shaping its structure and outline. This approach usually emphasizes the series of sevens that are so obviously a part of the writer's arsenal of symbols and concepts. Sometimes commentators have structured the material according to groupings of sevens not explicitly mentioned but stand behind the visions themselves. An example of this order would look something like:

   I. The Prologue (1:1–8)

  II. The Prophetic Call (1:9–20)

 III. The Letters to the Seven Churches (2:1–3:22)

 IV. The Visions (4:1–22:5)

     A. The Heavenly Court: The Glory of God and the Lamb (4:1–5:14)

     B. The Seven Seals: Judgment on Sin (6:1–8:1)

     C. The Seven Trumpets: God Calls to Repentance (8:2–11:14)

     D. The Seven Visions of Conflict: The Establishment of God's Kingdom (11:15–13:18)

        1. The woman with child: the birth of Jesus (12:1–2)

        2. The great red dragon: the enemy of peace (12:3–6)

        3. The war in heaven: the Cross (12:7–12)

        4. The dragon, the woman, and her children: the struggle of God's people (12:13–17)

        5. The seven-headed beast from the sea: the power of Rome (13:1–4)

        6. The war against the saints: persecutions (13:5–10)

        7. The beast and his mark: corruption of the emperor and the dragon's agents (13:11–18)

     E. The Seven Visions of Mt. Zion: Assurance to God's people (14:1–20)

     F. The Seven Bowls of the Wrath of God: Security amid Turmoil (15:1–16:21)

     G. The Seven Visions of the Fall of Babylon: End of the Evil Empire (17:1–19:10)

H. The Seven Visions of Recompense: Celebration of Victory (19:11–21:5a)

I. The Holy City: Kingdom of God in a New Heaven and New Earth (21:5b–22:5)

V. The Epilogue (22:6–21)[10]

As in the chiastic model, this approach usually does not accept a chronological flow of the material though it is possible to do so. The content repeats itself by way of a series of symbols and images. This technique often includes a method known as "recapitulation," the repeating of the same theme over and over under different headings.

LITERARY DRAMA

This relatively new approach to the book, often drawing upon modern literary critical tools, seeks to utilize the internal, existential features of the literature's story and drama. Those who would use this mode for outlining the book would seek to follow the action itself as the vision unfolds for John and the reader (or hearer), the vicarious participant. Understanding the apocalyptic genre is very important to this model, as the commentator believes rational insights in the book are secondary to the more non-cognitive and experiential styles of knowing.

The outline that we will use in this commentary is rather pragmatic in nature, but it does attempt to take into account the obvious repetition of the sevens used in the development of this drama.

A. Prologue and Vision of Christ (1:1–20)

B. The Letters to the Seven Churches (2:1–3:22)

C. John's Vision of God and the Lamb (4:1–5:14)

D. Opening the Seven Seals (6:1–8:5)

E. Sounding the Seven Trumpets (8:6–11:19)

F. The Conflict (12:1–15:5)

G. Pouring Out the Seven Bowls of Judgment (15:6–16:21)

H. Final Judgment of Babylon and the Beast (17:1–19:21)

I. The Millennial Reign of Christ (20:1–15)

As an introductory commentary on the book of Revelation, the hope is to use the apocalypse as a catalyst for engaging the world and understanding how a theology of the "last times" aids in an overall understanding of the Christian life at *present*. It is high time that eschatology be removed from the last chapter in systematic theology texts, and in biblical studies, as a novel interest to a few cranky exegetes. Revelation provides us with a prism into the world of God, and allows this world to break into our own. The lens should not distort our worldview, making it difficult to maneuver through our mundane affairs, but rather finally give meaning and insight into the malformed world that we experience. As a discipline, eschatology is coming of age, and one "Wesleyan-friendly" thinker, Jüergen Moltmann, has given us tools for taking back this area for the Christian. For Moltmann, eschatology is not about something apocalyptic—the end or "The Last Things" or "The End of All Things"—but rather about new beginnings. Moreover, it is about the "coming of God" and "the cosmic Shekinah of God." In *The Coming of* God, Moltmann tries to integrate the traditional diverged perspectives: the perspective of individual and universal eschatology, the eschatology of history and the eschatology of nature. This theme is developed through four spheres: personal eschatology (eternal life), historical eschatology (the kingdom of God), cosmic eschatology (new heaven-new earth), and divine eschatology (glory).[11] The modern church needs a biblical understanding of history and a wider understanding of the cosmic significance of Jesus Christ.[12]

When we stop using the book of Revelation as a catalog of "end times" events, we can recognize John's theological insights into the living Christ in history, a vision of God in the world.

ENDNOTES

1. Adv. Haer, 4.14.1; 5.26.1.

2. Robert H. Mounce, *The Book of Revelation* (New International Commentary on the New Testament; Revised edition; Grand Rapids: William B. Eerdmans Publishing Company, 1977), 14, 15.

3. Adv. Haer. 30.3.

4. Haer., li.12, 233.

5. Compare Tacitus, *History* i.2; Eusebius, *Historia Ecclesiastica*, III, 18.

6. Hist. Eccl. III, 18.

7. An amazing analysis of the variety of outlining approaches can be found in Gregory K. Beale, "The Structure and Plan of John's Apocalypse," *The Book of Revelation: A Commentary on the Greek Text* (Grand Rapids: William B. Eerdmans Publishing Company, 1998), 108–151.

8. This is the standard outline for most pre-millennial models of the book. See particularly that of Tim Lahaye, *Revelation Unveiled* (Grand Rapids: Zondervan, 1999). His three-part division of the book is (1) Christ and the Church Age (Rev. 1–3); (2) Christ and the Tribulation (Rev. 4–18); and (3) Christ and the Future (Rev. 19–22).

9. Elizabeth Schüssler Fiorenza, *Invitation to the Book of Revelation* (Garden City: Doubleday, 1981), 7.

10. This example is taken from an adaptation of the outline found in Richard L. Jeske, *Revelation for Today: Images of Hope* (Philadelphia: Fortress, 1983).

11. See Jürgen Moltmann, *The Coming of God: Christian Eschatology*, trans. Margaret Kohl (Minneapolis: Fortress Press, 1996).

12. A very good book which explores the relationship between the modern interest in eschatology as a systematic discipline and the field of New Testament studies in Revelation is that of Michael Gilbertson, *God and History in the Book of Revelation: New Testament Studies in Dialogue with Pannenberg and Moltmann* (Cambridge: Cambridge University Press, 2003).

OUTLINE OF THE BOOK OF REVELATION

A. Prologue and Vision of Christ (1:1–20)
1. Prologue (1:1–3)
2. Greetings and Doxology (1:4–8)
3. The Initial Vision of Christ (1:9–20)

B. The Letters to the Seven Churches (2:1–3:22)
1. To the Church in Ephesus (2:1–7)
2. To the Church in Smyrna (2:8–11)
3. To the Church in Pergamum (2:12–17)
4. To the Church in Thyatira (2:18–29)
5. To the Church in Sardis (3:1–6)
6. To the Church in Philadelphia (3:7–13)
7. To the Church in Laodicea (3:14–22)

C. John's Vision of God and the Lamb (4:1–5:14)
1. The Throne in Heaven (4:1–11)
2. The Scroll and the Lamb (5:1–14)

D. Opening the Seven Seals (6:1–8:5)
1. The First Seal: The White Horse (6:1–2)
2. The Second Seal: The Red Horse (6:3–4)
3. The Third Seal: The Black Horse (6:5–6)
4. The Fourth Seal: The Pale Horse (6:7–8)
5. The Fifth Seal: The Souls Under the Altar (6:9–11)
6. The Sixth Seal: A Great Earthquake (6:12–17)
7. The Sealing of the Tribes (7:1–8)
8. The White Robed Multitude (7:9–17)
9. The Seventh Seal and the Golden Censer (8:1–5)

E. Sounding the Seven Trumpets (8:6–11:19)
1. The First Trumpet: Hail and Fire (8:6–7)
2. The Second Trumpet: Mountain in the Sea (8:8–9)
3. The Third Trumpet: Wormwood Star (8:10–11)

    4. The Fourth Trumpet: Sun, Moon, and Stars (8:12–13)

    5. The Fifth Trumpet: Plague of Locusts (9:1–12)

    6. The Sixth Trumpet: Release of Four Angels (9:13–21)

    7. The Angel and the Little Scroll (10:1–11)

    8. The Two Witnesses (11:1–14)

    9. The Seventh Trumpet: Judgment/Rewards (11:15–19)

F. The Cosmic Conflict (12:1–14:20)

    1. The Woman and Dragon (12:1–13:1)

    2. The Beast from the Sea (13:2–10)

    3. The Beast from the Earth (13:11–18)

    4. The Lamb and the 144,000 (14:1–5)

    5. The Harvest of the Earth (14:6–20)

G. Pouring Out the Seven Bowls of Judgment (15:1–16:21)

    1. The Song of Moses and Seven Angels with Seven Plagues (15:1–8)

    2. The First Bowl: Sores (16:1–2)

    3. The Second Bowl: Sea Turns to Blood (16:3)

    4. The Third Bowl: Rivers and Springs Turn to Blood (16:4–7)

    5. The Fourth Bowl: Sun Scorches People with Fire (16:8–9)

    6. The Fifth Bowl: Darkness (16:10–11)

    7. The Sixth Bowl: Euphrates Dries Up (16:12–16)

    8. The Seventh Bowl: Earthquake (16:17–21)

H. Babylon, the Great Prostitute, Falls (17:1–19:10)

    1. Babylon the Prostitute (17:1–18)

    2. Babylon Destroyed (18:1–24)

    3. Babylon's Fall Praised—Hallelujah! (19:1–10)

I. The Reign of Christ (19:11–20:15)

    1. The Return of Christ: Rider on the White Horse 19:11–21)

    2. The 1,000 years of Christ's Reign (20:1–6)

    3. Satan Destroyed (20:7–10)

    4. Great White Throne Judgment (20:11–15)

J. The New Creation (21:1–22:5)

K. Epilogue (22:6–21)

INTERPRETING
THE BOOK
OF REVELATION

Before we enter into any attempt to read the Revelation of John we must come to grips with the methods of interpretation that are required for this unique style of literature. Unlocking the meaning behind the many textures of symbols, sounds, and signs almost requires a completely new vantage for the modern, scientific reader.

It might be best to read first through the entire revelation as quickly as possible in one sitting. The reader should resist any initial attempt to dissect and analyze the many dramatic and artistic representations until the entire sweeping drama is immersed into the senses. Much like standing in front of a Rembrandt, an appreciation for the artist's work is lost when one focuses too long on any one fleck of paint or crease of a brush print. All of the lighting, color, and texture come together to give an impression that is easily lost in such minute examination.

John has many clues along the way that he is recounting the vision as quickly as it is coming to him, and he wants to scan the entire event in a rapid succession of experiences for the reader. Certainly, though, many of the images will demand further analysis to make sense of them, sometimes because the images no longer have reference to the modern reader and sometimes because the images were cryptic even to the first century audience.

APOCALYPTIC LITERARY GENRE

The word "apocalypse"—the Greek word (*apocalysis*) meaning "revelation" or "unveiling"—is one of the descriptive words that the author John uses to title his book. This term has been associated with a genre or style of literature that appeared on the world scene sometime between 500 B.C. and the second century of the Christian era. Jewish writers became fascinated with this style around the events of their oppression by Antiochus Epiphanes in 167 B.C. and through the period of the Bar Kokhba Revolt in A.D. 135. Outside the canonical books of the Bible, we see this style represented in the Assumption of Moses, 1 Enoch (or the Book of Enoch), 4 Ezra (or 2 Esdras as it is called in the Apocrypha), the Testaments of the Twelve Patriarchs, the Psalter of Solomon, the Sibylline Oracles, the Book of Jubilees (sometimes called The Little Genesis) and the Apocalypse of Baruch.

Biblical scholarship has attempted to address the actual roots and formation of this literature, generally agreeing that the Jewish writers who utilized it did so by contact with the Persian worldview during captivity. Persian Zoroastrianism introduced Judaism to a dualistic understanding of the world filled with fanciful images of humans with animal heads and animals with human characteristics. Angels and demons filled this surreal world and gave explanation for the various powers that exhibited themselves in the world of mere mortals. By way of a wedding with their own wisdom and prophetic traditions, the Jewish apocalyptic form was born. Up until this point their worldview tended to be very "this-worldly," even world affirming. Questions concerning ultimate judgment—what the prophets called "the Day of the Lord"—were left unresolved on this side of life (cf. Job).

Perhaps one of the attractions apocalyptic literature held for both Jews and Christians was its ability to interpret world events and circumstances without being locked into the actual facts themselves. In other words, when the data of world events makes one appear to be on the losing side, the apocalyptic enables the reader to see beyond these truths to a more determinative or ultimate truth. For this reason, some have called apocalyptic writing a form of "protest literature." This would allow a people who held little control over the writing of history to write from a new perspective, even if from the underside of history. The winners of wars, the rich and the powerful, have written most of world history. So when people find their history unfriendly and destructive, the apocalyptic allows a different understanding of that history to emerge away from the obvious eyes of natural historians. It would take an "unveiling" of history for someone to see what really is happening.

In the case of the Revelation of John, those "without eyes" would believe that the Roman Empire was in ultimate control of the Church's success or failure. But this work shows the real history unfolding, one that shows martyrdom to fuel success and salvation as well as the demise of the seemingly indestructible Roman world. To the modern reader, imperial power is still alive and well and vying for our allegiance. We, too, would be tempted to succumb to worship human strength, projects, and schemes, if the faithful were not shown a deeper reality in our world.

The apocalyptic style of literature is found in rare instances in the canonical books of the Bible. The Revelation associated with John is the only such literature in the New Testament. In the Hebrew Scriptures, the book of Daniel and special sections of Ezekiel, Zechariah, and Isaiah represent the apocalyptic.

In the scope of the Bible, the literary style of apocalyptic adds to the diversity of expressions in God's Word. David's Psalms tend to tap into the emotional side of our experience; Paul's letters, the rational and logical. But the apocalyptic encourages us to use our imagination. When we try to use the same linear form of reasoning to unlock the meaning of John's Revelation that we might use to understand the Epistle to the Romans, we do this literature an injustice.

At the same time, some interpreters let their imaginations "run wild," something that is equally problematic. The symbols, drama, and action of the book of Revelation are rooted in a reality that guides our apprehension of the prophecy. When we read the Revelation, we are called upon to imagine, but our imaginations are to be shaped by the content of the revelation itself. Bruce Metzger describes this process as a "disciplined imagination."[1]

BIBLICAL NUMBERS, COLORS, AND SYMBOLS

The authors of the Bible, from the Genesis to the Revelation, have varied interests and usages for a specific set of numbers, symbols, and colors. Because the Apocalypse has an extensive array of metaphorical language some background in numerology and symbolism would be helpful to the reader. Some of the numbers found in the book of Revelation are numbers that have surfaced in other biblical contexts.

GREAT THEMES • NUMBERS IN THE REVELATION

Number	Usage	Concepts
7	54 times	John's favorite number, meaning complete or finished as in the days of creation
1/3	23 times	A large number, but not as bad as it could be
4	29 times	All encompassing (four winds, directions, etc.)
12	23 times	Israel, Apostolic Church, all of the people of God
24	2 x 12	Used only in the Apocalypse, often to describe both Israel and Church together
1,000	11 times	Used to depict a large host or time, as in 144,000 or the 1,000 year reign of Christ

The number seven—obviously a favorite of John's—had its earliest use in the first book of the Bible as it seeks to lay out the origins of the world that we live in by way of a seven-day week. It should not surprise the reader to see that the end of the chaotic world that we now experience will take place in series of sevens as well, as if reversing the creation to recover the complete and perfect cosmos that God had intended from the start.

Besides the number seven, John uses many other familiar numbers such as twelve and four. These numbers are sometimes used with a particularly distinctive Johannine creation, such as the number twenty-four (a multiple of twelve) to emphasize new situations in God's design.

The fraction one-third also carries with it psychological features that go beyond any attempt to give a literal meaning to the numbers. A plague that destroys one-third of the population is indeed horrid, but there is also an implied hope in the midst of great tribulation and sorrow that twice as many people and things were left untouched. (Recall that ages earlier, one-third of the angels, led by Satan, rebelled against God, but twice as many remained faithful.)

Colors also play an important role in the development of the ideas of the revealer and for informing the experiences of the reader. We are reminded that John is "seeing" this vision unfold, and he takes great care in describing those sights (and sounds) to us so that we can "see" it as well. Many times colors have multiple meanings. For instance, the color red, often associated with the devil or the beast, is also the color of blood

GREAT THEMES • APOCALYPTIC COLORS

Color	Concepts	Contexts
White	Holiness, victory, God's world	The Son of man's head and hair (1:14)
		The stone of the conqueror (2:17)
		The clothing of the faithful (3:4,5,18; 6:11; 7:9, 13; 14:14;19:14)
		The clothing of the twenty-four elders (4:4)
		White horse (6:2; 19:11)
		White horses of God's armies (19:14)
		White cloud of Son of Man (14:14)
		The white throne (20:11)
Red	Satan, blood	The red horse (6:4)
	War, violence	The fiery red breastplates of the angels that bring death (9:17)
		The red dragon (12:3)
Green	Death	The green horse (6:8)
Purple	Abominable	The great whore (17:4)
	Riches, power	The cargo of the Babylonian merchants (18:12)
		The city of Babylon (18:16)
Black	Horror	The black horse (6:5)
	Calamity	The blackened sun (6:12)

(either of the victims of Satan's murderous fury or of the blood of the saints and of Christ). By layering many different colors, sounds, and even smells into the landscape of the visions, the reader of the book of Revelation is given a full, theatre-style experience of God's final judgment and recreation of the cosmic scene.

The importance of understanding the pallet of John's artwork cannot be overemphasized when attempting to interpret this book. Many fundamentalist interpreters have forced literal readings of this text, usually to compress the complexities of this literature into specific contemporary events or end time scenarios. When this is done, the Bible student misses the greatest lessons and far-reaching meanings of the apocalypse, and usually deflects the prophetic message meant for them and the contemporary Church. As it is with most biased and self-serving interpreters, we tend to want to make literal what God meant to be symbolic, and symbolic, those obvious teachings that God meant to be literal.

APOCALYPTIC PROPHETIC LITERATURE

Some scholars have warned against making too close a comparison of the book of Revelation with traditional Jewish apocalyptic literature. Because the author himself also gives the writing a secondary description as **prophecy** (1:3; 22:7, 10, 18, 19), we must be careful not to be limited to the apocalyptic characteristics of the book. As apocalyptic literature arose out of a historical context of great turmoil, persecution, and oppression, it tends to see little hope beyond the present situation except for the end of all things. The prophets looked forward to God balancing the scales of justice within history; apocalyptic has given up on history and has become so pessimistic of change that it can only see God acting by bringing a radical end to history, destroying all evil, and beginning again with a new world.

It would appear that John also sees his writing as an oracle from the Lord, which, in the long history of Hebrew prophecy, has definite historic concerns related to judgment, warning, and promise. This quality seems to argue that the book of Revelation is some kind of new hybrid of the apocalyptic and prophetic style.

This relation to Old Testament prophecy also underscores the fact that the book of Revelation is related to a particular time in history, to a particular set of circumstances, and to a particular people. This does not mean it is irrelevant for us today; it just means we cannot make the book address the issues we want it to address directly without first understanding something about what it meant to the early church.

Before we conclude this section dealing with the literary nature of the book, it should also be noted that the book has been formed, by both its beginning and end, as an epistle. Standard Greco-Roman writing practices are used, and in the case of the internal letters to the seven churches, there is some evidence that some residue form of the imperial edict can be found. In summary, these three literary genres—the apocalyptic, prophetic, and epistolary form—have been mixed to create the most unique and imaginative style of writing that we find in the New Testament canon.

INTERPRETIVE SCHOOLS OF THOUGHT

It is at this point that certain modes of interpretation are brought to bear on the ultimate meaning of the book. There have traditionally been four schools of thought when it comes to interpreting the book of Revelation as a whole. In delineating these views, it should be noted that the type of apocalyptic literature that the book represents has not been adequately addressed by any one of these approaches. With the recent publication of some very important scholarly books and articles, the study of Revelation is coming of age with a completely new outlook for its use in preaching, theological reflection, and spiritual formation.

Up until this point, interpreters of the book could be placed in one of the following camps: the historicist, idealist, preterist, and a variety of futurist methods. These categories are still helpful for identifying the presuppositions of the interpreter of Revelation, but they should not limit the explosive nature of the literature itself. Being revelatory, in the strictest sense, our interpretive principles for the book should expand our vision of reality rather than merely to support and limit us to our preconceived hypotheses.

◨ KEY IDEAS • FOUR INTERPRETIVE APPROACHES

Historicist	Revelation is the history of the Christian Church from its beginning to end.
Idealist	The symbolic character of the apocalyptic limits the meaning of the book to universal abstract principles for all time and places.
Preterist	Argues that all of the events are completed in the time frame of the original reader in the first-century Church.
Futurist	The bulk of Revelation is about the end of the world. Gives little attention to how the original readers would have understood the book.

HISTORICIST

The first is the *historicist* method of interpretation. These interpretations tend to see the events described in Revelation as referring to actual events from the beginning of the church until the proximate time of the interpreter.

For rather selfish reasons, the sixteenth century Reformers introduced this model so that they might interject themselves into the work of God in history. Thus the Reformers, or any other historicist for that matter, could say that the Roman papacy was the Antichrist, propagating false doctrine and deceiving the faithful, just as the beast of the Revelation. The Reformers, of course, thought of themselves as the faithful witnesses called for at the end of time. This model continued to be popular after the Enlightenment and continues with this arrogant placement of the interpreter into the text.

The view had little to do with the time in which the author John wrote, but according to Mounce, "the Apocalypse was held to sketch the history of Western Europe through the various popes, the Protestant Reformation, the French revolution, and individual leaders such as Charlemagne and Mussolini."[2] The method had a seminal connection with Joachim of Fiore (d. 1602), a monastic who divided history into three millennial ages roughly corresponding to the Trinity. The age of the Father was the Old Testament period of prophets; the age of the Son was descriptive of the period of the Church from Jesus' birth until the middle ages. He wished to see the age of the Spirit (a renewal through monastic reform) usher in the Kingdom and replace the corrupt Church of his day. As was noted, many Protestants came to usurp this historical schema for their own.

The general outline used by most historicist interpretations of Revelation would look something like the following:

Ephesus: (A.D. 34 to 95) The church from the Apostolic age until the end of the first century;

Smyrna: (A.D. 95 to 313) The church under Roman persecution;

Pergamos: (A.D. 313 to 606) The church, now under Roman Catholic rule, in political power;

Thyatira: (A.D. 606 to 1517) The church under persecution by Roman Catholicism;

Sardis: (A.D. 1517 to 1793) The church of the Reformation;

Philadelphia: (A.D. 1793 to the Return of Christ) The true church from the Great Awakening to the end;

Laodicea: (present or future) The lukewarm church of the last days.

Some Protestants, though they were also historicists, differed with the spiritual-historical view of Augustinian heritage and continued in the pre-millennial tradition. They also saw the history of the church symbolized in the seals, vials, and trumpets of the book of Revelation, but to them the second coming of Christ was predicted in Revelation 10 (prior to what they saw as the millennium of Revelation 20).

Many such interpreters, though quite literalistic in their interpretation of the millennium of Revelation 20, were less literalistic in their understanding of the Antichrist. They did not expect a personal antichrist to appear at the end of the age to persecute the saints during a three-and-a-half-year period. Nor did they look for what has often been called "the Great Tribulation," but were convinced that the tribulation extended throughout the history of the church. The three and a half years, or 1,260 days, were often interpreted to mean 1,260 years of church history prior to the end times. Examples of pre-millennialists of this historicist type are Joseph Mede (1586–1638), Isaac

Newton (1642–1717), William Whiston (1667–1752), J. A. Bengel (1687–1752)[3] and Johann Heinrich Alsted (1588–1638).

Overall the historicist approach is open to several criticisms, but perhaps the most damaging critique is the fact that such a method leads to endless speculation and subjectivity in its interpretation. It simply is next to impossible to arrive at a consensus in the identification of referents in history for the symbols in the text. Whether it be a medieval monk, a sixteenth century Reformer, or a modern social critic, anyone with a bit of creativity is able to find personal meaning in the obscure and cryptic symbolism of the book's apocalyptic style.

The historicist model generally is found in most of the dispensational schemes popular today. Commentators appear to be quite skillful and ingenious when they are able to discover elaborate time schedules and symbols that match contemporary events. They often look like a religious CNN, watching events unfold in the Middle East and other world hot spots with their Bibles open to the Apocalypse on their desks. They love to point to "obvious" parallels between Scripture and the unfolding political images. The commentator's attitude often takes on the form of a Christian Gnostic, dividing the Church between those in the know and those who are unenlightened and ignorant of God's plan for the ages. In order to show this elite knowledge, the symbols and time frame of the book of Revelation must be sliced and diced to fit within elaborate artificial divisions of human history.

But when the events of history eventually prove the commentators wrong, they merely replace their fiction with new facts and move on. This was seen in a most obvious fashion when the many preachers of Bible prophecies, at its collapse, eventually gave up on the Soviet Union as the great Satan and replaced it with China, or Iraq, or North Korea. Many Western readers of Revelation are attracted to the *historicist* model because it resolves their curiosity for a rational and sensible answer to the very aesthetically expansive nature of apocalyptic literature.

Unfortunately it has also been used to overlay paradigms of hate on the geo-political landscape, often identifying America's enemies with incarnate evil and encouraging cross-cultural divisions and stereotypes.

IDEALIST

The second method of interpretation is known as the *idealist,* sometimes called the timeless, symbolic method. In this approach, the contents of the book are not seen to relate to any historical events at all, but only to symbolize the ongoing struggle between good and evil during the church age and until Christ returns.

It is more recent than the three other systems of interpretation (preterist, historicist, and futuristic) schools, but, that being said, is hardly distinguishable from the earlier allegorizing approaches of the Alexandrian School (Clement and Origen). In general, the idealist view is marked by a refusal to identify any of the symbolic images with specific future events, whether in the history of the church or with regard to the end of all things.

The primary benefit of this view is that it renders the Apocalypse quite understandable, as well as relevant, at its face value. It is simply a book that was written to encourage the persecuted Church with the knowledge that God will someday conquer all evil and make things right. This encouragement is accomplished through a fanciful story of God's victory over symbols representing opposition forces of evil (like dragons, beasts, and harlots) There are no secrets to be unlocked, other than to know that the symbols of one worldview and society are not always understandable to those of another.

One of the most significant criticisms brought against this view is the fact that Revelation is of the apocalyptic genre and apocalyptic documents generally are written to describe actual events in history. This also appears to contradict the clear language of the text when the writer says that Jesus will show him what must take place next (4:1). If there is no real chronology according to real historical events, then this statement seems to be superfluous.

Too, the section describing actual, historical churches (chaps. 2–3) seems not to be relevant to a real situation in history at all. To most experts, this book has a rather obvious historical context, and one is able to discern explicit and literal prophecies about the future, whether immediate or far-reaching.

On the other hand, the strength of this view is that it takes seriously the imaginative nature of apocalyptic literature. As Mitchell Reddish has said, "To 'literalize' is to trivialize."[4] Allowing this style of literature to express itself as literature gives readers the opportunity to involve themselves in the complexities of the drama and to probe it for its multifaceted meaning. Those who merely take Revelation as a literal prose are missing the dynamic quality of the way in which John first received the revelation. So much more could be gained from taking the teaching of Jesus literarily and allowing for a more figurative and expansive meaning to the drama of the book of Revelation. Some people demand a more literal reading of this fanciful vision than they do of the actual Gospels themselves!

PRETERIST

A third method of interpretation is the *preterist* method. The word "preterist" is Latin and means "pre (before) in fulfillment," i.e., [L. *praeteritus, gone by*]. It is expressing time fulfilled. Preterits believe that most or all of Bible prophecy has already been fulfilled in Christ and the ongoing expansion of His kingdom. They hang this belief of past-fulfillment on different verses, including the witness that Jesus and His apostles said that His coming (or presence) and the end of all things would occur soon (in that generation).

In this approach to the book, the symbols and content relate only to events and happenings at the time of the author. The beasts of chapter 13, for example, are related to Imperial Rome and the Imperial priesthood. There is no future eschatology in the book whatsoever. This method is based primarily on relating the book to Jewish apocalyptic tracts written at that time to encourage faithfulness during times of persecution. Therefore, the message of the book would seem to be that while the church is threatened by the state and the demand of emperor worship, those who endure will share in the final victory of God over the demonic powers which control and direct the totalitarian state.

Though the historical context for the book of Revelation was diminished early in the first years of the Christian era, the allegorizing techniques of the Alexandrian School relegated the Revelation to spiritual principles and meanings. The preterist system first appeared among

Renaissance scholars of the seventeenth century, with their "return to the sources," and revived new interest in the contemporary setting for the Revelation. The view is held by a great number of scholars today, including those from a more liberal perspective.

The benefit of this view is that it interprets the book in its primary historical setting first. Modeling serious study of the Revelation from its historic sources is to be encouraged and supported by Bible teachers today. But one of the most significant problems with the preterist view is that none of what was supposed to happen actually happened. Rome was not overthrown by God (though in some sense it was in A.D. 476) and the saints certainly did not share in any such victory.

In conjunction with this problem is the fact that much of what is in Revelation appears to be prophetic and speaking of a time quite distant from John's time (i.e. the return of Christ and the consummation of all things). For that reason many interpreters who see the events described by John as extending past the first six centuries of the church are not in agreement with this view.

FUTURIST

Most refer to the fourth method of dealing with Revelation as the *futuristic* method. In 3:10 the Lord says to the church at Philadelphia that they will be kept from the "hour of trial" to come upon the earth. This is a literary, programmatic statement wherein the *hour of trial* refers to the judgments described by John in chapters 6–18. According to John, the church at Philadelphia will not even enter that tribulation. Author John Walvoord argues that it is unlikely that just the church at Philadelphia is ultimately in mind here; surely it must be the Church as a worldwide body.[5]

Therefore, the seals, trumpets, and bowl judgments (chaps. 6–16), which in this system are referred to as a time of Jacob's trouble (Jer. 30:7), are all future and occur after the rapture (1 Thess. 4:16) of the Church. They relate directly to Daniel's seventieth week (see Dan. 9:24–27; a seven year period) and therefore concern Israel and not the Church. In Walvoord's system,[6] the seals, trumpets, and bowl judgments are chronologically sequential—that is, after the seal judgments, come the trumpet judgments and finally the bowl judgments. These all occur in the last three and a half years of the seven-year period of Daniel's seventieth week. The end result of this Great Tribulation is the destruction of ecclesiastical (chap. 17) and political (chap. 18) Babylon. Then Christ will return with the Church and set up His kingdom (chaps. 19, 20).

Scholar George Eldon Ladd is correct when he asserts that this interpretation relies heavily upon the distinction between Israel and the Church and the distinctive plan God has for both.[7] Ladd, as well as a host of other commentators, are extremely critical of this distinction between ethnic Israel and the Church, but there appears to be significant precedent for it in a post-cross setting (cf. 1 Cor. 10:32 and Rom. 9–11).

Finally, in this method, proper attention is given to the grammatical-historical context of the letter, and the churches in chapters 2 and 3 are generally taken as real, literal churches. Therefore, since the first three chapters (one might also add chapters 4 and 5) deal with "things" during John's lifetime and chapters 6–22 deal with "things" to come in the future, I have called this view the *mostly futuristic* view.

A view espoused by Ladd is sometimes referred to as a *moderate futurist* view. According to Ladd, an answer to the problem of the relationship of the seal, trumpet, and bowl judgments to one another could provide the solution to the view of history affirmed in the book. With that in mind, he proposes that the seal judgments represent "the forces in history, however long it lasts, by which God works out His redemptive and judicial purposes leading up to the end."[8]

Therefore, Ladd understands the seal judgments to be going on throughout the church age and the trumpet and bowl judgments (really from chapter 7 onward) to be concerned with the time of the consummation. The primary reason he argues in this fashion is because the contents of the book cannot be opened until the *last* seal and 6:17 explicitly says that the "great day of their wrath has come, and who can stand?" This text, according to Ladd, suggests that it had not yet arrived until the sixth seal was broken. Further, Ladd understands the seal judgments to parallel the woes outlined in Matthew 23 and that the white horse in Revelation should be understood to be the victories won by the gospel in an age characterized by evil and death.

There are several problems with this view of Revelation 6. First, it is unlikely for several reasons that the rider and white horse are to be associated with Christ and the gospel. It is true, as Ladd points out, that white is generally associated with spiritual victory in Revelation, but the identification of the rider in 6:2 rests partially on parallels with the rider in 19:11. They are similar in that they are both on white horses, but the parallel is difficult to maintain beyond this. The rider in 6:2 has a bow and a crown and is bent on conquest; the rider in 19:11 is judging to effect justice. Therefore, the purpose and contexts for their actions are different. Also, the language of "was given" is used of divine permission given to evil powers to carry out their destruction (9:1, 3, 5; 13:5, 7, 14, 15).

Therefore its use in 6:2 would tend to argue for the rider and his mission relating to some form of evil, perhaps military invasion, with the crown symbolizing eventual authority over the conquered peoples. Yet another thorn in the side of Ladd's theory is the fact that 6:2 is part of a series of judgments and calamities and it is difficult to believe that it could refer to the gospel going forth. Chapter 6 and the seals represent profound judgment, not salvation. Finally this interpretation of the rider in 6:2 seems to promote confusion between Christ opening the seals and also being the one sent forth as the first rider.[9]

CONCLUSION

In conclusion to our discussion on the various ways the book of Revelation is interpreted, it should be pointed out how each of these methods was historically conditioned and arose out of particular concerns by the Christian community. Even by the time the Church included the Revelation in its canon, the problems of interpretation were understood. Still, the Church in her wisdom knew that the epistle to the seven churches was still applicable to them as well. John himself, when writing down the account of the prophecy, was writing from a historical context to a particular set of problems and situations, and was doing so from a set of principles and ideas that could apply to future events as well. Whatever our method, we should be sensitive to those earlier interpretive principles and be true to them today.

Recognizing that people come to this book of the Bible with differing points of view should not limit the Church's openness to God speaking through it. The role that Revelation has played in giving hope and strength to Christians along the way was often independent of being placed in any of these categories of interpretation. Generally, the literary connection with history is tied to just a few pivotal points in the chain of chapters (such as chapter 20), and the significance that the bulk of the prophecy has comes through clearly.

WESLEYAN/HOLINESS THEMES

Although the book of Revelation is full of emphases that fit well within the systematic reflection of Wesleyan-holiness Bible students, there have been few attempts to think biblically from that perspective. Part of the struggle with developing a Wesleyan approach (called hermeneutic) to the book of Revelation is that, historically, Wesley and Wesleyanism were not that concerned about identifying themselves with any one position of the end of the world (see chapter 12 on millennialism). So quite often the curious who had questions concerning eschatology received their answers from the prevailing religious culture.

Wesley himself would be hard to pigeonhole. Many scholars would imagine that he was a pre-millennialist. (Premillennialism is the belief that Christ returns bodily before the thousand years of peace and righteousness over which He rules.) He was in dialogue with many preachers of his day representing this model, and his own notes on the New Testament were taken almost verbatim from the work of Johann Bengel, a noted pre-millennialist scholar. Still others, extracting from Wesley's own sermons and journals, would want to identify his thinking with that of post-millennialism—or at least to argue that he had seminal ideas for such a position.[10] (Postmillennialists believe that the world will eventually become Christianized and that the Millennium is a long period of righteousness and peace on earth before the bodily return of Christ.)

In the end, John Wesley, as a source for understanding a systematic treatment of the Revelation, must be understood within his own historical setting and with the constraints of his own inability to transcend that setting.

The disciples of Wesley seemed to extend the teaching of the Wesleys, with their optimism of grace, into the nineteenth-century American religious

WHAT OTHERS SAY

I said nothing less or more . . . concerning the end of the world. . . . I have no opinion at all on it: I can determine nothing at all about it. . . . I have only one thing to do, to save my soul, and those that hear me.
—John Wesley

scene. Phoebe Palmer was a type of post-millennialist. Another was the famed Methodist theologian Daniel Steele, who vehemently rejected the dispensational pre-millennialism being offered by his contemporary J.N. Darby.[11] Often any form of pre-millennialism was rejected as if it was a rejection of Calvinist teaching in general. It wasn't until the early twentieth century, with the rise of fundamentalism, that Wesleyans found themselves inundated with this approach to the Apocalypse. Even then, the various Holiness bodies tended to take no official stance on millennial views—or the approach to Revelation that was implied by them. An appreciation for diversity and freedom of opinion dominated Wesleyan eschatology while still holding to general orthodox positions on the Second Coming, the final judgment, and beliefs about heaven and hell.

Wesleyans do have a different reading of the book of Revelation. Some of the interpretive principles that may guide us as we approach the chapters ahead center on (1) the basic Wesleyan witness to a realistic optimism of world history in the face of current doomsday motifs; (2) an emphasis on the present victorious living of the Christian as a supplement to an understanding of salvation primarily as a future reward in heaven; and very important, (3) a Wesleyan view of history as a synergy between human endeavor and engagement with Divine providence.

As all the Gospel heralds wished to express, particularly through their report and theological reflection on the mission given to them at the end of Christ's earthly ministry, we do have something to do while we are awaiting our Lord's return. This work is significant, important, and effective in aiding the completion of the new city John saw coming down.

The historic emphases found in Wesleyan social ethics are easily highlighted in a reading of the Revelation today. Though concerned with the evangelical message of individual salvation, Wesleyans have always understood salvation in more holistic terms, and like the theology of the Revelation, have attempted to understand the role human works play in a salvation accomplished by faith alone. The book of Revelation too wants to draw its readers into the unfolding plan of God's salvation and make them *more* than overcomers.

A REALISTIC OPTIMISM DOOMSDAY SCENARIO

The book of Revelation, and the worldview that it depicts, has often been usurped by the pessimistic and doomsday scenarios associated with dispensational interpretations of history. (Dispensations are specific time periods in which God interacted in certain ways with His creation: law representing the Old Testament, and grace representing the New Testament) Generally, seeing world history divided into epochal dispensations helps us to make sense of it. Quite often this is done artificially, as when people describe American history by the decades—the "forties" were at time of patriotic zeal; the "fifties," the American dream; and the "sixties," a time of moral decay. This usually ascribes well-defined ideologies more than assigning meaning to history itself.

Dispensationalism as an interpretive approach to the Apocalypse is relatively recent in Church history. The Plymouth Brethren pastor J. N. Darby popularized this approach that sought to divide history into eras—or dispensations—of time, giving meaning for the present age to the divisions and groupings of events found in Revelation (and Daniel). Somehow, believing that we were living in some era of the "last days," the Church was seen to be in a unique vantage to understand the complexities of faith in a modern world. This seemed to neglect Luke's insight that with the coming of the Spirit, the last days had been inaugurated.

Historically, Wesleyan/holiness preachers were often swept up in this approach as well. During the early part of the twentieth century, the theologically conservative holiness movement tended to identify itself with the intellectual and cultural features of fundamentalism, a resistance to modern religious ideas, scientific evolution, and liberal social agendas. One of the tenets of fundamentalism was a pragmatic belief in the depravity of human history. Dwight L. Moody's "lifeboat" mentality tended to view the Christian church's role as getting as many people out of the world alive, while the rest of the world drowns and goes to hell. This "lifeboat" provided a powerful metaphor for evangelism, but provided little hope for staying behind and aiding in the world's recreation.

During this period of time, holiness pastors were trained with the dispensational exegesis of Revelation.[12] Though often noting an implicit antipathy with the Wesleyan optimistic theology of sanctification and perfection in love, the holiness movement's pastors made an uneasy alliance with fundamentalism. It seemed to them that the only other eschatological alternative, a view of the future as moving toward the modern vision of technological utopia, would be an acceptance of the liberal ideas of human endeavor and, later, of the materialistic view of history found in atheistic Marxism.

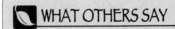

WHAT OTHERS SAY

I look upon this world as a wrecked vessel. God has given me a lifeboat and said to me, "Moody, save all you can."
—Dwight L. Moody

A charge to keep I have,
a God to glorify,
a never-dying soul to save,
and fit it for the sky.

To serve the present age,
my calling to fulfill;
O may it all my powers engage
to do my Master's will!
—Charles Wesley

The synergism—a view that God works with humanity to accomplish His will—found throughout Wesleyan theology was forgotten and replaced with the deterministic outlook of these hyper-reformed interpretations of history. Though this brief historical overview begs for a more developed analysis, a greater appreciation for how the Wesleyan doctrine of perfection applies to a theology of history is needed to offset the negative effects of reading history without hope.

This commentary employs a Wesleyan interpretive lens for reading the Apocalypse of John as an optimistic guide for Christians seeking to contribute to the growth and development of God's will in the world today. It is a realistic optimism in that a real sense of sin and depravity is taken into account, keeping a perverted reading of the Revelation from depicting

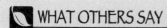

WHAT OTHERS SAY

The Revelation was a message of hope, grace, and comfort to early Christians as they faced persecution. The message has not changed. The hope God offers is still sure; the grace God is pleased to give is still sufficient.

—Marva Dawn

some form of utopist vision for the future. In the end, God is in control of the Creation. A vision of the end of the world must take into account our inability to see and discern fully what that shall be. To be sure, we believe the vision that John saw of the New City was meant to inspire and encourage contributions to such a community, not merely to look forward to the destruction of our present one.

NOW FUTURE OF SALVATION

Another Wesleyan key to understanding John's Revelation is how a view of the end of history aids one in living today. Quite often commentaries and studies of the Apocalypse appear to be a "road map" to the end of the age. We are not interested in the road we are on, only in the signs along the way that keep us on course. It is as if John had his vision of the future written down so that those at the end of history might pick it up and know that they were at the end of history when they got there. The question of why this knowledge makes a difference is of little consequence, not alone what it had to do with the interim years in between the first and Second Advent of Christ. In fact, the recurring theme of "overcoming" makes little sense if the purpose of the Revelation was merely to inform us of future events. We are asked to live in the present as people who overcome and have victory because we have such knowledge of the future.

When theology has relegated eschatology, or the study of "last things," to merely "add-ons" to our doctrines, the book of Revelation has been viewed as an interesting collection of oddities and speculations about futurology. Questions like "What will heaven be like?" "Who is the Antichrist?" or even "How will the end of the world come?" have little to do with the wide-sweeping issues of God, salvation, and humanity. Karl Barth spoke of this annexing of eschatology to the appendix of our thought as eschatology becoming "a harmless little chapter at the end of dogmatic theology."[13]

Believing that the theological continuity of John's writing can be described by this prophetic revelation, the interpreter will seek to discover what the "already" dimension of Christ's first coming has to do with the culmination in His second coming. It is the contention of this book that God has not developed a variety of plans for salvation, but only one, in Jesus Christ. This theological credo implies that the teaching of Christ's historical life is not divorced from His reigning, triumphant role in history. Once more, the book of Revelation must have a design for life in this world if it is to say anything of the world to come.

SOCIAL AND PERSONAL HOLINESS

Wesleyans have always understood God's redemptive plan to extend beyond mere piety and personal morality to include social, even cosmic, reform. Thomas Merton, the well-known Trappist monk turned social activist, once described himself as "the man who spurned New York, spat on Chicago, and tromped on Louisville, heading for the woods with Thoreau in one pocket, John of the Cross in another, and holding the Bible open to the Apocalypse."[14] "Holding the Bible open to the Apocalypse," for him, was a synonym for leaving behind a God-forsaken world. But to be a disciple of Jesus Christ, and an heir to the Wesleyan worldly parish, retreat from the world eventually gives way to a prophetic move toward the world, the world that God created and loves. We must be encouraged to see through all the smoke, ashes, and brimstone of Revelation to the purged world that Christ is heralding. Once we have seen such a world, the possibility of its completion is close at hand. Wesley wrote in the preface to *Explanatory Notes* that as the bulk of the New Testament dealt with the history of Christ on earth and the subsequent rise of the Church through His apostles after His ascension, "the Revelation delivers what is to be, with regard to Christ, the Church, and the universe, till the consummation of all things."[15] Wesley understood the whole of the New Testament as a message about Christ. It follows that Revelation completes this study of Christ's final work for all creation.

This is why Wesleyans took such (sometimes embarrassingly) unpopular stands against alcohol, gambling, dancing, and a myriad of other social vices. Unlike other church traditions that also tended to be against these same behaviors, Wesleyans often based their abstinence of these things on the potential destructiveness they held for those least able to defend against them. The acts by themselves were not thought of as evil, but as a collective, they could possess and destroy the fabric of families and societies, as well as individual lives.

John Wesley tended to see social reform as an accumulation of individuals transformed by conversion and holy living, but his optimism for the possibilities of human progress gave him occasional insights into the whole of life and the world. The optimistic belief in the creation of a new community living alongside the old dying world led historic Wesleyanism to stand against slavery, the subjugation of women in Church and society, and to the participation in urban renewal during the rise of industrial America.

Wesleyans tend to look at the world in much the way that John's gospel depicts it. We know from him that "God so loved the world [cosmos]" (John 3:16) that He gave His Son for it. The world is a tapestry woven of people, place, and Spirit. Because we are part of the very fabric of creation, we will never be redeemed if not to this whole. God has not planned salvation for humanity alone, but has included a renovation project for the whole of His creation. Wesley's sermon "The Scriptural Way of Salvation" depicted salvation as a restoration to what was lost in the garden of paradise, a theme that fits very well with John's vision of the New Earth. For Wesley, salvation even extended to the "brute world" of the creation, and not merely for the human individual. It is ironic that Wesleyans have spent so much time attempting to define themselves over against a "worldliness" when Wesley's understanding of holiness was so world-oriented. The Revelation provides a purifying lens into the redemption of the world and a helpful tool for engaging and incapacitating the destructive powers that stifle God's work.

There may be other specifically Wesleyan perspectives that may arise in our reading of the Apocalypse, but these general ideas would appear to come from the text itself and may be added to the general presuppositions of this commentary.

ENDNOTES

1. Bruce M. Metzger, *Breaking the Code: Understanding the Book of Revelation*, (Nashville: Abingdon, 1993), 11.

2. Robert H. Mounce, *The Book of Revelation,* (Grand Rapids: William B. Eerdmans Publishing Company, 1977), 27.

3. John Wesley's *Explanatory Notes Upon the New Testament*, being an abridgement/translation of Bengel's *Gnomon Novi Testamenti*, depicts this view as well. An example can be found in the notes on the seven trumpets, representing the various theological/doctrinal struggles from early Church history until the Reformation. For this reason, Wesley's own comments on the book of Revelation are instructive as a student of the Bible for his own age. See John Wesley, *Explanatory Notes Upon the New Testament* (London: Epworth Press, 1976), 976–979. A modern "Wesleyan" reading of the Apocalypse must take this into account.

4. Mitchell G. Reddish, *Revelation* (Macon: Smyth & Helwys, 2001), 31.

5. Walvoord, John F., *The Revelation of Jesus Christ: A Commentary* (Chicago: Moody Press, 1966), 939.

6. Ibid., 950.

7. Ladd, George Eldon, *A Commentary on the Revelation of John* (Grand Rapids: William B. Eerdmans Publishing Company, 1972), 673.

8. Ibid., 670.

9. Ibid., 672.

10. Clarence L. Bence, "Processive Eschatology: a Wesleyan Alternative," *Wesleyan Theological Journal,* vol. 14.1 (spring 1979): 45–59.

11. Daniel Steele, *A Substitute for Holiness* (London: Taylor & Francis, 1985), pp. 170, 195; *Jesus Exultant* (Salem, Ohio: HE Schmul, 1972), 15, 22.

12. A significant text used to train many of the holiness movement's ministers, often coupled with C. I. Scofield's *KJV Study Bible*, was Clarence Larkin's very popular *Dispensational Truths* (Chester, PA: 1915). His many charts and elaborately developed schemas whetted the appetite of any rational preacher wanting to be armed against the onslaughts of modernism and the questions posed by evolutionary views of history.

13. Karl Barth, *Der Römerbrief* (Munich, 1922), 486; cited in Zachery Hayes, *What Are They Saying About the End of the World?* (New York: Paulist, 1983), 5.

14. Thomas Merton, *Contemplation in a World of Action* (Notre Dame: University of Notre Dame Press, 1973), 159.

15. John Wesley, *Explanatory Notes Upon the New Testament* London: Epworth, 1976), 10.

2

THE PROLOGUE AND THE LETTERS TO THE SEVEN CHURCHES

Revelation 1:1–3:22

Though we are often most concerned with the visions and prophetic activity of the book of Revelation, the reader must move through a series of introductory chapters before the apocalyptic imagery begins. These chapters contain an epistle format made up of greetings and doxology normal to a letter and an initial vision of Christ, which offers up information that will be important to unlock the subsequent ideas surrounding God's eternal work in this passing world. They also include the famous series of letters to the seven churches of Asia Minor that seem to provide the ethical framework for motivation and encouragement to "overcome" the atrocities that are to be spelled out in the subsequent pages.

PROLOGUE 1:1–3

We are told from the initial words that this is to be an apocalypse (or **revelation**) **of Jesus Christ** (1:1). Unlike the confusion brought about by the title of the King James Version, this is not to be a revelation or revelations of St. John the Divine, as if it is a word or prophecy from God through a prophet of old, but a revealing of Jesus himself. This beginning statement sets the course for the whole of the book. Gerhard Ebeling puts it this way: "We do not by any means merely interpret Jesus in light of the apocalyptic, but also and above all, interpret apocalyptic in light of Jesus."[1] John truly believes that in the face of confusion and chaos, the only thing that will bring sense and meaning to the raging events taking place is a glimpse of the Messiah in history.

Christ gives John this revelation through the mediation of an **angel**. We eventually discover this angel is actually Jesus' **angel** (22:16). As with other apocalyptic texts, the disclosed message is often delivered by an angel. Angels will show up numerous times throughout the revelation, often to open seals, pour out bowls, and deliver specific messages or tasks from God or Jesus Christ. Even the churches themselves have their own angels that become their ambassadors for Christ. The result is that, despite the intimate experience that we have of God opening His secret places before us, we realize that we still do not have direct access to the mind of God. He delivers His revelation to us. Even in the great mystical expanse of the book of Revelation, transcendence is maintained so that there really is no unmediated experience of God.

The prologue to the book gives some description as to the contents that are to follow. Jesus was to show **what must soon take place** (1:1) through the **servant John**. The word "soon" has with it a psychological experience, meaning different things to different people.

In the early centuries of the Church, an emphasis on "soon," as well as an anti-worldly outlook, led many to quit their jobs and sit waiting for this return. These are the issues addressed by Paul in his early letters to the Thessalonians. People there had stopped working and were grieving the death of the first Christian disciples because they believed they were on the verge of Christ's coming.

Paul answered this problem by assuring them that various events must take place in the apocalyptic calendar before Christ returns and that the dead in Christ will actually go on ahead of those who remain to be with the Lord. Because a long period of time has passed since those first struggles with the timetable of God, many take heart in the concept in 2 Peter 3:8: "With the Lord a day is like a thousand years, and a thousand years are like a day." There, Peter wants to argue that the delay of Christ's coming is tied to His patient desire that people be saved from the wrath of God.

One should recognize this historic tendency to overstate the nature of "soon" in the revelation.

The recipients (**his servants**) were expected to receive a blessing through this revelation. **Blessed is the one who reads the words of this prophecy, and blessed are those who hear it and take to heart** (1:3) those words. As the letter made its rounds through the addressed churches, it was expected that a person would read the book to a group of hearers. The blessing should fall on both reader and hearer, but with the hope that the hearers take it to heart. The actual use may have been as a sermon, or, better still, as a liturgical format for worship in the early Church.

John gives his readers a blessing at the beginning of this book. Because of the perspective of doom that many interpreters bring to the book of Revelation, this repeated benediction is often overlooked. Some have even detected a hidden series of seven such blessings in the book as a whole.

KEY IDEAS

1. Blessed are those who hear it and take to heart what is written in it (1:3).

2. Blessed are the dead who die in the Lord from now on (14:13).

3. Blessed is he who stays awake and keeps his clothes with him (16:15).

4. Blessed are those who are invited to the wedding supper of the Lamb (19:9).

5. Blessed and holy are those who have part in the first resurrection (20:6).

6. Blessed is he who keeps the words of the prophecy in this book (22:7).

7. Blessed are those who wash their robes (22:14).

We would notice how many of these "blessings" are connected with the need to follow the ethical demands of the prophecy in this book. The context of those that do have this explicit ethical demand often points to the "deeds" and "righteous acts" of the people being blessed (14:13; 19:9). Those blessed people with washed robes in chapter 22 are contrasted with "the dogs" that "practice" all kinds of wickedness (22:15).

The real benefit to the book of Revelation is to provide encouragement to continue to walk in the way of Christ. By the third century, Dionysius had noted that the Revelation was being used to promote an anti-worldly attitude accompanied with overindulgence and sensuality. John would see that any legitimate eschatology for the present Church will have the by-product of holiness.

Some literary scholars have analyzed the prayers, hymns, and doxological poetry percolating from the main structure of the text and have suggested how worship may provide a key to understanding the work as a whole. The blaring trumpets, incense on altars, and bowls being poured out all conjure up images of Temple worship. After all, John himself, while **in the Spirit**, wrote the text of the revelation **on the Lord's Day** (1:10). The text helps us to see that when we worship, we find ourselves gathering with all the heavenly assembly around the throne of God. Worship on earth provides an insight into the meaning of the cosmos. As interest in the book has been mostly at the periphery of church life, being confined to backroom discussions and lecture halls, the Church has much to gain from discovering the practical use of Revelation today for devotion and worship. The spiritual formation that was to be garnered from the use of the Revelation of John has yet to be fully realized. If we **take to heart** (1:3) what is read and heard in this prophecy, structures of understanding will give rise to a new imagination for what God plans for His Church and creation.

GREETINGS AND DOXOLOGY 1:4–8

Following the letter-writing form of the ancient Greco-Roman world, the book begins with an address naming the author and its recipients: **John, To the seven churches in the province of Asia** (1:4). It then follows with the customary grace and doxology often seen in Paul's letters. The grace is given through an implicit Trinitarian formula. The Father is named **him who is, and who was, and who is to come** (1:4; repeated in 1:8; and, in similar form, in 4:8 and 11:17). Next, but out of traditional order, is the Holy Spirit, or **the seven spirits before his** [God's] **throne**. This phrase may also be interpreted "the sevenfold spirit," emphasizing the perfect spiritual power of this particular spirit. **Jesus Christ**, actually the second person of the Trinity, is probably mentioned last so as to emphasize and develop the role of this divine person in the verses that follow. The formulaic quality of the subsequent phrases is obvious to those who look for such fragmented hymns and creeds in biblical texts. Much as in the "Christ Hymn" of Philippians 2, the relative pronoun "who" is followed by a series of descriptive Christological statements. Jesus is **the faithful witness, the firstborn from the dead, and the ruler of the kings of the earth** (1:5). Joined to these statements is a beautiful doxology: **To him who loves us and has freed us from our sins by his blood, and has made us to be a kingdom and priests to serve his God and Father—to him be glory and power for ever and ever!** (1:6). It is interesting to note that, unlike Philippians 2, the emphasis upon Christ's humility is supplanted by His role as reigning monarch of the universe. The Christian identification with Christ as a **faithful witness** results in their sharing in the new Kingdom that He has established.

We are encouraged to **look** for God's advent into history by a piece of tradition that looks very much like that found in Matthew 24:30 (but in reverse order):

> **Look, he is coming with the clouds,**
> **and every eye will see him,**
> **even those who pierced him;**
> **and all the peoples of the earth will mourn because of him.**
> **So shall it be! Amen** (1:7).

THE INITIAL VISION OF CHRIST—ONE LIKE A SON OF MAN 1:9–20

John, at the start of the apocalyptic vision wants to remind his readers that he did not receive this vision as a mere bystander. He is a **brother and companion** (1:9) to all those who are suffering and who have experienced the **kingdom** through **patient endurance** (1:9). John was in the place he was (Patmos) because of his faithfulness to God's Word and his testimony to Jesus Christ.

The **loud** trumpeting **voice** (1:10) that commands John to write catches his attention, and, almost instinctively, he turns **around to see the voice that was speaking** (1:12). What an interesting thought in itself:

that John wants to see **the voice**. This is a good example of the multifaceted, swirling complex of images and experiences found in this literature.
The Apocalypse attacks the senses from every conceivable direction.
John's first vision is in fact a vision of Jesus Christ. The readers are not
told this explicitly, but if they were believing Christians, they would have
no problem identifying the person who now stands in view. This picture
of Christ, replete with numerous symbols, colors, and numbers, will be
focused upon in more detail in other parts of the Apocalypse, often
emphasizing characteristics of Christ needed for that setting. For
example, the addresses to the seven churches are said to be written by
Christ, referring to the specific images from this vision.

One more time, we are reminded that John must not just watch the
unfolding vision, but he must record what he sees. The loud voice
instructs him to **write on a scroll** what he sees and **send it to the seven
churches** (1:11) that are named. The vision was being given to aid the
Church in its confused existence in the world. After the body of the
prophecy, with its visions, stories, and theology, the writer will return
again to this letter form (22:7–22), concluding with its benediction. This
literary feature that holds the book of Revelation together like two book-
ends makes us aware that the revelation given to John was always meant
to be shared and used, not horded and dissected.

But actually the first thing that he sees—before he sees who is speaking—
is the **seven golden lampstands**. Eventually we are told that these lampstands are actually **seven churches** (1:20). **Someone "like a son of man"**
(1:13) was among them. The KJV renders the **lampstand** as a candlestick.
This is a poor definition for this Greek word. For one, candles were not
invented until the Middle Ages. But, more important, the lampstand
emphasizes the role of the Church as a mere holder of the Light, Jesus
Christ. It may be that John sees Jesus in the midst of these lampstands, but
He is the lamp whose **face was like the sun shining in all its brilliance**
(1:16). For this reason, a major warning of the angel to the seven churches
is that Christ will take their lampstand away (2:5). Through unfaithfulness,
the Church will give up her right to be a lamp bearer for Him.

Anyone looking for Jesus must first deal with the problem of the
Church. The person of Christ is disguised in the middle of the institution

and incarnation. These lampstands, representing the Church, provide the structure and support for the one who **walks among the seven golden lampstands** (2:1), but they will not supplant His brilliance. In an attempt to win back the thousands of secularized masses to Christianity, the modern church is often tempted to market itself and draw the religious consumer with a dazzling array of products. John knows that the only role the Church has, even in the worst of times, is to display the person of Christ. The Church, while in any historic role as lampstand, could lose its role as a presenter of Jesus Christ if she falls prey to the siren call of compromise and pride.

The fact that this person looked like **a son of man** connects the vision to Jesus, even if subtly. In the Gospels, this was Jesus' favorite way of describing himself. It was both incarnational and messianic as a technical term: incarnational, in that it could mean that the person was described as having the traits of looking human as in Psalm 8:4, "what is man . . . the son of man. . . ." It is also a term that begins to show what God's ultimate savior was to be—a Son of Man, a Son of God.

So we know that this voice is connected to someone that appears human. Who is it? What other features might help John discover His identity? Chapters 7 and 10 of Daniel appear to be in the background of the composite picture of this man. First, as in Daniel 10:5, he was **dressed in a robe reaching down to his feet and with a golden sash around his chest** (1:13). Generally, the kingly status of the person comes to mind. Commentators have also suggested that the individual is dressed in priestly attire. **His head and hair were white like wool, as white as snow**, probably symbolizing how wise and respected the person was, **and his eyes were like blazing fire**, a metaphor suggesting insight and clarity (1:14). The mixing of symbols, a trait of the apocalypse throughout, might allow the reader to see both priestly and royal characteristics represented here.

John knows this to be the Christ, even God, because the vision evokes immediate worship. At the sight, he **fell at his feet as though dead** (1:17). John was unable to stand before such an awesome spectacle of revelation. The mysteries of God are powerful to behold, but to have them explained may be too much.

Using His **right hand** (the hand of power), Christ reaches out and calms John. Reminiscent of the resurrection narrative, He tells John, "**Do not be afraid . . .**" (1:17). These words are as filled with as much irony here as on Easter morning. The sight of the resurrected Lord brings terror to the mortal living within the boundaries of life and death. But it is this very vision that brings peace to the persecuted Church.

John is then commanded to write **what you have seen, what is now and what will take place later** (1:19). Some have suggested this verse forms the outline for the book-as-a-whole: (1) what you have seen (this chapter); (2) what is now (the letters to the seven churches); and (3) what will take place later (the rest of the revelation).

Probably the sense here is to ensure the reader that John has been instructed to write down an all-encompassing report on the vision that he receives. God will open the mystery of all His plans for history; nothing will be left out. One English translation of this sentence might look more like: "When you're done with this experience, write what you have seen; it contains things that are happening now and in the future." This sentence structure offers a less forceful structure to our reading but fits the spirit of the purpose of the revelation as being intended for the first century reader as well as to those who follow.

THE SEVEN CHURCHES OF ASIA MINOR 2:1–3:22

Some have postulated that the seven churches mentioned here are in fact to be interpreted as the "universal Church," as the biblical number "seven" quite often depicts a completed state. This often leads to viewing the churches themselves and the details associated with them as fictional. The fact that we have here seven actual locales in Asia Minor, and each has historical viability, support the idea that the original Apocalypse was written to be circulated to these seven churches. This does not mean, however, that the universal consequences of these letters do not pertain to the contemporary settings in which the Church finds herself today.

Furthermore, any attempt to "spiritualize" these Churches, that is, to tear the letters away from their historic connection to a specific place and time, has led to many bizarre interpretations of their importance for the reader. The most notable (perhaps creative) interpretive device was to use the depictions of the seven churches as dividing up time into seven "church ages" thereby placing the contemporary reader in the last of these epochs—the period of the Church of Laeodicea. It is usually the case that these designs will manipulate the texts to fit the scheme that best places the "end of time" in the writer's own era.

Obviously, this model of interpreting the seven churches would make the letters nonsensical to the first-century reader. It would only make sense to those who have had enough history flow by so that they could notice the import of each of the subsequent Church periods. To confuse matters more, those who advocate such a "spiritual" reading of the letters to the seven churches will often turn around and demand a "literal" reading for the rest of the book of Revelation. Having said all of this, one cannot help but notice how John has intricately developed the history of salvation into the series of seven churches, starting with the tree of life in Ephesus, moving through various Old Testament themes, and culminating in the Laodicean period of religious crisis.

In looking at the geographic placing of the seven cities, a map would show the connect-the-dot pattern that it creates. This seems to support the theory that the message of the Revelation was meant to be carried from church to church and read to congregations along the way. The individual messages

delivered to each of the churches coincide with the historic description and context of the Roman city identified. These observations lead us to conclude that the seven letters probably should be treated not unlike the epistles that Paul wrote to his own mission churches, that they have a specific historical-grammatical interpretation but are instructive to Christian communities for all times.

TO THE CHURCH IN EPHESUS 2:1-7

The first church that John addresses is Ephesus. Ephesus is one of the most important churches in the early history of Christianity. Of the cities that are to follow, only Laodicea has been mentioned in the prior New Testament books (Col. 4:16), but the probability is that all of the churches came about because of the preaching of the Apostle Paul during his long stay in Ephesus.

In what is today modern Turkey, Ephesus was a bustling trade and port city, the inhabitants reflecting a wealthy and cosmopolitan lifestyle. Because of its location, the Romans had made Ephesus an administrative center for all the regional cities. Religious temples, a sporting arena, and a popular theater were among the beautiful buildings that offered the entire province an entry point into the cultural luxuries of the Empire. A city of over a quarter-million people, the largest in Asia Minor and ranking fourth in the Roman Empire, would warrant this privileged role as the first church to be addressed.

John approved of the church's **hard work and perseverance**, presumably as it is demonstrated in its lack of tolerance for **wicked men**, but reflected in the work ethic of the city they occupied (2:2).

The church at Ephesus was planted in the largest and one of the most religiously active cities in Asia. The exotic temple of Diana (or Artemis, as the Greeks called her) flourished there, not only by providing a pilgrimage site for all those who worshiped in that cult but also by contributing immensely to the city's economy and politics. Paul's visit to Ephesus records his Christian missionary confrontation with that city's silversmiths who made their living making small replicas of the Diana shrine (Acts 19:24–37). For fear that the Christian message would hurt their pagan business; the silversmiths started a riot attempting to stop Paul from proclaiming the gospel.

In just a few decades the Christians in Ephesus went from being the oppressed minority to being the aggressors, in control of the religious culture themselves. The fear of the silversmiths had come to its fruition:

they were out of work and the Christians were as vicious as they had been at keeping the status quo.

No wonder the angel indicts the Ephesians, **"You have forsaken your first love"** (2:4). The Ephesian Christians had to remember their own sinfulness, and their own past lives, **the height from which** they had **fallen** (2:5). This is reminiscent of Paul's admonition to "Remember that you were once . . ." (Eph. 2:11–12).

◣ KEY IDEAS • THE LETTER TO EPHESUS

To: The angel of the church in Ephesus
From: He who holds the seven stars in his hand, who walks among the golden lampstands

- Positive commendation: works, endurance, hate for the Nicolaitans

- Negative condemnation: forsaken first love

- Change needed: repent (twice)

- Reward for overcoming: the right to eat from the tree of life, which is in the paradise of God

- He who has an ear, let him hear what the Spirit says to the churches

---

This rigid intolerance manifested itself in two ways: from within and from without their ranks. The first was through weeding out **wicked men** and false **apostles** (2:2). They seemed fixated on correct teaching and uniformity of thought. This virtue can quickly turn in on itself. Being morally judgmental while crusading against the prevailing evils of society can lead to a lack of compassion and love for the very people that Jesus came to save. It is not enough to be intolerant of the wrong doers of society; the Church must also be active in enabling them to live righteous lives. Apparently the Christian community had succeeded at putting the silversmiths out of business, but they had not contributed to the economy in such a way as to find new livelihood for them. In a similar manner today, campaigning to stop abortions does not necessarily affect the climate that creates millions of unwanted children.

Commonly preachers have referred to this "first love" as a means of encouraging revival of some earlier pious sentiment toward God. We as individuals, or even as a church, are encouraged to go back to some earlier stage of our coming to God and renew that first feeling of affection, much like a married couple reminisces about their first date or early days of courting. This is possible, but given the nature of the history of the Christian mission at Ephesus, there is a need to see a larger social emphasis in the text. Actually, every church or Christian believer could examine his or her motives for evangelism as from the first. What brought about the original passions for ministry is often replaced with feelings of duty, disgust, or even one-upmanship. Love is the only motivator accepted by God for social or spiritual renewal. The Great Commission must never overshadow the Great Commandment.

The letter lauds the Ephesians for their attempts at getting rid of the false teachers from within. But, secondly, they are praised for resisting the influences on them from outside the faithful. Christ approvingly says, **"You hate the practices of the Nicolaitans, which I also hate"** (2:6). We are not called to love everyone! "Hate," in the

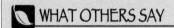

WHAT OTHERS SAY

The church is the church only when it exists for others.
—Dietrich Bonhoeffer

biblical sense, is always a state of separation and rejection. It has little to do with the emotion of disgust, but more to do with definition and refinement. The Nicolaitan group is unknown to us today, but undoubtedly were a part of the Ephesian culture's siren call to compromise. The Ephesians were quick to notice the claims of the gospel on their lives and rejected the advances of any attempt to derail them into paganism.

The letter ends with a promise to be realized at the completion of this church's successful perseverance: **I will give the right to eat from the tree of life, which is in the paradise of God** (2:7). This allusion to the Garden of Eden (Gen. 2–3) revives a frequent theme in Jewish apocalyptic writing, that the end will be a return to the intended beginning. The faithful overcomers are to have God's life-giving presence in their midst. This is a fitting reward for those who **have endured hardships** (2:3) in the name of Christ, even to the death. Gregory Beale also notes that a tree image was long associated with the goddess Artemis, and by extension, with Ephesus itself.[2] For the Ephesians, this right to eat from the true **tree**

of life is vindication for their reluctance to give in to this cult's empty promises.

TO THE CHURCH IN SMYRNA 2:8–11

Smyrna (modern Izmir, also in modern Turkey) is the next city we come to as we follow the trade route; it is just thirty-five miles north of Ephesus. It too was a very significant port city in Asia Minor, but for different reasons. This city had a long and industrious history, known for its commercialism at the time of the writing of the Apocalypse. The urban plan could be recognized in the way the streets and buildings move from the bay up the terraces of the hills the city sat upon. Aqueducts from these hills flowed into the city-state centers giving it its splendorous fountains and refreshment.

Loyal to Rome, the city was a center for imperial worship. Smyrna's national religious history also extends back to the eve of Roman culture. A temple was erected to worship Roma, the goddess of Rome, and, during the Christian era, the city even dedicated a temple to honor the emperor Tiberius.

The letter written to the church at Smyrna has in common with the Philadelphian church this rare claim: Christ only has commendation, and no condemnation, for Smyrna. "**I know your afflictions and your poverty—yet you are rich!**" (2:9). The general tone of this letter is one of understanding, that is, Christ knows the situation at Smyrna. Now we know why the characteristics of the one writing are **the First and the Last, who died and came to life again** (2:8). There is no prophetic concern for the Church at Smyrna to get its act together or even to be obedient. Christ tells the church that He knows their **afflictions** and their **poverty**. People living in extremity know what it is to have pain and suffering buffet them (affliction) and to have no resources to do anything about it (poverty). Christ tells those believers in Smyrna that He knows as well. Some might suggest that the afflictions and poverty that they were experiencing were brought on by a refusal to participate in the imperial cult. This could very well be the case.

We see later in the Revelation that refusing the mark of the beast—the worship of Babylon's power—brings about such deprivation as well. The intricacies that exist between the exercise of religion and economic prosperity are often subtle but vicious. Even in those countries, like America, where the separation of Church and State is a constitutional fixture, prejudice and alienation exist. In any case, the Christians in Smyrna were not in a position to help themselves, even if it meant buying into the system.

On top of this extreme poverty, the Christians at Smyrna also had to

---

 KEY IDEAS • THE LETTER TO SMYRNA

To: The angel of the church in Smyrna
From: Him who is the First and the Last, who died and came to life again

- Positive commendation: afflictions and poverty

- Negative condemnation: none

- Change needed: do not be afraid, be faithful

- Reward for overcoming: will not be hurt at all by the second death

- He who has an ear, let him hear what the Spirit says to the churches

---

endure the abuse or accusations by a group of Jews He calls **a synagogue of Satan** (2:9). They probably were bringing the Roman authorities down on them. If they were a true Jewish people they would have been a support for this messianic sect in Smyrna. Instead this synagogue had learned a technique for continued existence—attack those who the prevailing power attacks. The Jewish alignment with Rome against the Christians appears to have continued into the second century. *The Martyrdom of Polycarp*, a letter describing the death of Smyrna's bishop (circa. A.D. 156), shows the Jews of Smyrna joining in his persecution, even helping to pile up the firewood for the execution. Prohibitions against the alignment of God's people with the enemies of this world go back to the earliest of Old Testament teachings.

The revelation of John seeks to describe God's prophetic fulfillment as a New Jerusalem, one that fulfills the promises to Israel and places the Christian community in that fold. According to Christ's condemnation, the Jews at Smyrna are not a true synagogue, but are working on behalf of Satan. The condemnation is not meant for all Jews, but for those selling out to Rome and the safety that provided.

If the church at Smyrna understands Satan to be the source of their punishment, and not the Jews, they will better understand the suffering that is to come by way of the devil. This affliction will last **ten days** (2:10), a harsh, but endurable period of time. The reward that Christ promises for enduring these hardships is a **crown of life** (2:10). A crown (*stephanos*) was symbolic in the Roman period, generally for victory and status. Often they were awarded to the winners of athletic contests, worn by politicians and dignitaries in processionals, and adorned VIPs at celebrations such as weddings, promotions, and anniversaries. Here those enduring the persecutions of the devil will wear a victor's crown that signifies their victory over death and their new status as accomplished and wealthy.

The encouragement of the letter written to the church at Smyrna should still be felt by the Church today. For one, suffering is given meaning through Christ's words, and those who are poor are shown the true nature of their resources. Furthermore, the picture we see of God's identification with the plight of the marginalized critiques a triumphal view of Christ who wins by worldly ways. As Christianity becomes increasingly competitive with others in the religious market, we must be reminded that Christ's Church is successful by other standards.

We may ask who the current synagogues of Satan are, those who attempt to win over our present powerful cultural forces by attacking the true witnesses of God. The hierarchical pecking order of society has often encouraged those along the strata to step on those beneath it to rise to the next level. Christians and Christian organizations are to understand that lifting up the weaker below makes one stronger. The new satanic synagogue could take many forms: supporting a male dominant church by putting "women in their place," the growth of super-sized churches at the expense of closing the poorer, smaller ones with fewer resources, or even the political alliances Christians make with certain ideological groups to oust differing minority opinions. The Church is always the most dangerous to authentic faith when it has the power to dictate and rule over others.

TO THE CHURCH IN PERGAMUM 2:12–17

Traveling forty-five miles north of Smyrna, we come to the capital city of Pergamum. Dating back to the third century B.C., the city was an important political and military center for the Attalid kingdom. Eventually coming under Roman control by the will of Attalus III in 133 B.C., the city prospered and built numerous buildings on a thriving acropolis complex. The city boasted of one of the greatest libraries in the world, second only to that of Alexandria. Christ locates Pergamum as the place **where Satan has his throne** (2:13). He could be referring to Pergamum's role as a center for emperor worship, depicted through a temple built there for that purpose in 29 B.C. by Caesar Augustus. It could also be a phrase connected with a beautiful altar erected to Zeus or a pantheon of other worship centers for Roman gods (Dionysus, Athena, and Demeter). Regardless, Christ knows Pergamum as a place where Satan is at work. And, as we will see in the drama about to unfold, Satan is not some faceless force or even a myth-like creation of our imaginations. He resides in the real world and, particularly, enjoys setting up shop wherever we build his throne.

Unlike Smyrna before it, Christ is not completely happy with the church of Pergamum. Because the words of this message come from **him who has the sharp, double-edged sword** (2:12, see 1:16), Christ is able to address the church's heretical doctrines with clarity and truth. After affirming their steadfast faith, He declares, "**Nevertheless, I have a few things against you**" (2:14). In this precarious place to live, having

 KEY IDEAS • THE LETTER TO PERGAMUM

To: The angel of the church in Pergamum
From: Him who has the sharp, double-edged sword

- Positive commendation: steadfast in faith, Antipas' martyrdom

- Negative condemnation: some hold to teachings of Balaam and Nicolaitans

- Change needed: repent

- Reward for overcoming: some hidden manna, also a white stone with a new name written on it, known only to him who receives it

- He who has an ear, let him hear what the Spirit says to the churches

Satan's throne in your neighborhood, there are many opportunities to compromise. They have not yet renounced their allegiance to Christ, but they are already dancing around the edges of apostasy.

Despite the possibility of failure, the Pergameme Christians were encouraged to hold fast, even as they were presently resisting the false teachers. **Antipas**, called Christ's **faithful witness** (2;13), is the only named martyr in the book of Revelation. If the rest of the church there were to follow Antipas as faithful witness, Christ promises them **some of the hidden manna** and **a white stone with a new name written on it, known only to him who receives it** (2:17). These cryptic gifts (being **hidden** and **known only to him who receives it**) are both eschatological symbols from Jewish Midrash. Second Baruch taught that the miracle of God's manna would appear again at the end of time. Receiving **hidden manna** would insure the suffering Christian's survival through the wilderness wandering of that confusing time. **White stones** were probably associated with some form of approval process, either judicial or commercial, allowing entrance into God's kingdom at the end of time. As names were thought to have power, even magical, the **new name** written on the stone would provide access for the individual, and for that one alone. The newness would come in the status and character that has occurred through faith in Christ. Throughout the book of Revelation the color white is associated with the final and pure state of victory over sin and death.

Doctrinal indifference usually gives way to heretical acceptance. The city of Pergamum looks much like our modern culture today with its thriving urban life full of cultural wonders and a variety of intellectual pursuits; the pluralism of ideas, both religious and philosophical, calls from all directions. Christ's answer to faithfulness in a world like this was to develop a greater sensitivity to the Word of God and its sword-like swath.

We must not miss the intricate relation that exists between holding fast to sound theology and resisting the ideas of heretics. Too often the Church has responded to an intellectual culture by creating a ghetto of insider beliefs and practices. Teaching our children that education is dangerous to faith or that spiritual people are led astray by too much thinking will not strengthen the Church against the mires of relativistic belief. If Christianity is to exist in the world, it must engage the mind as well as the heart. The Christians at Pergamum were collecting around them people who were well versed in the teaching of Balaam and the Nicolaitans. Apparently they did not know Scripture as well. Christ himself was soon to come to **fight against them with the sword of [his] mouth** (2:16). Despite the numerous war scenes in the book of Revelation, the sword, which proceeds from the mouth of God, is the only offensive weapon available to the army of God. The Church of any age must also be reminded where it must invest its intellectual capital.

TO THE CHURCH IN THYATIRA 2:18–29

The city of Thyatira does not rate very high with most students of ancient Rome. Though it lacks the same luster of its auspicious colleagues of the seven churches, Thyatira's reputation as a commerce center should be noted. Located just a short distance inland from the Aegean Sea, the city was situated at the crossroads of a number of trade routes. The textile industry and its secondary services were quite strong, particularly the production of a rich, purple dye. We remember that Paul while ministering in Philippi discovered a woman from Thyatira named Lydia, who was selling purple cloth (Acts 16:14–15).

The description of the one writing to the church located at Thyatira was **the Son of God, whose eyes are like blazing fire and whose feet**

 KEY IDEAS • THE LETTER TO THYATIRA

To: The angel of the church in Thyatira
From: The Son of God, whose eyes are like blazing fire and whose feet are like burnished bronze

- Positive commendation: love, faith, service, perseverance

- Negative condemnation: tolerate that woman Jezebel

- Change needed: Jezebel and her followers repent; others hold fast

- Reward for overcoming: authority over the nations, the morning star

- He who has an ear, let him hear what the Spirit says to the churches

are like burnished bronze (2:18). A God who is able to see with such purifying focus and who stands on an unwavering platform calls this church to a level of faithfulness that is presently missing. The accumulation of their deeds—**love and faith, service and perseverance (2:19)**—is acknowledged to have progressed for the better. But God is not happy with mere progress, particularly when that progress is mixed with problems. This particular judgment keeps the church from falling into any possibility of works righteousness. As the blazing eyes of the Son of God falls upon such works, any level of compromise is isolated and exposed.

This church has the opposite problem of Ephesus: tolerance. The **woman Jezebel, who calls herself a prophetess** (2:20) was leading the congregants of Thyatira to participate in sexual immorality and other abominations associated with idol worship. An infamous Old Testament woman, Jezebel was the foreign wife of King Ahab who led Israel into Baal worship and pagan practices. The language of sexual immorality blurs the images of idolatry and unfaithfulness so that those who go after her teachings **commit adultery with her** (2:22). And so they will share the same bed of suffering. The woman in this congregation was a type of Jezebel, an insider who is able to be used by the prevailing world order to distract the believers away from God after idolatrous cults.

Tolerance can be taken to an extreme, as with the Corinthian church and their lenient treatment of one of its members who was engaged in some form of sexual incest. Tolerance often becomes an occasion for arrogance. The Thyatirans could say, "Look at how open we are to foreign ideas! We are a liberally-minded city, accepting all manner of customs and cultures!" Sometimes modernity has brought about its own struggle for clarity. The Church, while supported by His feet of bronze, must look through Christ's eyes to show them a pure vision of the world. As they persevere and join the unwavering Christ who rules **with an iron scepter,** they can picture also that **he will dash them to pieces like pottery** (2:27). Perhaps the Christians of Thyatira would remember their past as a city greatly damaged by an earthquake during the reign of Caesar Augustus (27 B.C.–A.D. 14) and recently repaired through Roman aid.

TO THE CHURCH IN SARDIS 3:1–6

Since the seventh century B.C., Sardis (originally the capital of Lydia) was well known for its wealth. Much of the gold that fed into the campaigns of the Lydian, Persian, Greek, and Roman empires was mined in the region. During the Persian period, the city of Sardis functioned as an important outpost, connecting the western part of the empire to the Persian cities of the east by a "royal road." An earthquake ravaged Sardis, along with many other cities of Asia Minor, in A.D. 17, with records showing the emperor Tiberius allotting funds for its rebuilding. By the time of John's writing, Sardis again had become a successful commercial center and had a sizable number of Diaspora Jews living there.

When John writes to the **church in Sardis** he gives them **the words of him who holds the seven spirits of God and the seven stars** (3:1; see also 1:4, 16, 20). If Christ holds the very presence of God himself, and shines that light through the cosmos, He would also be able to recognize a church that no longer had God's presence and life. This church at Sardis sent out a **reputation** for having activity and life in it, but God judges it **dead**. This indicative is followed by an imperative—**"Wake up!"** (Gk. *gregoreo*—"to watch, to be alert"). They are, in fact, **about to die** (3:2). This church, as all faithful churches in this interim time, has something that can be strengthened, remembered, and obeyed. If they repent of their present incomplete state, they can be **dressed in white** (3:5). Their names will be kept inviolate in the book of life, the book that refuses to hold the names of those belonging to dead churches. At this point, the Christ's warning is all-encompassing to this church. The question as to whether anyone in Sardis could find salvation outside of the whole church's repentance is not addressed.

But Christ does acknowledge that not all in Sardis have **soiled their clothes** (3:4). Sardis was a very important city and thought to have been one of the first to have discovered a means of dyeing wool. The production of clothing was connected with this process. Perhaps being dressed in white (no dye) is better than the prideful wearing of the clothes made in Sardis. Certainly having their fashionable garments considered soiled clothing would offend people who prided themselves on wearing only the best.

◤ KEY IDEAS • THE LETTER TO SARDIS

To: The angel of the church in Sardis
From: Him who holds the seven spirits of God and the seven stars

- Positive commendation: a few of them have not soiled their clothes (are worthy)

- Negative condemnation: appear alive, but are actually dead

- Change needed: repent

- Reward for overcoming: be dressed in white, names not blotted out from the book of life, but will acknowledge his name before the Father and His angels

- He who has an ear, let him hear what the Spirit says to the churches

Of all the seven churches, the denunciation of the church in Sardis could be considered the worst. There is really no mention of heretical teachers or specific historic enemies. This church has fallen without a whimper. A form of secularization had stripped the life from the church without any explicit attack, inside or out. Accommodation to the culture itself—akin to falling asleep—is the most dangerous threat to any Christian church. This church does not even have the obvious vices found at Laodicea, the vices of wealth and arrogance that are indicative of her downfall.

The church at Sardis could look like any modern Christian church. From the point of entry into the church's narthex, the visitor might be impressed with the building, the friendliness, and the throbbing excitement of the church's program. But activity and reputation are never the proper indicators of an authentic community of Jesus. Western culture, especially, has developed a view of success and prestige, mostly coming from the exploits of the corporate world alongside the development of the church. If a religious consumer discovers a local church having a full wardrobe of programs, then it is valued as a place of life. It follows that ecclesial marketers will often attempt to extend the church's reputation into the community they wish to attract. Surveying the non-church-going public, they look for positive initial responses: "That's the church to be at!" "There's a lot happening there!" "That church has it all!" Activity alone will not prepare the Church for Christ's coming. But there will always be a loyal opposition within the organization of the church that remains faithful to God's demands. **They will walk with me, dressed in white, for they are worthy** (3:4). Others may join them, but the worthy of the Church knows Him now. Authentic life-giving Christianity is marked by the righteous living of those walking with God.

TO THE CHURCH IN PHILADELPHIA 3:7–13

Just thirty miles southeast of Sardis, the city of Philadelphia was a fertile agricultural region situated in a valley at the base of a mountainous highland region of modern Turkey. The city received extensive damage by the A.D. 17 earthquake. The church in Philadelphia is addressed by the one **who is holy and true, who holds the key of David** (3:7). This description has departed from the literary norm by not taking a phrase out of the previous depictions of Christ in chapter 1. He is **holy and true**. These words often used of God in the Old Testament, and later in 6:10, are used of Jesus Christ. The **key of David** is found in Isaiah 22:22 where God gives Eliakim the authority to have access to Hezekiah's palace. The revelation had started with a vision of Christ with "the keys of death and of Hades" in His hands (1:18). Having such keys, Christ is able to open doors that have been barred to mortals.

Similarly to the church at Smyrna, the church at Philadelphia was facing persecution from a group of Jews who is called a synagogue of

 KEY IDEAS • THE LETTER TO PHILADELPHIA

To: The angel of the church in Philadelphia

From: Him who is holy and true, who holds the key of David; what He opens no one can shut, and what He shuts no one can open

- Positive commendation: faithful to Christ and true to the Word

- Negative condemnation: none

- Change needed: hold on to what you have

- Reward for overcoming: pillar in the temple, the name of God written on them, the city of God, the new Jerusalem, and a new name

- He who has an ear, let him hear what the Spirit says to the churches

Satan, **who claim to be Jews though they are not, but are liars** (3:9; see also 21:8). We may ask again if the sectarian character of the Christians had caused the Jewish community to isolate them or if there is even more foundational issues at stake. How Israel relates to the newly formed community of Christ is at issue throughout the Apocalypse. Jewish resistance to any paternalistic theology would have been expected, but Christ would eventually force them to fall down at the church's feet and acknowledge that He has loved them (3:9).

The reward for this church's perseverance is an **open door** that no one will be able to shut (3:8). Generally, in the Bible, an "open door" refers to a divinely appointed opportunity (1 Cor. 16:9; 2 Cor. 2:12), but in this case it is an invitation to join in God's fellowship. They will become a pillar in that fellowship. This City of Brotherly Love will become a place of belonging for these overcomers. Their impoverished and weakened state will not remove them from this city. One of the most painful human drives is that of the need to belong. Social status and cultural divisions have created a world where the marginalized—those having **little strength** (power)—are unable to find a place to belong. The promise to this church is that God will finally provide such a place.

Many are seeking to understand this powerful reason for being for the Church today. We know more about the nature of mass psychology than ever before. Architectural aesthetics, small group activity, and the process of assimilation are all used to bring the socially unattached into the fold. But for God, community is more than the experience of belonging; it includes Kingdom content and order. It is a gift from God. As in the Sermon on the Mount, we are aware that most people of this world have a place to belong, but the poor are given the Kingdom, specifically because they have no place in this world to live. This nameless group of people will be given **the name of my God** (3:12). They will have a home that is new, where no one can take away their crown.

TO THE CHURCH IN LAODICEA 3:14–22

The city of Laodicea was just ten miles from another biblical city in the same Lycus River valley—Colosse. The city was self-sufficient, boasting of a strong economic community, a reputable medical school, and, like a few of the other Asia Minor cities, was skilled in textile manufacturing. The city's location made it a crossroads for merchants traveling to and from Ephesus to western Asia Minor, and between the north-south points of Pergamum and Sardis.

Laodicea was known for its courts that heard many legal cases throughout the region and the use of the city's banks for depositing significant imperial economic funding. History records a number of earthquakes hitting cities throughout Asia Minor (besides the A.D. 17 quake, the city was hit again in A.D. 60—near the time of the writing of the Revelation). Laodicea is noted for having refused financial help from the Empire, repairing the extensive damage by means of its own coffers.

The church of Laodicea receives much press by contemporary preachers. It is the poster child for laziness and worldliness. Conversely, the one who writes to it is **the Amen, the faithful and true witness, the ruler of God's creation** (3:14) and, therefore, is the most credible judge to assess a church's authenticity. The Hebrew word "amen" is, in fact, appositional to the phrase that follows—"faithful and true." In the midst of this crumbling world, Jesus Christ, the unshakable foundation, writes to His Church.

The Laodicean Church is full of arrogance and pride, and yet Christ sees them as having no stable character. The church is **neither cold nor hot** (3:15). He is about to **spit** (3:16) them from His mouth. What an indignity to see the Lord Jesus spitting, the Greek word being closer in spirit to the act of vomiting. Many preachers have reminded us of the water supply at Laodicea that would give special meaning to the readers of this letter. Six miles away, hot springs, with health inducing mineral deposits, were found in the mountains visible to the inhabitants of that city. On the other hand, the city of Colosse, just a few miles in the other direction, contained an ever-bubbling stream of clear, cold water for its drinking supply. Laodicea's water was neither; it stunk and its stagnant warmth caused an immediate revulsion. This **lukewarm** quality of this church is in direct contrast to the one who is **the faithful and true witness** (3:14).

This lukewarm character of this church is described in detail. They view themselves self-sufficient, rich, healthy, and well clothed. Since they no longer have to fight and scrape for sustenance, they have lulled themselves into a mediocre existence. On the other hand, Christ knows them to be **wretched, pitiful, poor, blind and naked** (3:17). Despite the many sermons that have been preached to imply that this church's lukewarmness was

---

📖 KEY IDEAS • THE LETTER TO LAODICEA

To: The angel of the church in Laodicea
From: The Amen, the faithful and true witness, the ruler of God's creation

- Positive commendation: none

- Negative condemnation: lukewarm, think they are rich but they are poor

- Change needed: repent

- Reward for overcoming: the right to eat and sit with Christ on His throne, just as He overcame and sat down with His Father on His throne

- He who has an ear, let him hear what the Spirit says to the churches

---

being judged for a lack of pious luster or vibrant worship, the rebuke of the Lord is related more to their self-serving social status. These people did not need a revival of the camp meeting kind as much as they needed a jolt to their conscience and a passionate return to a faithful and just way of living.

Christ has an antidote for their problem. If this church is desirous of riches, Christ will sell them a refined gold so that they can **become rich** (3:18. But the fire that refines this gold is probably associated with a more difficult life than they would seek for themselves. The refining process usually requires intense persecution and suffering, but from this will come a reward more enduring than economic gain.

If fashionable clothing is what they want, then Christ will give them **white clothes to wear**, with the result that it covers their **shameful nakedness**. Again, white clothes are seen throughout the revelation as a symbol for the rewards of those who have stained their clothes with the blood of martyrdom.

Finally, the **salve** that Christ gives freely is far better than the medicinal salve that the Laodiceans were reputed for all over the world. This salve will allow them to **see**. Churches, like the one at Laeodicea, enjoy their privilege and cultural acceptance so much that they forget that the norm for Christian existence is to be experienced in the extremes. The suffering church is where Christ takes up His residence.

The Christian people at Laodicea could have answered Christ with a sense of incredibility. After all, this church was not skirting with doctrinal heresies or involving itself in overt idolatry. Their worst confession before God is that they **do not need a thing** (3:17). To Christ's ears this is even more repulsive than if the Laodiceans were apostate. Being self-sufficient is the most grievous of idolatries because it is worship of the self. Those churches that claim to have everything lack the most important ingredient to ecclesial success: dependence on Christ. They have taken no risks; they have banked on their full accounts and resources.

Laodicea is the only of the seven churches to receive no credit for any good virtue. Even the church of Sardis, who had a reputation for being alive but Christ called "dead," had within it a remnant of faithful that could be strengthened. The church at Laodicea was not a mixture of hot and cold, faithful and unfaithful, but was made up of a bland constituency of cultured Christianity. Christ's taste buds are repulsed by such food. But even this church is given a chance to change. Christ will not only enjoy the after taste of this converted church, but He will invite them to eat with Him and to experience the feast of the overcomers.

The reward for the Laodicean church is compared here to that of Jesus' victory over death: **the right to sit with me on my throne, just as I overcame and sat down with my Father on his throne** (3:21). The church that is able to repent of its gluttony, arrogance, and pride, will find itself seated on the heavenly throne with Him. But just as in Philippians 2, the means by which Christ ascended to sit at the right hand of the Father is a downwardly progression of emptying and humility. This church must learn that God will elevate those who are cast down and bring down those who are elevated.

As we have seen, the seven ancient churches of Asia Minor have many of the same concerns we still have today. With all of the new means of "doing church," we are in need of a message to the angel of the Church to keep her on course until the end of the age. While our churches seek to respond to the desperate needs of our society, they must continue to remain faithful to the apostolic message as it was from the beginning. The right blend of tolerance and intolerance is crucial if we are to help our hurting world without soiling ourselves in the process. Cultural accommodation and belonging are issues of relevance that must be addressed in every age.

The only two churches to receive no condemnation from Christ are Smyrna and Philadelphia. Both of these churches were poor alongside their contemporary standard. The church in Smyrna had no wealth; Philadelphia had no power (little strength). God's priority for the poor is noted in this theology of the Church. When Christ's Church reflects the worth that comes with the good news of the Kingdom, the Church is closest to being an authentic witness for the gospel. The other five churches, from one degree to another, found themselves in some form of accommodation to the world, whether religious or secular. They viewed themselves as successful by measurements always known to humankind: wealthy, prosperous, and creatively constructive. Churches like these would have had spreadsheets with positive balances and growth charts with climbing graphics. Their bank accounts and endowments would be safeguarded from any sporadic stock market swings. Others would have spoken well of them, and they would have counted themselves among the smug and proud. Living in a hostile world should not hinder the Church from holy living. This prophecy stands as a warning to all churches that find themselves successful alongside their worldly counterparts.

ENDNOTES

1. Gerhard Ebeling, "The Beginnings of Christian Theology in *Apocalypticism*," ed. Robert W. Funk, *Journal for Theology and the Church*, 6 (New York, 1969), 58.

2. Gregory K. Beale. *The Book of Revelation: A Commentary on the Greek Text* (Grand Rapids: William B. Eerdmans Publishing Company, 1998).

3

THE THRONE
IN HEAVEN

Revelation 4:1–5:14

The initial vision of a magnificent being sitting on a throne in heaven first appears as a parenthetical image before the actual revelation itself. This, however, becomes the source from which all other statements about the character of God are revealed.

Jürgen Roloff identifies four thematic sections to Revelation (1–3; 4–11; 12–19:10; and 19:11–22:21); the last three grow out of the throne vision in 4:1–5:14, which he calls "the theological fulcrum of the entire book."[1] Many works of art have attempted to grasp the splendor of this scene, but they have either succumbed to a bazaar literalism or to an abstraction unable to fully exhaust the symbolism.

The role that this section plays as an introduction to the rest of the vision (chapters 6–20) is obvious. A peek into the "war room" of the Lamb prefigures the ultimate control that God holds over the end of all things when righteousness is victorious and evil is condemned to utter destruction. We certainly do not see a throne room in chaotic disarray, in desperation or confusion. The Lamb is on the throne, and all are worshiping God. Things are as they should be—and prefigure things as they soon will be.

THE THRONE IN HEAVEN 4:1–11

After this (4:1), marks a new division of material where John now begins his prophecy of **what must take place** (4:1). Many commentators, when trying to discern an outline in the book, have used this line of demarcation to separate what they believe to be what was taking place during the time of John (chapters 1–3) and what is to take place in the future (chapter 4 on). This obviously supports a futurist view of the book, but it does not take into account that even the first three chapters have impending judgments attached to them.

What we are to notice is what John noticed, **a door standing open** (4:1). An open door, as with rolled back-heavens and open clouds, often carries with it the idea of an epiphany of divine revelation. What was once hidden is now open for all to see. We are not being told something that must wait some future disclosing. Like Moses being called to the top of Mount Pisgah, the church is given a roof top view. Some have attempted to interpret this vantage as connected to a rapture of the Church prior to the tribulations that are about to occur (**what must take place after this**, 4:1). This phrase—"**Come up here!**"—is used again when the two witnesses are called up to heaven in the sight of their enemies (11:12). For John and his fellow Christians, the door to the future is open, and we are invited to come up to it in order that we might behold all.

Along with this strong visual revelation is the sound of a voice **like a trumpet** (4:1). Besides being a blaring, unquestionable sound, the trumpet is generally associated with the heralding of messianic events in the Bible. We are reminded by the trumpet quality that we have heard this same voice before (1:10). This has the effect of grabbing John's attention and directing him deeper into the mystery.

John is at once **in the Spirit** (4:2). The experience described by the phrase "in the Spirit" occurs four times for John in the Revelation. Once it is a part of the initial setting describing the entire revelatory experience of John (1:10). The other three uses are at the beginning of significant visions: a vision of the throne of Christ (4:1–11); a vision of Babylon the Prostitute (17:3–6); and then of the Holy City Jerusalem (21:9–14).

Because the phrase describes a particular manner by which John is capable of interpreting large, expansive ideas, some commentators have found the formula "in the Spirit" instructive to the literary structure. The themes might divide along these lines: (1) from 1:10, an introduction to the book; (2) from 4:1–11, a view of God in history; (3) from 17:3–6, the true nature of evil in the world; and (4) from 21:9–14, a hopeful glimpse of a redeemed world.

Scholars have pointed to two different styles of apocalyptic mediation. One is usually a direct discourse with a divine agent, such as an angel or prophet. We have seen this style of apocalyptic up to this point. The second, often called an "otherworldly journey," takes the seer to secret places, such as the heavens or the ends of the earth or history, places normally left inaccessible to mortal beings. The Apostle Paul referred to such an experience in 2 Corinthians 12:2.

The apocalypses with otherworldly journeys generally have the seer taken up into various vantage points, and then whisk him away to new and varied sights along the way. In the case of the Revelation, John's journey is very truncated, the literature only mentioning his being carried "in the Spirit into the desert" to see the Great Prostitute Babylon (17:3), and then being taken "in the Spirit to a mountain great and high" from which to see the Holy City, Jerusalem (21:10). John may need a "spiritual" insight at these points for a reason. He wishes to show that a proper vision of Christ as Lord includes insights into the world powers as well as the kind of world God is calling us to inhabit. Being "in the Spirit" does not call us out of the world and into some surreal plane, but rather it gives us a vision of the way the world is and can be in Christ.

The throne room of God holds a prominent place in the Revelation of John (4–5; 7:9–17; 11:15–19; 19:4–8; 20:11–15; and 22:3). The Old Testament often depicted God as ruling the world from such a place (Ps. 47:8). Thrones were symbols of power and authority. Christians faced with bowing to an omnipresent Roman throne are given a view of the true Sovereign of the world. As great as Roman power could be, this throne room is a multiple of such power, as **surrounding the throne were twenty-four other thrones** (4:4). A perpetual problem of the first-century Christians was their inability to see the proper role that human thrones had over them. The book of Hebrews said it this way: "Yet at present we do not see everything subject to him. But we see Jesus" (Hebrews 2:8, 9).

Seeing Jesus as Lord over the entire world, and yet experiencing persecution, poverty, and hunger at the subjugation of earthly powers, must have been a very confusing experience for these Christians. For people not in these extreme situations, this revelation may pose other problems of allegiance. Because we sense ourselves being in subjection to earthly powers, we believe Christ is as well. We now see who really sits on the throne, and we must soon choose whom we are going to bow before.

A vision of Christ seated on the throne becomes the key to unlocking all of the mystery of life for Christians in any age. But wait! As we are seeing the vision along with John, we do not yet know the identity of this honored one. We notice along with him **a throne in heaven with someone sitting on it** (4:2). Since the throne is in heaven, our interests are piqued, but if we were taking this picture of the one sitting on the throne literally, we would have a very strange sight indeed. It is obvious that the sensory language being used by the writer is one that seeks to pull from images well known to the reading audience. Many of them are taken directly from Old Testament references used generally by the synagogue-going public.

Twenty centuries later, the meaning of some of those images may be lost to us; some may have been esoteric even to the contemporaries of John. Just as we have many different metaphors to invoke psychological responses today, so did the first century reader. When we say, "He has nerves of steel," we do not imply that a man has actual metallic elements making up the synapses of his physical body. Clichés such as "She has a chip on her shoulder," or "He has his nose to the grindstone," have idiomatic meanings that do not communicate cross-culturally without added explanation. In the same way, a person would be wise to be immersed in the world of the Hebrew Scripture, as well as have a good background in Roman social life, before letting the imagination loose on the ensuing visions.

John first notes the **appearance** of the one sitting on the throne as **jasper and carnelian**, even around the throne was a **rainbow, resembling an emerald** (4:3). The obvious connection made with rare, shining, and crystal-like jewels is to evoke a sense of God's splendor and awe-inspiring appearance. Rather than trying to discover a meaning found in the actual jewel or rare material, more important is the connection made with its source in the throne or chariot of God found in Ezekiel 1. There the language of "sparkling" gems (Ezek. 1:16, 22) is highlighted. And though it may be tempting to make a connection with the rainbow in the Genesis account, emphasizing the mercy of God in His coming judgments, the source in Ezekiel shows the role it plays in supporting the glorious image of the throne. "Like the appearance of a rainbow in the clouds on a rainy day, so was the radiance around him" (Ezek. 1:28).

Our gaze cannot stay on the center for long. We begin to notice the surrounding area, with its twenty-four thrones. **Seated on them were twenty-four elders** (4:4). These elders are found in various settings worshiping God in heaven (4:10; 5:5–14; 7:11–17; 11:16–18; 14:3; 19:4). The number **twenty-four** may represent the universal Church as it is discovered in the addition of the twelve tribes of Israel (Old Testament) with the twelve apostles of Christ (New Testament). They wore the **white** clothing of the redeemed, and victory **crowns of gold on their heads** (19:4).

The atmosphere of the throne room is charged with **flashes of lightning,** and **rumblings and peals of thunder** (4:5) hit the ears. These are the biblical sounds associated with the might and power of God Almighty (refer to Mt. Sinai descriptions in Exod. 19) and are used throughout the book of Revelation to set the proper tone for activity within the heavenly temple (see 8:5; 11:19 and 16:18).

In front of the throne **seven lamps were blazing** (4:5). We are told that **these are the seven spirits of God** or sevenfold Spirit (4:5). Many have tried to write significance into the number seven here, but we must remember, seven is a number of wholeness, completion, and perfection. Rather than viewing this as a seven-part spirit of God, it symbolizes the absolute perfection of the spirit of God.

Before the throne **was what looked like a sea of glass, clear as crystal** (4:6). Again, we can find the source for this image coming from Ezek. 1:22.

In the center, around the throne, were four living creatures (4:6). The image of being in the center, yet around the throne, is a bit difficult to imagine. These creatures appear to be as close to God as the inner circle of worship allows in this heavenly scene. They provide the extension of God's *shekinah* glory into the temple proper but allow us to participate in that worship by virtue of their earthly connections.

Ezekiel's angelic beings had four faces (a lion, an ox, a man and an eagle, Ezek. 1:6, 10); the apocalyptic quartet here has only one face (the man), but each living creature had the qualities of these various animate creatures. Each **living creature was like** a **lion**, an **ox**, a **man**, a **flying eagle**. All attempts at getting at the scope of the created world by way of interpreting the sphere—that is, the wild, the tame, the civilized, the air—that each of these animals represent falls prey to mere allegory. It is enough to know that the Creator has extended into the creation the qualities of strength and power that now pay homage to its origin. Because they are completely covered with eyes (even under their wings!), these creatures are shown to be all-knowing and perceptive to the things of God. Their multiple wings allow them to be swift in carrying out this known will of God. Their lone purpose and duty is to state a perpetual creed of God's being and quality. This ancient understanding of God is tied closely to the most holy name for God—Yahweh, "the one who is (or will be). All the creation, represented by these four, resonates with the song of the universe:

> **"Holy, holy, holy is the Lord God Almighty, who was, and is, and is to come."**

Every time **the living creatures give glory, honor and thanks** (4:9), the **twenty-four elders** prostrate themselves in front of the throne. But unlike the song of the heavenly creatures, which was sung into the air filling the throne chamber with the holiness attributes of God Almighty, the elders sing their praise directly to God. The first words out of their mouth—**"You are worthy!"** (4:11) were the welcoming words to the emperor as he processed into the Roman polis. The next phrase, **"Our Lord and God,"** was language created by Domitian to celebrate his divine status in the Imperial cult.[2] It is also of interest that these twenty-four elders add the word **"power"** (4:11) to the heavenly creatures' earlier offerings of "glory and honor" (4:9). Given the coming chapters describing the horrific events that are about to take place, it is important that the readers know who truly has the power to control their fate. Hence, the elders **lay their crowns before the throne** (4:10) acknowledging where the source off all power and authority resides. If even the Church's apostolic authority is seen to come from the throne of God, then certainly the authority of Rome must be submissive to God as well.

> **"You are worthy, our Lord and God,**
> **to receive glory and honor and power,**
> **for you created all things,**
> **and by your will they were created**
> **and have their being."**

The emphasis upon God's role as Creator in this hymn settles all questions of ultimate authority. Just as God silenced the whining Job with the query, "Where were you when I laid the earth's foundation?" (Job 38:4), all would-be contenders for authority are checked just as the ultimate depiction of God's control over the cosmos is to be shown.

THE SCROLL AND THE LAMB 5:1–14

ONE CANNOT LIVE WITHOUT HOPE 5:1–5

At the start of this chapter, our focus is immediately taken to a scroll. It is held by God (**him who sat on the throne**) and is controlled by Him (**in the right hand**, 5:1).

The image of a scroll containing God's hidden plans in history has been used before in Scripture. Daniel, in particular, had mentioned a prophecy remaining sealed until the end of time (Dan. 12:4–9; also see Isa. 29:11). John uses this imagery now to describe Christian history as representing this revealing time, the Last Days. It may also be important to note that the scroll was written **on both sides** (5:1), signifying the completion of all things hidden. But also, it would appear, that some of the writing was visible to the human eye, without the breaking of the seals. To be able to read the outer wording of the meaning of history is not enough; we must have the hidden, inner meaning if we are to live. But still, God does not hold even this inner meaning hostage. It is not some secret left only to Him. He holds it out in His hand for all to see.

The actor in this revelation has been spinning around, searching for clues to the secrets that are about to be disclosed. He is like a dizzy child in a cyclorama at Disney World, trying to take in all of the visuals and audios at once. The frustration comes to a climax with this weeping prophet as the elders call out: "**Do not weep! See . . .**" (5:5).

It is not important that the prophet—or anyone else for that matter—knows the contents of the scroll. Even though, by knowing, he would no longer feel anxious about the past, present, and future of God's will. It is enough to know that someone is able to break the seals, open the book, and put his mind at ease.

Emile Durkheim, the father of modern sociology, wrote in his classic study of suicide, "If therefore industrial or financial crises increase suicide, this is not because they cause poverty, since crises of prosperity have the same result; it is because they are crises, that is, disturbances of the collective order."[3] People will despair if they are given no cohesive social meaning. History without meaning is too painful to bear. Durkheim argued that religion provides society with this cohesive meaning; the Apostle John tells us that it is Christ alone that does this.

CHRIST ALONE IS SUFFICIENT FOR LIFE 5:6–8

The elders had announced to John that the "Lion of the tribe of Judah" was worthy to open the scroll. But as John is spun around one more time to see his redemption, he does not see a Lion, but a Lamb. And not just any Lamb. A Lamb **looking as if it had been slain** (5:6). We are reminded of another John, the Baptist, earlier in the life of Jesus pointing at the Savior and proclaiming, "Look, the Lamb of God, who takes away the sin of the world!" (John 1:29). Typical of Christians, we go looking for lions and find our salvation in a Lamb.

The strength of Christ's position is emphasized through His death and resurrection. The picture of a lamb **standing**, even though it appears to have been slain carries this strange belief in a Messiah who, though thought dead, is now at **the center of the throne**. The spatial limitations of God, the Father, being on the throne, and the Lamb now standing at the center of the throne are not logical. But the imagery conveys the idea that the Lamb is worthy of the same adoration as the former occupant of that seat. Therefore, the Lamb is God.

This Lamb motif certainly brings to mind the atoning sacrifice of the paschal lamb. Paul made this connection as well: "For Christ, our Passover lamb, has been sacrificed" (1 Cor. 5:7). The costliness of that act, and His substitution for us, permits Him to be the only one worthy to open the scroll in our place. We discover this in the later praises to Jesus as His "blood has ransomed people for God" (Rev. 5:9, NLT).

The Lamb is a sacrifice for sin, but the Revelation also focuses attention on the resurrected side of the power of the Lamb. He only appears to have been slain. He has **triumphed** (5:5). The horns symbolize power (potency) and eyes, His all-seeing knowledge, both of which He possesses in the fullest of power indicated by the quantity of seven. The seven spirits that emanate from this power indicate the fullness of the Spirit with which Christ is endowed and which He passes on to His Church.

When one's despair gives way to a vision of the Christ of history, worship is the only legitimate response.

A NEW SONG 5:9–14

The major sections of the Apocalypse are framed in a liturgical setting. We find the book of Revelation erupting in praises and adoration to God in the midst of the signs of the decay of history. Some commentators have noted a move in these worship settings from that of a celestial choir to that of common humanity. Eventually the Church, and all creation, joins in the songs of heaven, what John calls a **new song** (5:9).

Because the risen Christ alone can disclose the secrets of life to the believing Church, He alone can be praised. He is praised by the four living creatures, by the elders (5:8–10), by a whole host of angels (5:11–12) and by all creation (5:13–14.) The church's first theology was sung. Long before the Church developed conceptual categories for the Trinity or for Christology, the believers expressed their theology through doxology. In other words, as the Church prays, so it believes.

One of the central beliefs spelled out in John's revelation is that Jesus Christ is God. The same sevenfold virtue given to the Father Creator in chapter 4 (4:11) is now given to Christ as the one worthy **to receive power and wealth and wisdom and strength and honor and glory and**

93

praise (5:12). These virtues are the prize for which human destiny claws its way through history to achieve. We are now aware that Jesus Christ is the only one worthy to receive them.

Worship has become the church issue of the age. Just how we do it has preoccupied pastoral table talks for a decade. New technologies and a keener sense of mass psychology have created a powerfully seductive environment for worship. We must be careful that these fixations on method do not replace the substance of the worship experience. We have become acutely aware of the psychology of human experience. Worship, from the human side, is deeply experiential and subjective. At the same time, it must be rooted in the real history that such deep experience evokes, the object of our worship, Jesus Christ.

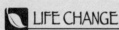

LIFE CHANGE

THE OBJECT OF OUR WORSHIP

A danger the church faces is the temptation to emphasize the individual experience over worship of God. It is easy to put so much emphasis on the setting or the technology that we forget the reason we have gathered. Music, technology, and even the building are merely tools to aid us in worship; we need to be sure the methods do not distract from worship. Worshiping the One to whom all glory, honor, and praise is due must always be our purpose. However from our perspective, worship is deeply experiential and subjective, so we have different tastes and preferences as we worship. What sights, sounds, and smells help you focus on God?

If there is one thing that can be learned from these major worship sections in the Revelation of John, it is that worship is not a programmatic issue: it is a response to our experience of Christ in history. True worship, as Jesus said, is not confined to church buildings or mountaintops. It is found wherever God is active—in the plain of human history. True worship does not come about by removing ourselves from our mundane lives, but rather it is discovered in the midst of it.

Wouldn't it be a great application of this lesson if during this week you found yourself—while reading the newspaper or watching CNN—breaking out in praise to Jesus Christ? After a week of worshiping Christ in the midst of the flow of world events, your personal worship next Sunday could not help but be affected!

ENDNOTES

1. Jürgen Roloff, *The Revelation of John: A Continental Commentary* (Minneapolis: Fortress Press, 1993), 15–17.

2. Suetonius, *The Life of Domitian*, 13. "With no less arrogance he began as follows in issuing a circular letter in the name of his procurators, 'Our Lord and our God bids that this be done.' And so the custom arose of henceforth addressing him in no other way even in writing or in conversation."

3. Emile Durkheim, *Suicide* (Paris: Alcan), 1897.

4

OPENING
THE SEVEN SEALS

Revelation 6:1-6:17

The breaking of the seven seals initiates the first of three series of sevens depicting the eschatological woes of the book of Revelation. Jewish apocalyptic expectations for an outbreak of catastrophic events preceding the Day of the Lord and the coming Messiah come from a variety of Old Testament and apocryphal texts. Sometimes these woes are to be experienced only by the wicked oppressors of God's people; sometimes God's chosen would need to go through the tribulations as a way of testing their true endurance and faithfulness. By unleashing these woes with the opening of the scroll, John is shown that he and his fellow persecuted believers are about to see the end to their wait for vindication. The vision may carry with it a sense of dread even for the righteous, but these events were now signaling a hope to the culmination of their present suffering.

The first interpretive question to be addressed by this literary phenomenon is whether the three series are to be taken as a successive, chronological order of events, or if the three (seals, trumpets, bowls) represent the same events repeated with variations on a theme. When one studies the literary sources of these three symbols of end-time tribulation, the latter appears to offer a better explanation for the literary approach used by this series of seven. When one compares the succession of woes found in the seals with those eschatological texts of the Gospels we see that both appear to rely heavily upon a pool of readily available beliefs about the catastrophes at the end of the world.[1]

THE FIRST FOUR SEALS: THE FOUR HORSEMEN 6:1–8

Finally John gets to see what he was longing for: the opening of the seals that would unlock the knowledge that he so desperately desired. John **watched** as the Lamb began the countdown of the breaking of the seals. In parallel sequence, each of **four living creatures** surrounding the Lamb commands a horse and its rider to "**Come!**"(6:1). (Perhaps the better translation is "Go!") The four living creatures function as announcers and initiators of each of the horrid events that unfold. The difficulty of attributing the command that brings such trouble to the world to God has led to numerous variants in the manuscript tradition. The phrase "Come and see" (the reading of the NKJV) redirects the command to John. Because it is more difficult to reconcile with the narrative, the reading that understands "Come!" as directed to the four horsemen is probably the original meaning. Elsewhere in the book of Revelation, the invitation to come is formulaic, especially as John is invited into the great reward at the closure of the prophecy (22:17). It may also carry with it the idea of a separation from the visionary's present vantage or even the way of Babylon and the world (18:4.) We are constantly told that the Lord will come, and the benediction says, "Come, Lord Jesus!" (22:20).

Throughout the book an invitation to participate in the vision is seen as a graced experience, one that makes the hearer whole and well. In this instance, the command is merely a means of directing the script. The horses thunder onto the stage at the beckon call of God. The most obvious Old Testament antecedent for these four horsemen is found in Zech. 6:1–8. In that context God sends out four groups of different colored horses to roam throughout the earth bringing punishment to those nations afflicting Israel. God is in control of all things, even this punishment of the world.

When the first seal is opened, a **white horse** comes galloping onto the scene. The color **white** may suggest that this horse carries its rider with holiness, righteousness, and purity. Since this is the way the color white is used throughout the book of Revelation, we are on tiptoe to see who this might be. We quickly discover that **its rider held a bow, and he was**

given a crown, and he rode out as a conqueror bent on conquest (6:2). These attributes have caused many commentators to suggest that this rider is Christ himself. The white color, the crown, and the title of "conqueror" are all suggestive of the Risen Christ, riding as the gospel truth through history.

Adding to this interpretation is the reappearance of a rider on a white horse in chapter 19 who is explicitly identified as "Faithful and True." He, too, "judges and makes war" (19:11). Those who make this connection presuppose that when the Revelation uses a symbol, such as a color or a theme, it must always be interpreted the same way throughout. With apocalyptic literature this is an unproven, even risky, assumption. But, in most cases, it is a way of allowing the book to interpret itself.

The difficulty of interpreting the symbolism here with the same person in chapter 19, however, is that Christ is then lumped together with the subsequent three horsemen of war, famine, and death, a rather motley crew for Jesus to be riding alongside. If one is inclined to believe that the providence of God carries with it the pestilence and death that is now wreaking havoc on the earth, then this situation may make sense. But perhaps the better line of reasoning is to accept this horseman as just the beginning of a series of horribly destructive powers coming at the Christian community—as well as the whole world. In this case, we might see the "conqueror" as representing militarism and power in general, holding his **bow** and wearing a victor's **crown**. The bow is a common Old Testament symbol for military might. Jeremiah prophesied that the Babylonian armies would be captured and "their bows [would] be broken" (Jer. 51:56). The crown might better be thought of as a wreath worn after battle by victorious Caesars. Bruce Metzger has suggested that this cluster of symbols fits well with the depiction of a Parthian warrior.[2]

On the eastern border of the Roman Empire, Parthia was always a military threat breathing down the neck of Rome. The readers of the Revelation would have recognized the first horse as the constant fear of military invasion, now happening before their eyes. As with any generation of nations, an "axis of evil" feeds the fear of impending war. Real armies with weapons and strength are always waiting to be unleashed on the world.

The idea that this conqueror **was given** his crown might lend some support that God's sovereign will allows the success of this rider even before he goes on his mercenary adventure. Usually the use of the passive "given" in Revelation implies that God allows and initiates this power. Once these four horsemen are all in full attack mode, we are told that they are given power **to kill by sword, famine and plague** (6:8). This methodological trilogy coincides with the second, third, and fourth horsemen; the first horseman may be the general spirit of "killing" or conquest. Of course, it might also lend credence to the former interpretation that the first rider is to be identified with Christ, being different in kind from the trilogy that follows.

A further development of our thinking on this theme might suggest to us that the later literary connection with chapter 19 is not irrelevant. The revelator likes to expose counterfeits to the Risen Lord, and in the first seal, we could be beholding a "Christlike" figure. As the Lamb opens the seal, at first glance, John might be led to say, "Hurray! The Christ is now coming!" But soon he is driven into the realities of this revelation: suffering must precede redemption. Unlike the Lamb, who appeared to be slain, this rider holds a bow, a symbol of strength and military prowess. This rider is also given a mere crown, significantly less than the horseman of chapter 19 who has many crowns on his head. The rider of the white horse may look like Christ, but its way of doing things is quite different. All power comes from God, but the misuse of power brings about disturbing consequences.

Military power will never be the answer the Christian Church desires because it only brings with it more devastation and violence. Those who go out **bent on conquest** (6:2) will do so by riding their horses of righteousness. Few wars have been fought that the bureaucracies and governments that sent their soldiers did not believe they were doing so with the full support of God. During World War II, the allied forces were reading the same Bible that Hitler's troops were reading. Both had chaplains praying them into battle. The spirit of militarism rides hard throughout history and, when coupled with religious zeal, is the vilest of human evils.

The second horse, **a fiery red one** (6:4), arrives with the opening of the second seal. The significance of the color **red** could be associated with its satanic origin. We will discover this to be the color of the dragon (who is Satan) in chapter 12. But it must also be noted that this is the color of the blood of the martyrs, showing the murderous wake of this horse's trail. The color red probably is emblazoned on this horse because it thrives on blood and seeks to spill it wherever it may.

The rider on this horse was given power **to take peace**

LIFE CHANGE

BLESSED ARE THE PEACE-MAKERS

Jesus reminds His disciples that those who live by the sword will die by the sword and, most important, "God blesses those who work for peace, for they will be called the children of God" (Matt. 5:9, NLT). The days recorded in Revelation show there will be no peace. As a Christian, how can you bring peace even when the rest of the world seems to be full of unrest, evil, and violence? In what ways can you encourage peace even in chaos?

from the earth and to make men slay each other. This is represented by the presentation of a **large sword**, the means of this slaying. Because the symbol of the sword is such a powerful one in the book of Revelation, one must be careful not to apply too much to this particular instance. The sword coming from Christ's mouth (1:16; 19:15) utilizes the same metaphor found in Eph. 6:17, representing the penetrating and winsome power of God's Word. This is in contradiction to the use of the sword by this rider. He uses his sword to kill and to make others kill. We will note that the message of Revelation takes the same non-violent stance taught by the historical Jesus. "If anyone is to be killed with the sword, with the sword he will be killed. This calls for patient endurance and faithfulness on the part of the saints" (13:10). A bigger and better army will not beat the armies that are formed against God's children. Armageddon has received much attention from this literature, reflecting a grand battle of good and evil taking place on the earth. What is more striking to the reader is the constant redirection of our attention to the throne room in heaven where peace and calm reign. God is never fearful of losing a battle; so neither should the Church.

Immediately the third seal is opened and so comes the next wave of suffering. A third rider appears mounted on a **black horse . . . holding a pair of scales in his hand** (6:5). **Black** has often portrayed the psychological correspondence to evil, darkness, and death. At the opening of the sixth seal, the sun turned black (6:12), probably suggesting the opposite of the life-giving light of the sun. It is no wonder that darkness is the motif of this rider. He carries with him the economic depression that all humanity fears. What sounds like a voice coming from the four living creatures gives the stock report for that day, showing ten to twelve times less worth than normal. For a day's work a person could buy a parcel of wheat, feeding only himself. If he bought the less desirable barley, he might feed two others. The scales and this haunting economic report point to famine in the land, undoubtedly brought on by scarcity and imbalance.

The cryptic phrase, **do not damage the oil and the wine**, is difficult to recognize in this time of want. Possibly it is a statement of limitation as found in other places related to destruction and devastation. Because the roots of the olive tree and grape vines go deep, God will not allow a total famine to destroy God's people. Or perhaps this is the meaning behind the symbol of the scales. In times of famine, the poor cannot buy enough food for their families, while the rich continue to pour out lavishly their oil and drink good wine to their fill. This is the nature of such economic disasters; it usually affects those who are already suffering enough. The parables of Jesus often uncovered the social and economic issues of His day. Through them Jesus instructed the poor working class in the discipline of macroeconomics. In that world, most vineyard workers worked for an owner who lived in a far-away country (Rome). The worker was forced to work for shamefully low wages in obscene workplace environments. Instead of using the prime agricultural areas of Palestine for food and local sustenance, grapevines were planted and its fruit was used to provide the luxuries of taste to the Romans back home. Olive oil took up the remaining precious acres. Even if the poor are found hungry in this uncertain time of want, they still are forbidden to usurp **the oil and the wine** (6:6) needed by the Roman aristocracy.

With the numerous technological advances of our day, the production of food and the quantity of resources are rarely the problem. However, the distribution of those resources to all in need and the economic parity of the world are often in question. Crops are left to rot in first world countries while people in other parts of the world starve. South American fields are full of cash crop coffee plants, or worse, illegal poppy and cannabis plants to satiate American drug needs, while not growing enough food for its own population to meet basic calorie intake. Faceless, multi-national corporations sell products at ridiculously low prices to rich consumers at the expense of the inhumane treatment of the workers living well below sustenance. John Wesley noted that in the England of his day.

The global economy seems to be a fact of our age. Some have protested the rise of this phenomenon as mega-corporations have stepped beyond the confines of their national borders. These protests tend to attack the perceived injustice that comes from their profit motives, using and defrauding poor countries and small, community-based companies. Often, they attack the global market without offering much organization in return. The impact of the horror of this third horse is felt mostly by the victimization felt by those under its thundering hoof beats. The Christian response must be to humanize the facelessness of the distant market forces. Undoubtedly, globalism is here to stay. The revelation warns us that the destructive qualities of unjust scales affect people at their most basic living. When people feel that their sustenance and future security is in the hands of a beast-like organization that has no heart or concern for their workers or them, then the despair of the third horse is understood.

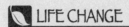

LIFE CHANGE

THE RIDE OF THE BLACK HORSE

Jesus used parables to address some of the social and economic issues of His day. Today we still wrestle with such issues. Good, fair distribution of earth's provisions is questionable though there are adequate resources and production of food. Faceless, multi-national corporations sell products at ridiculously low prices to rich consumers at the expense of the inhumane treatment of the workers living well below sustenance. These are the black horses of our times. So what ought we do now? Should we battle the corporations? Should we find ways to care for the poor and hungry? How can we make a difference to those being trampled by the black horse?

At the opening of the fourth seal, a rider seated on a **pale horse** captures John's attention (6:8). The Greek word here for pale is "chloros," the yellowish-green color of the dead. "Pale" is as good a word as any, denoting the lifeless character of the rider's hue. In fact, we are told, this rider's name is **Death**. John noticed that following very close behind him was **Hades**. One kills, the other completes the task. The role that this last rider plays with the other three is given through a description of their unified given purpose: **to kill by sword, famine and plague** (6:8). **Plague** completes the themes. **Death**, then, is alternatively called Pestilence, noting the biological nature of his attack. Biological death can be seen at both the microscopic (disease) and environmental (ecological disaster) levels. Unlike the first three horsemen, this rider, and his friend Hades, touch the entire human matrix. The world as it was meant to be is hostile and in disarray.

Added to this group of destructive tools is the ravaging of humanity by the **wild beasts of the earth**. The creation's original design for human and animal interdependence is replaced with a violent chaos. We are reminded of Mark's truncated temptation narrative, "He (Jesus) was with the wild animals, and angels attended him" (Mark 1:13). In the narrative, the results of the Second Adam's temptation are different than that of the First Adam. Because Jesus was successful in His wilderness experience, the wild beasts are again our friends and no longer an adversary. The effects of the pale horse are to destroy humanity's ecological friendship with the animal kingdom; the earth is now theirs.

If there is a progression or interdependence between the four horsemen, the spirit of conquest and power is the underlying force that initiates all the suffering unleashed on humanity. This leads to warring (the sword,) economic upheaval (unequal distribution of food and human goods), and ultimately the physical death brought about through global imbalance and an unsustainable environment. These four henchmen have been galloping their way through human history since the dawn of civilization. At the end of everything, they are exposed for what they are and we see them in all their awful glory. The four of them work as one cohort to dismantle and pillage all that is good in the world. The name "Death" summarizes the entire four quite well.

THE SEALS CONTINUED 6:9-17

The invitation to "Come!" stops here. John is now a captive audience. Perhaps he has seen enough. The Lamb continues to open **the fifth seal** that allows John to see the **souls** of the martyrs of the Church **under the altar**. They were slain **because of the word of God and the testimony they had maintained** (6:9). This is the very reason that John was on Patmos (refer to 1:9). Certainly he would identify with their plight. It is not enough to know that they are now (as we often speak of the deceased faithful) in "a better place." Or even to know that their life blood (their **souls**) has poured out over the altar and onto the floor as an offering to God. (Paul also called his life a poured "drink offering" in 2 Tim. 4:6.) There is unfinished business for these who have died in the faith. They must be vindicated. And, perhaps more important, God must be vindicated, since God had called them to that witness. Their death now gives the martyr a privileged place from which to speak.

From this safe position from under the altar, they call out, **"How long, Sovereign Lord, until you . . . avenge our blood?"** (6:10). The ethical concerns surrounding this question are a stumbling block to many modern readers of the Apocalypse. The violence that is suggested by the martyrs' cries is thought to be out of sync with the earthly teaching of Jesus. Jesus taught His disciples to turn their other cheek when struck and to forgive the enemy. Certainly it does not sound like the Savior on the cross saying as He died, "Father forgive them" (Luke 23:32). Even Stephen, the first martyr of the New Testament Church, mimics our Lord in that resolve (Acts 7:60).

On the contrary, these souls from under the altar are more like the psalmist of the Hebrew Scriptures demanding in the face of God to be vindicated for their faithfulness to Him. The great American philosopher C.S. Peirce speaks for many as he dismisses the book of Revelation — and God — for its gleeful insensitivity to those receiving retribution and vengeance.

But little by little the bitterness increases until in the last book of the New Testament, its poor distracted author represents that all the time Christ was talking about having come to save the world, the secret design was to catch the entire human race, with the exception of a paltry 144,000, and souse them all in a brimstone lake, and as the smoke of their torment went up for ever and ever, to turn and remark, "There is no curse any more." Would it be an insensible

smirk or a fiendish grin that should accompany such an utterance? I
wish I could believe St. John did not write it. . . .[3]

Peirce has missed the main point of the saints' cry. The **holy and true**
(6:10) character of God is at stake. The Christian martyrs are not so much
concerned with seeing their enemies suffer as they are in seeing God's
purpose fulfilled.

The answer to their question comes quickly. But instead of bringing
down fire from heaven on the enemies of the gospel, God directs His
attention to the saints themselves. **Each of them was given a white robe**
(6:11). The white robe undoubtedly covers the color of red that marks their
lives at the present. Their perseverance in suffering for the claims of the
gospel is now repaid with an innocent verdict by God. We know this not
to be, as some have thought, the "glorified bodies" of the dead in Christ,
because this gift is only an initial response to the saints' demand. The final
vindication for their lives would come only if they **wait a little longer.**

Perseverance is to be followed with patience. Assurance of God's
response to their woeful death is given through the new clothing that they
were given, but a time lapse is not to be taken as reason to doubt the full
answer. Furthermore, this period of waiting and resting is for a purpose.
They are to be joined in martyrdom by **their fellow servants and brothers**
to complete a predetermined **number**. This number is later to be disclosed
as the amount of 144,000, itself needing interpretation of its significance.

It does not take John long to see the description of that vindication
that was alluded to in verse 11. With the opening of the **sixth seal** (6:12),
all the glue that holds the cosmos together lets loose. Earthquakes, a
blackened sun, the blood-red moon, and a variety of other cosmic signs
of upheaval accompany the breaking of this seal. Jesus' Olivet Discourse
comes to mind (Matt. 24:3–25:46). These two descriptions of the time of
God's final judgment are consistent with the metaphors described in Isa.
34:4, particularly associated with the time indicator of when leaves that
"drop from a fig tree" (6:13). Jesus used this reference to encourage His
disciples to practice watchfulness. He pointed to the twig's tender
period, when the leaves first come out, as a sign that the figs prophesied
to come will soon be here. Revelation places the time of **late figs** as the

KEY IDEAS • END-TIME WOES

Matthew 24	Mark 13	Luke 21	Revelation 6, 7
Wars	Wars	Wars	Seal 1: Wars
International Strife	International Strife	International Strife	Seal 2: International Strife
Famine	Earthquakes	Earthquakes	Seal 3: Famine
Persecutions	Persecutions	Persecutions	Seal 4: Death
Cosmic eclipses	Cosmic eclipses	Cosmic eclipses	Seal 5: Persecutions
Cosmic eclipses	Cosmic eclipses	Cosmic eclipses	Seal 6: Cosmic Eclipses
Cosmic eclipses	Cosmic eclipses	Cosmic eclipses	Seal 7: Earthquakes

Source: R. H. Charles, *A Critical and Exegetical Commentary on the Revelation of St. John* (The International Critical Commentary; 2 vols.; Edinburgh: T. & T. Clark, 1920), 1:158.

imminent moment in God's judgment. All it takes is a strong wind to knock them down.

This dramatic portrayal is the stage that is set for the drama of the final judgment. **Kings**, **princes**, **generals**, **the rich**, and **the mighty** are joined with slaves and free men shivering and shaking with fear and hidden in mountain caves (6:15). Such an inclusive group of people shows that God will be no respecter of persons when judgment comes to the earth. A similar list of people, "the rich and the poor, the free and the slaves," take the mark of the beast in chapter 13 and the composite of the armies destroyed in the final battle (19:18). We are to understand this group of people to be the unbelievers who are in need of the reckoning that the saints asked for in the breaking of the fifth seal.

Mountains are very important geographies in the Jewish world. Looking to the hills is where salvation can be found. In their time of need, these hapless people do what comes naturally. They go to the mountains. But these did so to be enveloped by those hills, and to hide from God (6:16). They call out, **"Fall on us and hide us from the face of him who sits on the throne and from the wrath of the Lamb! For the great day of their wrath has come, and who can stand?"**

ENDNOTES

1. The eschatological teaching of Jesus is known as the Olivet Discourse found in Matthew 24 (Mark 13 and Luke 21). Like the Revelation of John, this teaching is dependent on the prophecies of Daniel and seeks to answer the questions of Jesus' disciples concerning the second advent of the Messiah and the coming new age of the Kingdom.

2. Bruce M. Metzger, *Breaking the Code: Understanding the Book of Revelation* (Nashville: Abingdon, 1993), 58.

3. Charles S. Peirce, "Evolutionary Love," *The Essential Peirce: Selected Philosophical Writings*, Vol. 1 (1867–1893), Nathan Houser and Christian Kloesel, eds., (Indiana University Press, 1992): 365–366.

5

AN INTERLUDE AND THE SEVENTH SEAL

Revelation 7:1–8:5

Chapter 6 ended with a question: "For the great day of their wrath has come, and who can stand?" (6:17). After the breaking of the first six seals, the obvious question facing the followers of Christ is whether they too are experiencing the woes described by this vision and whether they will be able to endure. Before the breaking of the seventh seal, their question is mercifully answered. The interlude and the breaking of the last seal turns their attention to the faithful, those on earth (7:1–8) and those in heaven (7:9–17), to reassure them that God holds them in His divine providence.

In answering the question of the prior chapter, "Who can stand?" (6:17), this chapter contains two visionary answers: (1) the sealing of the tribes (the 144,000) and (2) the happy reception of a great multitude before the throne of God. Many commentators have attempted to define the nature of both of these groups as well

 WHAT OTHERS SAY

Under the crisis of persecution and under the urgency of an imminent end, reality is revealed suddenly for what it is. We have supposed our lives were so utterly *ordinary*. Sin-habits dull our free faith into stodgy moralism and respectable boredom; then crisis rips the veneer of cliché off everyday routines and reveals the side-by-side splendors and terrors of heaven and hell.

—*Eugene Peterson*

as differentiating the one from the other. Apparently the Church is in view in both visions, but different concerns are addressed.

The first vision is an encouragement to those who are passing through the tribulation on the eve of the final trumpet blasts. They are sealed and protected from any ultimate destruction.

The second group, a larger and more inclusive gathering, is made up of all those who find their reward in heaven after a long history of faithfulness. This picture is a fitting chorus of praise and blessedness befitting the final home of the believer.

THE SEALING OF THE TRIBES 7:1–8

John sees **four angels standing at the four corners of the earth** (7:1). These angels, representing the authority and hand of God within the world, are shown to have full authority over all the earth by where they are standing. No part of the world is outside the control of God's command. From their four positions, the angels are able to keep **the four winds of the earth** (7:1) from unraveling the fabric of the world. The four winds of the earth are connected with the picture of Elam's punishment of being scattered by "the four winds" (Jer. 49:36). The use of this set of four could easily point back to the disasters brought by the four horsemen before them. Zechariah (6:5) even identifies his four horsemen (chariots) as the "four spirits of heaven." Nevertheless, the sealing of the faithful protects them from the vindictive wrath of God that the unbelieving world will now experience. The biblical words "tribulation" (*thlipsis*) and "wrath" (*orge*) are never used synonymously. As in this case, the people of God are expected to go through times of tribulation, but they are excluded from the wrath of God reserved for the enemies of God and His Church.

Then John sees **another angel coming up from the east** (7:2), perhaps an illusion to hope bearers from the east, as in the magi of the nativity. Or as Mitchell G. Reddish has said, "from the rising of the sun."[1] This angel comes halting the winds from doing their damage on the **sea, land, and the trees**. The damaging of trees is the visible symbol that the earth is being hit hard. In storms, the trees are first to fall. God now is showing His control over this chaotic windstorm by this pause. A pause long enough to insure protection to His own.

John is told, in the midst of the unleashing of calamities beyond imagination, that **a seal** or protection is to be placed upon God's select people. The angel from the east has **the seal of the living God** (7:2). The ancient process of sealing a letter or contract is behind this action. A document would be rolled or folded, tied in some way, and adhered with a piece of clay or wax. The sender would press a signet ring or stamp into the hardening sealant leaving their imprint. In this case, the imprint of God is left on the faithful Christians, usually symbolized by a mark on their foreheads (9:4; 14:1; 22:4).

As an aside, this same concept is used in the Revelation to identify those faithful to the evil one, by taking on the "mark of the beast" (15:2; 19:20). Far more is said in the Apocalypse concerning the "seal of God" than this infamous mark on the foreheads of the devil's followers, yet we are fascinated by the possibilities this mark poses. With the advent of various technologies for credit card usage, grocery store scanners, and even tattoo parlors, we have been encouraged to keep watch for such a mark arising in our culture. Perhaps we should be more vigilant in assuring that we, the followers of Christ, are carrying the mark of God's seal on our lives.[2]

The number of those who were sealed was **144,000 from all the tribes of Israel.**

Literal interpretations of this group have created many problems.

First, some have understood the number 144,000 to represent an actual number of people. The obvious symbolism of multiples of 12 and 10, numbers representing completeness, the tribes of Israel, and the apostles of Christ, would expand the meaning of an actual, limited number.

Second, the limitation of the tribes of Israel to Jews or even Jewish Christians misses the vital point that the Revelation never makes a distinction between Jews and Gentiles, but understands a newly formed people of God incorporating both.

The symbolic richness of the number 144,000 shows how God is still the Good Shepherd who knows each of His sheep by name and has even the most insignificant and lost sheep in His purview. None of God's faithful will be lost. As the amassed people are given greater amplification, the description becomes clearer. The multitude is made up of those who have gone through the great tribulation and survived to praise God.

KEY IDEAS • COMPARISON OF TRIBES LISTS

Revelation 7	Exodus 1	Numbers 1	Deuteronomy 33
Judah	Reuben	Reuben	Reuben
Reuben	Simeon	Simeon	Judah
Gad	Levi	Judah	Levi
Asher	Judah	Issachar	Benjamin
Naphtali	Issachar	Zebulun	Joseph
Manasseh	Zebulun	Ephraim	Ephraim
Simeon	Benjamin	Manasseh	Manasseh
Levi	Dan	Benjamin	Zebulun
Issachar	Naphtali	Dan	Gad
Zebulun	Gad	Asher	Dan
Joseph	Asher	Gad	Naphtali
Benjamin	Joseph	Naphtali	Asher

Often it is questioned whether the order and makeup of the tribes here has any significance. Each tribe, numbering a multitude of twelve thousand, is listed as Judah, Reuben, Gad, Asher, Naphtali, Manasseh, Simeon, Levi, Issachar, Zebulun, Joseph, and Benjamin (7:5–8). Normally Reuben would have been at the head of the list, being the oldest, but Judah may assume that position due to his family lineage carrying the Messiah into history. Conversely, some Jewish traditions believed the tribe of Dan to be the line from which the Antichrist would be born, so this tribe was replaced with Manasseh, one of the two tribes of Joseph's family (Ephraim being omitted) making up twelve tribes. It has been suggested that in enumerating a collection of twelve tribes to make up a complete Israel, the list excluded both Dan and Ephraim because of their association with idol worship (Dan, Judg. 18:16–19; Ephraim, Hos. 5:9). In any case, the result of all these arguments is to take note of the attempt to show the complete sealing of God's faithful (perhaps also to show that God's protection will not be applied to the "unfaithful," even of Israel).

THE WHITE ROBED MULTITUDE 7:9–17

After all of this preoccupation with numbers, John sees before him **a great multitude that no one could count** (7:9). Contrary to those sectarian groups that would claim some connection with the limited number of 144,000 elect people, we now know that the heavenly population is expansive and inclusive. The incalculable description of this great assembly not only tells us that it is large beyond our ability to fathom; it also encourages the Church not to think of herself as a puny and ineffective institution. You can almost feel the elated response that the isolated and lonely John felt when his gaze fell upon his fellow saints. He is not just one of a ragtag remnant of those who made it through. He is a part of a victory throng whose numbers are not of human comprehension.

With all of the modern preoccupation with growth accounts of local churches, even the largest of these little kingdoms have little significance for any given locale. A church of 30,000 people in a secular urban community may be tempted to view itself triumphantly. But a church of 30 in the same place may have the same spiritual impact over eternity. It is to the latter group that the importance of John's vision is amplified. To those who think they have or are of little importance, whose numbers are small, they are a part of a throng of people that cannot be counted. Particularly to those who suffer in isolation, who believe their influence to have little impact, look: these are your fellow workers!

Too, the heavenly population is made up of individuals **from every nation, tribe, people and language** (7:9). The great assembly is less described by its quantity than its quality. This succession of Greek words is a beautiful way of wrapping our arms around the entire world. Today we are becoming more aware of how the concept of a nation is far more complex than we ever thought. Whether we like it or not, globalization has become the common human experience. In the relatively recent experience of just a century ago, most people treated their national identity as an allegiance to a sporting club. We held pep rallies, wore our colors, and competed with other nations as if at a football game. We went to war to prove that we were better than the other nations. Multi-national corporations have begun the dissolution of these borders. Religion itself has shown us that there are higher allegiances than those given to nations. Within nations, tribes continue to vie for power; outside of nations, language groups tie people together without the constraints of borders. The fact that there will be some **from every** people group teaches us to resist thinking of any splintered human history as having a special destiny in the history of the world.

We are to discover from this vision that all of the different ways that describe our differences are now unified by the place where this group is gathered: they are all **standing before the throne and in front of the Lamb** (7:9). They also were unified by their common experience of having gone through the tribulation (**wearing white robes**), and worshiping the Lord of lords (**holding palm branches in their hands**). Given this communion found in suffering for the One Lord, all other differences found in the Church are of little significance.

The heavenly scene develops as the multitude breaks out in song: **"Salvation belongs to our God, who sits on the throne, and to the Lamb"** (7:10).

The description of God as the one **who sits on the throne** (7:10) continues the literary device of focusing on the imperial application of the revelation. The multitude in heaven has received its deliverance from the Roman tormentors and persecutors, not by Rome, but rather from God. The throne room, as a recurring scene in the book, is not a "situation room" full of warlords and sages scurrying about to address the Church's suffering. The picture of God is not developed in any humanlike fashion to show anger, anxiousness, or even impatience. The throne room has one activity: worship. Those who inhabit this holy space are calm, at peace, and focused on God. This is often in stark juxtaposition to the picture of earth below, going through its various throws of convulsive violence.

Around the throne, the elders, and the four living creatures stood all the angels. The whole assembly bowed before the throne and said in worship to God, **"Amen! Praise and glory and wisdom and thanks and honor and power and strength be to our God for ever and ever. Amen!"** (7:12).

This seven-fold list of attributes exhibits a complete offering of praise to the eternal God. This doxology has been building exponentially since the living creatures first offered praise to "him who sits on the throne" (glory, honor, power in 4:11; power, wealth, wisdom, strength, honor, glory, and praise in 5:12). It begins and ends with an "Amen!" Perhaps this "amen" at the beginning of the heavenly host's praise was an acknowledgment of the martyrs' own praise to God in verse 10. In mirroring Jesus' use of the "Amen" ("verily, verily" KJV) at the beginning rather than the end of a pronouncement, John may also be emphasizing the unusual authority of this statement as compared to other such claims to our worship.

John, who has been a spectator up until now, is brought into the throne room and the unfolding story, when **one of the elders** asks him, **"These in white robes—who are they, and where did they come from?"** (7:13). John himself answers, **"Sir, you know"** (7:14). This brief exchange shows a rare moment in the revelation—John is now directing the script. It may be that John knows the answer himself, meaning by this, "Sir, you know as well as I do who those people are!" The **white robes** are the symbols of blessing and purity throughout the revelation, worn by those who have weathered the storm of persecution and martyrdom. John and the elders around the throne are very aware of the kind of people who wear such robes. Or the question may show that John has come to recognize the source of all answers in this revelation from God, meaning, "Sir, I don't know who they are, but you do." In either case, John is now about to hear the answer to the question.

The elder responded: **These are they who have come out of the great tribulation; they have washed their robes and made them white in the blood of the Lamb** (7:14).

The roots of the questions, "who" and "where" have been answered. These came out of the "great tribulation" and they have washed and made their robes white (active verbs) **in the blood of the Lamb** (7:14). The worldly activity of the martyrs is seen as the answer to why these people are now in the throne room of God. But the death of Jesus Christ still is the agent by which this activity results in holiness.

The elder, having answered his own question, feels the need to explain their new activity in the throne room of God. He continues: **they are**

115

before the throne of God and serve him day and night in his temple. . . . Never again will they hunger; never again will they thirst. . . . For the Lamb at the center of the throne will be their shepherd; he will lead them to springs of living water. And God will wipe away every tear from their eyes (7:15–17).

This description continues the themes of protection and sealing found in this interlude. There are sixteen references to the temple in the book of Revelation. When we see it, or are invited into the activity found there, we are in the presence of God and out of the clutches of this world's power. God himself will place **his tent** of comfort over these who have come from such a dangerous journey which included **hunger**, **thirst**, and **scorching heat**. Echoes of Psalm 23 are found in this affirmation, calling the Lamb now **their shepherd**, leading the flock to **springs of living water** (see 22:17). What a beautiful picture of God! Not only providing such a holy place of shelter for the beaten and downtrodden, but He is seen wiping **away every tear from their eyes**! (7:17) God is not only the holy presence of the temple; God is the nurse who comes by the bedside and cares for the sufferer's every need.

Since God's people are assured protection, and because we have peeked into the holy chambers to see that God is indeed in control of all things, we are now ready for the seventh seal to be broken and the contents of the scroll to be revealed.

THE SEVENTH SEAL AND THE GOLDEN CENSER 8:1–5

What a dramatic pause! One after another, the seals have been broken. John is about to see what lies hidden in the book of prophecy. But **when he opened the seventh seal**—nothing (8:1). Perhaps the silence speaks louder than any of the previous cacophonies. John can only watch as the stage is set for the seventh and final drama of the seals. The angels before God are readied with seven trumpets. Another angel serves before the altar with a censer first filled with the cries of the saints and then fire that would soon pummel the earth with thunder and rumblings. But for **about half an hour** there is silence in heaven.

Silence is often the means of reverence before God in worship. And yet, such stillness is a rare commodity these days. Our congregants come into their worship centers to the sounds of loud and raucous music; they leave with the swell of sounds and conversation. Joyous and lively worship runs through any authentic church, just as it does in the scenes of Revelation, but a moment of silence gives the participant a chance to reflect and give meaning to the whole experience. There is little opportunity to sit and listen to the quiet of God's still small voice.

It is worth noting that within the history of the Church there have been those religious orders that have taken a vow of silence—a discipline of Christian virtue—but records no such vow for noisemaking or talking. Silence is a spiritual discipline because it so unnatural to the human tongue. Though much theological and ecclesial discussion over the charismatic gift of tongues has occurred, little thought for a gift for silence, a much-needed supernatural manifestation of the Holy Spirit, has preoccupied churches today.

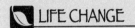

LIFE CHANGE

SILENCE

Mother Teresa said, "We need to find God, and He cannot be found in noise and restlessness. God is the friend of silence. See how nature—trees, flowers, grass—grows in silence; see the stars, the moon and the sun, how they move in silence . . . We need silence to be able to touch souls." Do you agree or disagree with her? Listening in silence is challenging to us. Some seem to fear silence, yet we need it in order to hear God's still small voice. We need silence to allow our souls and spirits to soak in that which God would teach us. How can you bring the discipline of silence into your life? What will you need to do in order to find a time and place for silence?

This time of waiting before a silent heaven could be identified with the experience of the imminent return of Christ. The Church has always lived in a period of silence. We have seen the seemingly next-to-last events ride by like galloping horses; we know something of the pleas of the saints and the tribulations of life. Often in the Old Testament, silence precedes judgment of God Almighty on the earth (Hab. 2:20; Zeph. 1:7; Zech. 2:13). We know the time is at hand for the final Day of the Lord, when He comes to make all things right and vindicate the faithful. But we see nothing happen, and we feel the silence.

Some scholars have suggested that this silence is more than a mere dramatic device.[3] It might also point to the eschatological atmosphere as recorded in the Apocryphal book 2 Esdras. "Then the world will be turned back to primeval silence for seven days, as it was at the first beginnings . . ." (7:30). The idea that the end would be like the beginning, as a depiction of a new creation, arises often in the Revelation. The fact that this silence is followed with scenes of destruction does not have to negate this possibility.

The preparation that is taking place during this period of silence then is for a reason. **The seven angels who stand before God** and **were given seven trumpets** (8:2) were preparing for the events of the seventh seal. The trumpets will blow and, eventually, the bowls of God's wrath will be poured out. In the verses that follow, **much incense**—which represents **the prayers of all the saints**—will reach God's nostrils (8:3–4). He will respond, and He will do so with a dramatic culmination of history. The golden censer that is held in the angel's hand to lift up this incense before God is secondarily used to scoop up burning embers from the altar. When the angel hurls this fire to the earth it causes **peals of thunder, rumblings, flashes of lightning and an earthquake** (8:5). These actions are often found in the areas surrounding the temple. They represent the awesome reality of a holy God, and they serve to prelude the judgment that is soon to come to those who have not recognized this God. The golden censer is used to connect the saints' prayers going **up before God** (8:4) and the action of judgment **on the earth** (8:5). Though the causality is still in God, the saints are involved through worship and prayer in the in-between of heaven and earth. The subtle nuance of the nature of prayer in the book of Revelation is one of its key encouragements. We are exhorted to pray to God because God acts; and because God acts, we are called to pray.

 WHAT OTHERS SAY

For many people, waiting is an awful desert between where they are and where they want to go. And people do not like such a place. They want to get out of it by doing something.
—*Henri Nouwen*

This interlude, which follows the opening of the sixth seal, accomplished two things in answering the imploring question of the faithful on earth, "How long will we have to wait before we are vindicated for this suffering?" (cf. 6:10). One, it offers assurances that the faithful community of God will be protected from ultimate harm, as if they are marked with divine protection as in the Exodus. And, second, the silence in heaven only serves to test the patience of those already seeing the escalating pattern of history. This patience will be stretched even further as the seventh seal only serves to unleash a new series of seven horrors. But the Church now knows that they are in view of their reward and the opportunity to enter heaven's rest. Like someone holding his or her breath while waiting for a finish, the Christian is on tiptoe to spy the promised respite.

ENDNOTES

1. Mitchell G. Reddish, *Revelation* (Macon: Smyth & Helwys, 2001), 142.

2. The Old Testament has a number of instances in which God's people carry on their foreheads a mark or symbol identifying their allegiance to God. One such text is where the forehead of the High Priest was marked with golden letters proclaiming that he was now HOLY TO THE LORD (Exod. 28:36) or in Deut. 6:6–8 and Ezek. 9:4–6, when the servants of God are "marked" on the hand and forehead with the law of God.

3. See, for instance, Reddish, *Revelation* (Macon: Smyth & Helwys, 2001), 159, 160.

6

SOUNDING THE SEVEN TRUMPETS

Revelation 8:6–9:21

The interlude that makes up chapter 7 has now come to a conclusion. The last of the seven seals has been opened. The use of the series of sevens only serves to usher in yet another series. With the breaking open of the seventh seal, when we would expect to see the culmination of the revelation, we are awakened by the glaring reality of the ongoing revelation.

THE SEVEN TRUMPETS

Following the pouring out on the earth the mixing of the saints' prayers and burning embers, **the seven angels** (8:6) place their trumpets to their lips readying for the instrument's blast. These seven angels are those **who stand before God** (8:2). Sometimes referred to as the archangels, the Jewish apocryphal book of Tobit speaks of them as angels "who stand ready and enter before the glory of the Lord" (Tob. 12:15). The group includes Michael and Gabriel, the great announcers of divine action and epiphany.[1] They play the trumpet, the most popular apocalyptic instrument, because its glaring sound cuts into the hearer's noisy life, demanding a halting attention. We might also notice that they stand **prepared** (even in the Tobit text) as if reminding us that they take their commands from God and do not work out their own designs.

The seven trumpets of judgment that follow are primarily in response to the prayers of the saints for some form of vindication for their suffering and witness. As in the last group of seven, there appears here as well, to be a division in kind between the first four from the last three trumpet blasts. As the trumpets are sounded, a series of calamities begins to hit the earth. The subsequent terrors follow on the heels of the tribulations described in the opening of the seven seals, what is referred to as the "great tribulation" (7:14).

Because these trumpet judgments serve in the book of Revelation to warn the unbelieving tormentors of God's people to repent, the sequence follows, in some fashion, as the plagues recorded in Exodus.

KEY IDEAS • TRUMPET JUDGMENT PARALLELS PLAGUES ON EGYPT

Trumpet	Plague
First Trumpet (8:7)	Exodus 9:22–25
Second/Third Trumpet (8:8–11)	Exodus 7:20–25
Fourth Trumpet (8:12)	Exodus 10:21–23
Fifth Trumpet (9:1–11)	Exodus 10:12–15

Just as the plagues were used to try to get Pharaoh to soften his hardened heart toward the captive children of Israel, these judgments are poured out on the earth to warn persecutors of Christians to stop their actions and follow God. The story of the Exodus shows us that the use of the plagues is somewhat problematic toward our understanding of God's providence. God hardened Pharaoh's heart at the same time He was trying to get him to let His people go. In the end, the main purpose of the plagues was to glorify God and to make His might and name known on the earth.

In the same way, we might believe the text here to mean what it says: that God is seeking to jar the senses of those who would sin against the Christian people. The hope is that they will learn and turn from their wicked ways. The probability is that they will not. The view of providence in the book of Revelation can be somewhat problematic. Still, we can only take the purpose of the revelation at face value. God is showing what will soon take place as a way of encouraging right action, but there is a subtle acknowledgement that those bent on evil will no doubt continue their course of action only until they are stopped by God.

FIRST TRUMPET

The first angel sounded his trumpet (8:7). The horror that follows, **hail and fire mixed with blood** falling **down upon the earth,** proceeds to **burn up a third** of the earth, **the trees,** and **all the green grass** (8:7). The image here is derived from the seventh plague enacted upon Egypt (cf. Exod. 9:23). Generally, the fraction of a third is used to describe the horrible extent of the destruction. **A third** is quite a bit of damage to inflict on the earth and trees, but we should remember from chapter 1 the hopeful ratio of God's judgment on the earth: two-third are *not* destroyed. Or the one-third could represent that the final consummation of God's judgment has not yet been felt. We will eventually see that full devastation in the pouring out of the bowls of God's wrath in chapters 15 and 16.

In the past, God placed a rainbow in the sky to show His restraint in judgment, even though people still die in floods today. In the same way, God retrains His ultimate judgment on all the earth by affecting only a third of the earth and allowing two-thirds of the earth to survive. Not withstanding, the third element to be burned up, **all the green grass**, is a complete destruction. The scorching of the earth leaves behind this brown, scorched, visible reminder. The luxury of walking on the soft carpeted texture of the ground is now gone; the earth is livable, but no longer hospitable.

SECOND TRUMPET

When the **second angel**'s trumpet is sounded, it is accompanied by **something like a huge mountain, all ablaze,** being **thrown into the sea** (8:8). This image may bring to mind the description of an erupting volcano, perhaps connecting the first century reader to the Vesuvius volcanic display at Pompeii in A.D. 79. This eruption poured molten lava into the Gulf of Naples, putrefying the water and sinking docked ships.[2]

Besides this first-century contemporary reference, the Old Testament often connects the picture of a great mountain with that of a great kingdom. Jeremiah 51:25 speaks of Babylon in this way: "I am against you [Babylon], O destroying mountain . . . I will . . . make you a burned out mountain."

In this case, the mountain is **thrown into the sea** (8:8). Reflecting back to the first plague on Egypt (Exod. 7:20–21), **a third of the sea**

turned into blood. The sea in Revelation is often a symbol of the politically chaotic world of unbelievers, but perhaps here it is to be connected with the Exodus plague that poisoned the life-giving flow of the Nile's water. Again, all that exhibits the life of the sea—its water, its fish, its vessels—are proportionately destroyed according to a third.

THIRD TRUMPET

The **third angel**'s trumpet sounds (8:10). With it comes the falling of a great blazing **star** continuing the ravaging of the earth's waters as was in the second. Again, the image of a blazing star falling from the sky has a literal correspondence with the falling of a meteor into the earth's atmosphere. Such an event in the ancient world was to be taken as an omen of impending doom. The star's name is called "Wormwood" (8:11), which means "bitterness." In fact, wormwood is a bitter herb that if found in water in large enough quantities can poison its drinkers, making it an undrinkable cauldron of death. Perhaps, too, the reader is to remember the Old Testament's use of wormwood as a symbol of bitterness, sorrow, and the judgment of God. Because Israel had turned her back on God, God would make them "eat bitter food [wormwood, KJV] and drink poisoned water" (Jer. 9:15).

As the prior trumpet plague had brought about a natural disaster on the sea (salt water), this plague primarily effects the fresh drinking water sources of the earth—**the rivers and . . . the springs of water** (8:10). Unlike Moses' miracle at Marah, when he cast a tree into the bitter waters making them sweet (Exod. 15:25), this event turns the refreshment of the earth's waters into a source of sorrow, even death.

FOURTH TRUMPET

The **fourth angel** brings with its trumpet blast a type of summary of all of the first three trumpets. **A third of the sun, the moon**, and **the stars** were deprived of their light, **so that a third of them turned dark** (8:12). The cosmos itself has been touched. The earth, the sea, the universe—we might say the entire natural cosmos—has felt the terror of God's judgment: a third of **the day was without light** and also a third of the night.

The actual description is strikingly like that found in the initial out-pouring of judgment found in 6:12–13.

More important, the fourth trumpet judgment points to the role that light plays as a depiction of the goodness of the creation and the moral character of God as the backdrop for this plague on the earth. Before God created the world, He said, "Let there be light" (Gen. 1:3). Light is the mystical quality representing God's ability even to call something "good." Extinguishing the light jeopardizes the moral quality of the world. The parallel with the Exodus plagues that has been noted in the previous comments continues with the darkening of the world. The ninth plague brought darkness over Egypt for three days (Exod. 10:21–23) and foreshadowed the final liberation of God's people. In the midst of this next-to-the-last horror, we are aware that we are on the eve of such cosmic redemption.

In fact, these first four trumpets have been merely a prelude to the three that are to follow. The circling of an eagle calling out in a loud voice heightens the warning: **"Woe! Woe! Woe to the inhabitants of the**

KEY IDEAS • SEALS AND TRUMPETS PARALLELS

	Seven Seals		Seven Trumpets
6:1–7	First Four Seals	8:6–13	First Four Trumpets
6:9–11	Fifth Seal	9:1–12	Fifth Trumpet
6:12–17	Sixth Seal	9:13–21	Sixth Trumpet
7:1–17	Interlude	10:1–11:14	Interlude
8:1–5	Seventh Seal	11:15–19	Seventh Trumpet

earth, because of the trumpet blasts about to be sounded by the other three angels!" (8:13). Because of the three-woe condemnation, and with the knowledge that three more trumpets are yet to blow, many literary scholars have sought to connect each woe with the subsequent plague sections (9:12; 11:14; and what appears to be the last trumpet blast commencing the total of seven bowl judgments in chapters 15 and 16.)

Perhaps the more important observation is that of the recipients of the warning: **the inhabitants of the earth** (8:13). Some have wished to limit the scope of this phrase to the wicked of the world, but the ominous vulture-like bird, circling in the space between heaven and earth, is calling out a warning for all living on this now barren and bruised earth.[3] What John has been watching crash down on the natural order is now about to fall on humanity directly. The whole of creation is coming apart at its seams.

FIFTH TRUMPET

And so **the fifth angel sounded his trumpet** (9:1). Again **a star** falls from **the sky to the earth**. This star has animated qualities, being **given the key to the shaft of the Abyss** (9:1). In chapter 20, this key again shows up in the hand of an angel, enabling him to lock up the beast who makes his home in the Abyss. The cataclysmic events taking place here now unlock this evil place and release all manner of evil from it. A great billowing cloud of smoke coming from the Abyss darkens the **sun and sky** (9:2).

Demonic locusts flow out of this smoke, but instead of hurting **the grass of the earth or any plant or tree** as earthly locusts are known to do, these creatures go after **only those people who did not have the seal of God on their foreheads** (9:4). Judgment has come! The unbelievers are to be punished, and like the Passover in the Exodus account, God restrains His wrath from those who are sealed with a mark. The cries to God coming from those who are the target of this attack (looking much like those in the sixth seal—that death may release them from this terror) are still not answered.

These scorpion-like locusts are not able to kill them, but only **torture them for five months** (9:5). The period of five months coincides with the lifecycle of the locusts, and the agricultural threat during the spring and summer months. This limits the time of the terror but focuses the threat. The reaction of the victims is much like that of those affected by the opening of the seventh seal, those who call to the mountains and rocks to fall on them. **During those days men will seek death, but will not find it; they will long to die, but death will elude them** (9:6).

The description of their agony is graphic. Few anymore can read the descriptions of these demonic locusts without seeing in them a reference to Hal Lindsay's comparisons to modern Apache helicopters and chemical warfare. Preachers have been known to identify these with the dreaded "killer bees" invading the United States and Mexican border to arouse fear in their congregations. Verse 9:7 brings the world of symbolism together with human qualities. As **the locusts looked like horses prepared for battle**, they also had faces that **resembled human faces**. The detailed features of the locusts combine technological advancements (helmets, iron breastplates, thundering wings with power greater than horses or chariots) and animalistic ferocity (uncut hair, lion's teeth, scorpion poison) to create a dreaded and invincible opponent.

One does not have to limit the horrible symbolism of these murderous creatures to twentieth-century war machinery to see the destructive possibilities of evil in the world. Some hybrid of the locust, a feared destroyer of the crops, with the scorpion, a venomous creature of the region, conjures up a nightmare for those living in any age.

The close observation of the locust show a horrible killing machine like never seen before, but a wider look at the battlefield shows who directs them in their assignment. The **king over them** was **the angel of the Abyss** (9:11). The Hebrew (**Abaddon**) and the Greek (**Apollyon**) name for the angel are given, both meaning "destroyer." The Hebrew derivative of Abaddon, meaning "ruin" or "destruction," is found in Job (26:6; 28:22; and 31:12), Proverbs (15:11 and 27:20), and in Psalm 88:11. In each of these contexts, Abaddon is connected with death and the Pit, just as in the personified form here. To enhance the importance of the destructive qualities of this leader, the Greek name is also given to the reader. The striking similarity between the name Apollyon (one Greek word for "destroyer") and the name of the Greek god Apollo may hold a key to a deeper intended meaning. Besides indicating that the religious culture of the Greeks is the enemy of the Christian, Apollo was the favorite god of Domitian—often identifying himself as a reincarnation of that deity. John's vision makes sure that the Christians understand the true source of their torment and the destructive quality of his reign. Domitian, and his idolatrous religious trappings, may be the one that is striking terror on the present lives, but the Christian knows that its source has risen from the Abyss of Satan's domain.

To keep the powerful drama moving along, the Revelation injects a movie-like segue, **The first woe is past; two other woes are yet to come** (9:12). The foreboding and foreshadowing of these woes serve to connect the previous set of trumpets with those to follow. This device keeps the story moving along, while the reader is left to ask, "If the torture of the locusts was not enough, what horrors lie ahead?" We are quick to discover the answer to that question. The three woes correspond to the three trumpet blasts heralding plagues that are to follow (9:12; 11:14 and chapters 15–16). The strange interlude of 10:1–11:13, with its stories of the angel and the little scroll and two witnesses, breaks up the woes that are to follow.

We see the second segue at 11:14. Various commentators have assessed this break in the literary structure, either seeing it as connected to the second woe (as 11:14 appears to do) or as a sidebar discourse on the imminence of Christ's return. Beasley-Murray feels that the interludes between the number six and the number seven of each of the successions serves to develop two eschatological questions: The first deals with the question posed by those living in the next to last times, "How long?" (cf. 10:7) and the second answers the concerns of the Great Commission: "What should the Church be doing in such a time?" (cf. 11:1–13).

When **the sixth angel sounded his trumpet** (9:13), John **heard a voice coming from the horns of the golden altar that is before God: "Release the four angels who are bound at the great river Euphrates"** (9:14). The horns are projections from the four corners of the altar (Exod. 27:2). The function of these horns is described in 1 Kings. If a person was seeking asylum, they could cling to these projections and plead for mercy from God (1 Kings 1:50–51; 2:28). Perhaps, as God is about to unleash the hellish war on the world, the voice from this location on the altar is a sign of such mercy.

But the four angels release their pent-up fury on the human inhabitants of the earth. The usual third is destroyed. These four angels unleashed at the sixth trumpet blast parallel the four angels holding back the winds of the earth of the sixth seal, but they are not the same nor do they function in the same way. In 7:1, these four angels are emissaries of

God, holding back destruction on God's sealed. Here we find four angles, apparently evil, who have been held back until God now allows their destructive mission to be used for His own judgment on the earth.

Their place at **the great river Euphrates** (9:14) gives us more insight into their role in the vision. The river, running through old Mesopotamia, was the home to an array of Israel's enemies (Assyria and Babylonia), and now modern Iraq. It was the dividing line that held back the enemies "of the north" that in the Old Testament often boded ill wind for Israel. When God set the boundaries for the Promised Land (see Gen. 15:18), this river was its northern most side. Many prophetic scriptures spoke of a swarm of armies invading from this natural wall (Isa. 8:5–8; Jer. 1:14–19; Ezek. 38:6). When the four angels are unbound from this great river of protection, it is equivalent to the unleashing of all the mounting fears of God's people, a massive military invasion from the north. Besides knowing that God has used such military force in the past to bring judgment on Israel, the Roman citizenry of the vision's present feared the encroachment of the armies of Parthia to their east. This vision combines both the fears of Israel and of Rome together in this one dreaded force. Rather than just have a visual experience of this vast array of power, John **heard their number**: two hundred million mounted troops alone (9:16). This number sounds incredulous, but merely points to the devastating and immeasurable destruction that is to follow.

Having heard the immensity of the number, John describes the powerful force through the depiction of **the horses and their riders** (9:17). The reader or audience, hearing that combination of words, could not help but remember the victory song of Moses (Exod. 15:1–18), "The horse and its rider he has hurled into the sea." The faithful witnesses are given a foreshadowed hope that God might do this again. These riders have breastplates (a coat of mail protecting the vital organs) of **fiery red, dark blue, and yellow as sulfur** (9:17). The colors were symbolic of the punishment they were bringing: fire, a constant for punishment in the apocalypse; the sapphire blue, looking like the smoke, and the sulfur color, the smell of the Pit—the very breath that came from the horse/lions' mouths (**fire, smoke and sulfur).** One third of humanity was destroyed by the three plagues coming from these beasts, inflicted by the mouth, and a particularly deadly tail that, like a snake, kills its prey with a deadly blow (9:19). There is no place to go to get away from their fury, neither in front or behind these deadly animals.

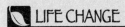

LIFE CHANGE

"THEY DID NOT REPENT"

The wrath of God poured out on the wicked serves only to harden them. Fear and, in these apocalyptic cases, absolute terror have never been effective motivation for repentance. It is only as people are drawn by God the Father (John 6:44) that they come into a saving relationship. Today is the day (2 Cor. 6:2) to respond to His quiet offer of salvation. Who do you know that has not yet come to the Father? What is your role in helping them hear God's offer of salvation?

Our attention now is placed on those that survive this attack. Surely they will fear God and change their ways! But we are sadly told that those **who were not killed . . . did not repent of the work of their hands** (9:20). As we will discover in the seven parallel bowl plagues, the wrath of God poured out on the wicked serves only to harden them to their activity. The list of their work is the occupation of those who worship **demons, and idols of gold, silver, bronze, stone and wood** (9:20), putting their faith in a lifeless and powerless worldly system. But this activity has its concrete form in murder, trusting **magic arts**, **sexual immorality**, and the theft of that which belongs to God (9:21).

ENDNOTES

1. The Greek text of the book of Enoch (chapter 20) lists them as Raphael, Uriel, Raguel, Michael, Sariel, Gabriel, and Remiel.

2. Bruce M. Metzger, *Breaking the Code: Understanding the Book of Revelation* (Nashville: Abingdon, 1993), 64.

3. This seems to be the understanding found in Rev. 6:10. There "the inhabitants of the earth" are seen as deserving God's judgment.

THE SEVEN TRUMPETS CONTINUED

Revelation 10:1–11:19

THE ANGEL AND THE LITTLE SCROLL 10:1–1

Chapter 10's actor is **another mighty angel** (10:1), like the one who had asked the looming question, "Who is worthy to break the seals and open the scroll?" (5:2). One more mighty angel is to come in 18:21 where, in announcing the destruction of Babylon, he throws a heavy boulder into the sea as an object lesson. Because the Hebrew word for mighty (*gibbôr*) is in the root of the name for the archangel Gabriel, some have suggested that the book of Daniel's angel Gabriel is in the background of this anonymous angel. The angel's clothing—a **cloud** for a robe, **sun** for a **face**, and a **rainbow over his head** (10:1)—is very similar to the descriptions of the Son of Man in the initial vision (1:12–16) and the décor of the heavenly throne room (4:1–6). This overlaying of descriptive sources from both the Old Testament and previous visions places the angel in the midst of a divine epiphany, but it does not identify him with any one player. He has come **down from heaven** and speaks for God.

The **mighty** angel was holding a **little scroll** (10:2). The play on words may be intentional. God's mystery and power is greater than any revelation that the human can receive. Unlike the first scroll of the Lamb (5:1), the little scroll lies open in his hand, representing the offer of God to see the secrets of His plan. The angel is indeed mighty because he places his **right foot on the sea and his left foot on the land** (10:2), showing the extent of his control and depicting the universal nature of the message he holds.

Yet before John is able to see what this new revelation discloses, the angel **gave a loud shout like the roar of a lion** (10:3). A further sign of the angel's mightiness, the shout breaks loose **the voices of the seven thunders**. John wants to record the message of these voices, but a **voice from heaven** (10:4) forbids him, as if the words are too awesome for anyone to understand or receive. In fact, the voice told him to **seal up** what was said as well as not to write it down. Some have compared this with Daniel's use of sealing as a way of speaking of things left unknown until the last days (Dan. 8:26; 12:4, 9). Since these voices were not recorded, this has led to great speculation as to what was said. Perhaps this tickling of our curiosities was just what the vision was seeking to accomplish. We are encouraged to come even closer so as not to miss another mystery that might explode onto our senses.

The angel who is **standing on the sea and on the land** (10:2) swears an oath (see Dan. 12:5–10) before God. **"There will be no more delay! But in the days when the seventh angel is about to sound his trumpet, the mystery of God will be accomplished, just as he announced to his servants the prophets"** (10:6–7). Remembering the answer "to wait" given to the saints' original question (6:10), God now says, **"There will be no more delay!"** The sign of the end will be the sounding of the seventh trumpet. The foreshadowing effect now is cast. Even if the next six trumpets bring with them what we have just experienced in the seals, we know that at the sounding of the seventh trumpet **the mystery of God will be accomplished** (10:7).

The same **voice from heaven** (10:8) that had kept him from disclosing the previous thunderous revelation now offers an invitation to receive the contents of the little scroll. Though a voice told John not to write the message of the thundering voices in 10:4, the same voice encourages him to accept what is being made available to him in this offering. **"Go, take the scroll that lies open in the hand of the angel who is standing on the sea and on the land"** (10:8).

As in the disclosure of the first scroll held by the Lamb (chapter 5), the little scroll is open and available for John to examine. Scholars have debated the relationship between the sealed scroll (*biblion*) of chapters 5 and 6 with this open "little scroll" (*biblaridion*). Some have suggested that the same scroll, originally sealed and now open, was meant. Others feel that a second, distinct scroll means a second revelation of God. What is clear is that God is moving from an all-inclusive disclosure of the Lamb's role in history, to John's specific purpose within that revelation. The question as to whether the visionary is able to stand the message is all that is unknown.

The strange command to **take** and **eat** (10:9) the little scroll has an antecedent in the commissioning of the prophet Ezekiel (2:1–3:3). In that story God instructs Ezekiel to eat the message that he is to deliver to Israel. The two stages that a preacher must go through in preparing a prophetic sermon, the spiritual formation that allows the message to permeate the messenger and the communication of that message to others, may be envisaged in this image. When Ezekiel ate the message given to him, he found it sweet. John found the scroll **as sweet as honey** in his **mouth,** but soon after he ate it, his **stomach turned sour** (10:10). John may find the message to be **sweet** upon receiving it, but when it comes to the actual application, the message has painful implications for him, the hearers of the message, and all of subsequent history. The sweet message of salvation would be mixed with tribulation and doom for all that would soon hear it.

The interplay that John has with the mighty angel of chapter 10 gives us insight into the Christian's role in the revelation. Unlike the concerns of the first "great" scroll, the emphasis is not upon the contents of the scroll, but rather on the reception and delivery of the scroll itself. John **was told, "You must prophesy again about many peoples, nations, languages and kings"** (10:11). In swallowing the scroll, John never shows us what was written upon it, but he does describe his internalization of the message and the nature of its taste. Even now we find this flavor to the book of Revelation. Preachers and teachers of this text must struggle to offer its bittersweet qualities to their students. Quite often one or the other, the sweet or the sour, is offered. But to the variety of listeners of the revelation—the **different peoples, nations, languages and kings**—there is also a mixed hearing. Salvation and judgment, tribulation and safety, persecution and victory make up the experience of all who "eat" the message that the mighty angel delivers on behalf of God. Too, we might take heart in knowing that the details of the message (what is written on the scroll) are not as important to us as the reception of the intent of the message (the offer of God's hope to us in the revealed Jesus Christ.).

THE TWO WITNESSES 11:1–14

Chapter 11 begins a series of strange events that are sometimes difficult to connect structurally with the flow of the text. Even if we were able to understand the sequence of events, the strange characters and actions of these two witnesses is a mystery to our eyes.

First, John is instructed to take a **reed** and measure the dimensions of **the temple of God and the altar** (11:1). A reed was often used as a standard measurement in the ancient Near East. With its jointed stalk, like bamboo, reeds grew to between 15 and 25 feet and looked like a natural measuring stick. Ezekiel 40:1–42:20 and Zech. 2:1–5 appear to be in the background of this action. But beyond this Old Testament imagery, the purpose and meaning of this measuring is in dispute.

The interpreter must first decide if John is being instructed to literally measure the Temple in Jerusalem. Those who argue for an actual measurement must deal with the timing of the destruction of the Temple by the Romans which occurred in the year A.D. 70. The extent of that destruction is also in debate, but certainly more damage was imposed on the Temple proper than merely the Court of the Gentiles. Others, who still want to hold for a later date (in the 90s), do so by ascribing an earlier source to this command to measure the Temple. Usually this demands that John used a tradition credited to an earlier Zealot author. This literature would have encouraged their rebellion against Rome by prophesying that God would only allow the "outer court" to be destroyed, but that the Temple and its holy remnant would remain intact.[1] It would seem more probable that John's vision is symbolic in nature, making use of the image of the temple as referring to God's faithful community as he has done on other occasions in the Revelation (3:12; 7:15).

Also, as in the Epistle to the Hebrews, John seems to understand the need for the temple to be limited in scope and function since Jesus Christ has become the ultimate temple and priesthood of God. John observed at the conclusion of the revelation: **I did not see a temple in the city, because the Lord God Almighty and the Lamb are its temple** (21:22). Certainly John's theology does not necessitate an actual literal temple and encourages a more spiritual reading of its Old Testament usage. But certainly this does not stop modern commentators from desiring the rebuilding of the temple in Israel as an eventual fulfillment of this text.

In measuring the temple and altar, the protection of God's faithful people in the face of persecution and calamity is assured. This image has the same effect as the sealing of the 144,000 in chapter 7. This divine protection is not stated directly, but is implied in the exclusion of such protection for **the outer court** (11:2). As this court **has been given to the Gentiles**, it will be trampled on by the unbelieving nations.

This action will take place for a period of **42 months** (11:2)—or the equivalent of three and a half years. The suffering that the Jews experienced under the Syrian emperor Antiochus Epiphanes (168–165 B.C.) appears to be behind this recurring period of time. His horrible deeds of desolation and defamation of the Jewish temple lasted three years, perhaps now viewed through the lens of Daniel's division of the seventieth "seven" into two parts (Dan. 9:27). This number occurs in other instances in the Revelation as "a time, times and a half of time" (12:14) and as 1,260 days (11:3; 12:6). The remembrance of this time frame had such a traumatic effect on the collective psyche of Israel that it becomes symbolic of any time of an unrestrained sadistic violence on the elect of God.

This time, the forces about to be unleashed on the world will punish those people who are outside the true community of God, whether they are Christians who are compromising their allegiances or whether they are unbelievers in general. As is understood throughout the Revelation, God's people are not to escape suffering and persecution in the days of trial, but they should know they are sealed and marked off for their ultimate spiritual protection. Just as the time is limited, so is the tribulation that they must endure.

During this same time frame (**1,260 days**) God will **give power** to His **two witnesses** who will **prophecy** while **clothed in sackcloth** (11:3). The three and a half year period is used often in the book of Revelation as a technical device for a period of unrestrained persecution. It not only mirrors the duration of the abomination of the temple by Antiochus Epiphanes (168–165 B.C.) but also divides the seventieth seven in Daniel into two equal parts. In this case, **anyone who wants to harm them must die** (11:5) by fire coming from the mouths of the prophets. We are always aware that "fire" in the apocalypse designates punishment, and here may be associated with the story of Elijah calling fire down from heaven to consume his enemies—or may represent the "prophecy" that they are called to pronounce. Either way, during this time protracted period of 1,260 days, the two witnesses are empowered to testify without restraint or opposition.

Teachers and preachers of the Revelation have discussed the identity of the two witnesses at length. The clothing is associated with penitence (Joel 1:13; Jonah 3:5–6) and worn by the prophets of old when they sought to encourage repentance in the nation. One thing that is certain is that John's vision has obvious connections with the two biblical prophets who the Jewish people thought would return at a latter time in salvation history. The prophet Elijah is associated with having **the power to shut up the sky so that it will not rain** and the great liberator Moses would **turn the waters into blood** and **strike the earth with every kind of plague** (11:6).

Too, both of these prophets made their exit from the earth through unconventional deaths. Through the apocryphal *Assumption of Moses*, we learn of the belief that God took Moses from the earth in a cloud, just as Elijah was taken up to heaven in a chariot of fire. At the divine epiphany of Christ's first advent, we would find both of these men showing up with Jesus on the Mount of Transfiguration.

Now they have come to testify to Christ before the days of His return. They are the **two olive trees** (signs of the coming end) and **the two lampstands** (holding the light of Christ to the nations) and represent the very presence of the Lord on earth (11:4; Zech. 4:11–14). If anyone would want to harm these witnesses, the powers represented by Moses and

Elijah will be used to kill them. Besides the obvious importance that these men have for messianic events, the biblical injunction for the necessity of two witnesses to authenticate a testimony in court or settle a dispute may be behind the need for this dual prophetic witness. Some have suggested even more importance to this dual character: priest and king; the Old and New Testaments; Israel and Church; the Law and the prophets, and the list goes on.

Regardless, these two witnesses are, without doubt, the most trustworthy prophets the earth could receive. But as the history of prophets to Jerusalem has proven, they are maliciously murdered and left to die in the most ignoble of ways. Like all ordeals and trials in the book of Revelation, once the purpose for the event is complete, God releases His protection and control so as to allow the flow of history to continue. So **when they have finished their testimony, the beast that comes up from the Abyss** attacks, overpowers, and kills them (11:7). This is the first occurrence of the beast. He comes from the Abyss, so we know of what type he is.

After they have accomplished their mission, and they are killed, **their bodies will lie in the street** (11:8) and all the people of the earth **will gaze on their bodies and refuse them burial** (11:9). Through our television screens, in modern times of war, America has witnessed the act of dragging our soldiers' bodies through the streets and knows what an indignity this is to all humankind. In Eastern culture, it would be hard to imagine a more disgraceful treatment of a human being than the public humiliation given to the two witnesses of God. The duration for this act of disgrace is a mere three and a half days (compared to their prophetic activity lasting three and a half years), so it does not negate the work that they have done.

Moreover, the place for this activity is **in the great city** (11:8), presumably Jerusalem. This is the city that Jesus wept over for its propensity for killing God's holy prophets and priests. It is the city where the Christ was crucified. But in this text, Jerusalem finds itself alongside the more stereotypical names of places hostile to God, **Sodom and Egypt**. Presumably, we are to extend this list to include all cities of the world that reject the witness of God in the world.

The hazing of the bodies of these holy witnesses will be cause for a festive spirit, where all the people of the earth will celebrate by sending each other gifts and take pride in their deeds. These two faithful witnesses to God are a link in the line of faithful witnesses from Christ, through Stephen, through all the martyrs, to these eschatological giants. We noticed that they died in the city where **their Lord was crucified** (11:8). Jesus was **their Lord**, and they followed Him in His death. People representing all the nations of the world will take part in this celebration, thinking that the ministry of God's prophets was a "torment" to **those who live on earth** (11:10). The word "torment" is used at various places in the Revelation, but here it is a claim of the wicked that they have been tormented by the two faithful prophets. Finally, the revelator is able to see who is really being tormented—and that the Word of God is having its effect on the world and will eventually show itself to be a more powerful and fearful adversary.

But after this relatively short period of shame **a breath of life from God entered them, and they stood on their feet** (11:11). As in the resurrection of Jesus after three days in the grave, God's raising them from the dead is a warrant for their testimony and life on earth. As they have followed their Lord into Jerusalem and received the same treatment and shame, they are now following Him in the exaltation. For the world, the party is over, **terror struck those who saw them** (11:11). A heavenly voice calls to them to **"Come up here."** The resurrected prophets are taken up **to heaven in a cloud** (11:12), the biblical transportation for all God's servants.

The discipleship path with Jesus is now completed; the prophets of God have mimicked Christ in His entire ministry. Three years of earthly ministry with unrestrained effect, three days in a disgraceful and shameful grave, and now exaltation to heaven. Whereas the Gospel writers depict Jesus' disciples "looking on" as Jesus went up into the clouds, the enemies of God's faithful (the two witnesses) are the ones left looking in this setting.

After watching this hopeful scene, John watches consequentially as **a severe earthquake** causes **a tenth of the city** to collapse. **Seven thousand people were killed in the earthquake, and the survivors were**

terrified and gave glory to the God of heaven (10:13). This response appears to be one of the few instances in the book of Revelation where a terrible act of punishment results in the repentance of the wicked. Robert H. Mounce believes this not to be a true repentance but only an acknowledgment of God's terrible power. He quotes Kiddle, saying, "the great mass of mankind [sic] will have committed the unpardonable crime of deifying evil."[2] As these people had just witnessed the resurrection of the two witnesses, and now have seen the terrible earthquake wipe out their city and friends, it just may be that they were willing to worship and give **glory to the God of heaven** (11: 13).

Many, fearing a type of universalism in this text, are not willing to allow this to be a true conversion to the Christ. Perhaps we should allow this one crack of hope in an otherwise devastating scene. Truly it is rare that any of the acts of terror in this book leads to the turning of the wicked from their routine, but here the power of the two witnesses' life, death, and resurrection eventually is too much for even this remnant.

But even this small opening of possibility closes quickly as the revelation offers its solemn observation: **the second woe has passed; the third woe is coming soon** (11:14). The second woe, having started at the blowing of the sixth trumpet, seems to have culminated with this last opportunity for responding to the prophets of God with faith. As we await the last trumpet blast, we know that the wicked will finally find their punishment for a continued attack on God's chosen.

THE SEVENTH TRUMPET 11:15–19

Finally the last of the seven trumpets is sounded. An interlude (10:1–11:14), as also used in between the opening of the sixth and seventh seal, had postponed the blast. The succession of events—from John's initial vision of Christ and the scroll of sealed mysteries, the removal of those seals, and now the heralding of the trumpets—has led to a mini-climax for the book. Many commentators have suggested that the book could have easily ended at 11:19, with the summary verse found in the first refrain called out by the **loud voices in heaven** (11:15): **"The kingdom of the world has become the kingdom of our Lord and of his Christ, and he**

will reign for ever and ever." The seventh trumpet brings with a very different atmosphere than the six that preceded it. Where the first six trumpets all signaled terrors upon the earth, the seventh trumpet is the first note to tune up the heavenly chorus for a jubilant celebration.

When we see **the twenty-four elders, who were seated on their thrones before God** (11:16), we know where we are again: the throne room of chapter 4. The elders, as in that initial vision, **fell on their faces and worshiped God**, saying:

> **We give thanks to you, Lord God Almighty,**
> **the One who is and who was,**
> **because you have taken your great power**
> **and have begun to reign.**
> **The nations were angry;**
> **and your wrath has come.**
> **The time has come for judging the dead,**
> **and for rewarding your servants the prophets**
> **and your saints and those who reverence your name,**
> **both small and great—**
> **and for destroying those who destroy the earth** (11:17–18).

The development of the series of sevens, and how it relates within and without to the other sections thus far, is sometimes difficult to follow. For one, in 8:13 we were told that last three angels were to unleash woes on the earth. Two of the trumpets (9:12 and 11:14) are specifically called woes and point to the coming of the next. But the third is not announced as such and, as we have noticed, the last trumpet is very different than those that preceded it. Some have suggested that the third woe is the next series of sevens (the bowl plagues). Others have felt that the third woe, though not called as such, is to be discovered in the interlude between the sixth and seventh trumpet. It is more likely that we are looking at the third woe in the blowing of the seventh trumpet.

Each of the two before used some form of foreshadowing to speak of the next (11:14 said, "the third woe is coming soon"). However, because this is the last woe, there is no need to use this type of formula. Though the tone of the seventh trumpet is jubilant and full of praise, the theme of woe-fulness comes through. As the chorus is heralding God's reign on earth, it acknowledges that **wrath has come** (11:18) along with God's blessings. As the earth is now in the hands of God's sovereign control, it is a time for **destroying those who destroy the earth** (11:18). Our view of the destruction has changed, but the results are still the same. By the time of the seventh trumpet, we are no longer thinking of the punishment and penalty for the wicked; we are addressing our praise to God—as we should.

John has one last view of the throne room before being given a novel **great and wondrous sign** in heaven (12–14). **God's temple in heaven was opened** (11:19). This heavenly temple is a much greater one than its earthly parallel in Jerusalem. As this chapter began with the measurement of the Temple, we are struck with the realization that the temple in heaven is now where we have direct access to the presence of God. Seeing the Ark of the Covenant is proof of that presence. The **flashes of lightning, rumblings, peals of thunder, an earthquake and a great hailstorm** seem to offer its final crescendo to the concert hall assembled in this closing scene. We noticed how this display was a common one in the book of Revelation, accompanying the throne room description (4:5) and usually giving an awe-inducing spectacle to the majesty of God. There are other places in the apocalypse where these natural activities, much like at Mt. Sinai, accompany the heavenly temple (see 8:5 and 16:18).

ENDNOTES

1. G. R. Beasley-Murray, *The Book of Revelation* (Grand Rapids, Michigan: William B. Eerdmans Publishing Company, 1978), 176–77.

2. Robert H. Mounce, *The Book of Revelation* (Grand Rapids: William B. Eerdmans Publishing Company, 1998), 224.

8

THE COSMIC
CONFLICT

Revelation 12:1–14:20

A t first observation, the structure of the book of Revelation takes a
wild turn at this point. Many have felt that the book has a beautiful
climax at the point of the last verse of chapter 11.[1] In many ways, the revelation could have ended with the blowing of the seventh trumpet and the
heralding of the finished kingdom at the end of that major section. But **a
great and wondrous sign** (12:1) breaks the flow of the series of sevens.
If we were attempting to make a chronology of these events, we would
be in desperate need of a signpost at this point. It makes better sense to
see this movement as starting over, attempting to get at a deeper look at
the prior conflict's history and causes.

The images that we are about to see are torn from any dateable features
and actually take us back to some primal period of cosmic clashes. These
cosmic clashes are even imbedded with features that look like the nativity
of Jesus Christ, but a story that we rarely hear at Christmastide. We can
see behind these storiesm various Old Testament and pagan myths that the
Jewish-Christian reader would have recognized in some form. The strange
uses of symbols, numbers, and creatures that are brought into the revelation have grabbed the attention of many creative interpreters of the
Revelation. Perhaps the reader should resist the temptation to stop at every
such text and read these chapters in the dynamic manner in which they are
written. The activity is compelling; the story drives us to look deeper into
the reasons for the struggle of good and evil that was described in a more
sweeping manner in the first half of the book.

THE WOMAN AND THE DRAGON 12:1–13:1

The sign we are directed to see is that of **a woman clothed with the sun, with the moon under her feet and a crown of twelve stars on her head** (12:1). "Signs" in the book of Revelation often point to the completed work of God in history. Much like in the gospel of John, the spectacular aspect of the sign is diminished in favor of its meaning and insight into the incarnate, hidden work of God. Without any further development in the story, we would wonder who this woman might be. She has just enough description to send our imaginations in specific directions. She has **the sun** for clothing, **the moon** for shoes, and a crown of **twelve stars on her head.** Aside from her cosmic significance, the number twelve serves to encourage further inspection.

She could be Israel, represented by the twelve tribes. Or she could be the New Israel, the Church, with her twelve apostles, or the sun, moon, and stars of Joseph's dream (Gen. 37:9). We soon discover that **she was pregnant** and **was about to give birth** (12:2). Now we're wondering if we are watching Mary in the birth pangs for our Lord. Or we can push the messianic character of Israel birthing her savior, a theme often found in Scripture. Isaiah spoke of Israel's pending freedom from bondage as "a woman with child and about to give birth writhes and cries out in her pain" (Isa. 26:17). Perhaps all of these images are layered in such a way as to give universal and ageless significance to the gospel story of Christ's first coming.

As the child is being born, another sign appears in the sky: **an enormous red dragon** (12:3). In this case, we are eventually told who this dragon represents. He is **called the devil, or Satan** (12:9). But before we get to that description, we are encouraged to use our imaginations to think more intuitively about this sign. He is **red** (12:3), as red as the blood that flows from the martyrs. He had **seven heads and ten horns and seven crowns on his heads.** The symbol of numerous heads dredges up the ancient depiction of the Canaanite dragon, Leviathan (Ps. 74:14). Often the Old Testament uses the image of these ancient dragons to represent Israel's enemies. John gives him seven heads, probably emphasizing the all-encompassing power of this monster. The ten horns presses the virility and power of those heads. The **crowns** that he wears are the diadems (*diademata*) of a presumed authority. Satan never wears the "victory crowns" (*stephanoi*) because he is never victorious in the book of Revelation.

This ancient enemy of all things good and godly has come on the scene just as the salvation of the earth is to be birthed. As we see the dragon's **tail** sweep a **third of the stars out of the sky** (12:4), we are tempted to think of the fallen angels that Jesus saw fall from the sky (2 Pet. 2:4). The drama is probably more descriptive of the massive size and power of this dragon, causing such cataclysmic damage with just the sweep of his tail. He positions himself **in front of the woman who was about to give birth, so that he might devour her child the moment it was born**. This dragon has a vested interest in not allowing God's messianic salvation to come to fruition.

The Israelite mothers while in captivity in Egypt found themselves in a similar situation, as Pharaoh's troops sought to kill their immediate born children. Matthew's nativity shows the historic jealousy of Herod seeking to kill the child Jesus. He too sweeps along other innocent bystanders in his murderous rage. It would appear that any time a savior is born, many innocent children are included in the carnage. It is no wonder that the Christian church calendar has historically used the first Sunday following Christmas to remember the Holy Innocents. As Israel cries for her children, so the Church weeps for those caught in the evil clutches of the devil.

In the midst of this danger, the woman gives **birth to a son, a male child** (12:5). We are not sure as yet why Satan wants so desperately to kill this child, but since we know him as the one **who will rule all the nations with an iron scepter** we are aware of the jealousy that exists. Before anything can happen, however, **her child was snatched up to God and to his throne.** The child is not seen again in this story. If it is the Christ Child, we are not led to wonder where He is, but only that he is safe with God and exalted. Perhaps we are to see in this exalted state the post-resurrection work of Jesus. Though there is little in the book of Revelation that carries with it substitutionary understandings of the atonement, the victorious component of Christ's work on the cross is often emphasized. Because Christ is victorious and with God, so shall those who persevere overcome.

On the other hand, **the woman fled into the desert to a place prepared for her by God** (12:6). The woman's plight continues while the child has now vacated the stage. In this wilderness sojourn the flight to Egypt is recalled. God has always prepared a place of escape for His people. She will **be taken care of for 1,260 days**, the same length of time that the persecution will occur (11:3; 13:5). Jesus left to prepare a place for His own just as God prepared this place for His people.

And there was war in heaven (12:7). The concept of war is a repeating theme in the Apocalypse. In fact, there are more instances of the Greek root word for war (*polemos/polemeo*) in the book of Revelation than in the rest of the New Testament books combined. Essentially the war pits the beast and its hoard of evil accomplices against God himself. Those people who align themselves with the beast are heard to ask: **"Who is like the beast? Who can make war against him?"** (13:4). This boast has been the boast of all those who make war. Their hubris and power make them feel invincible.

Because of this war motif, many have felt the book of Revelation too violent to have real application for Christians today. The prophecies of Revelation are a dangerous time bomb in some people's hands. It must be said that some actually develop schemes of interpretation that would lead to self-fulfilling prophecies of the end of time.

For example, if one can surmise that the final battle on earth appears to be made up of Israel and her enemies, we can hasten the last day by developing a political agenda that encourages such an Armageddon. Consequently, any group working for peace—which Jesus commands us to do—is viewed with suspicion. They are accused of aligning themselves with an evil network of shadowy antichrist figures seeking to short-circuit God's design for war and destruction. World organizations that promote cooperation and mutual understanding, such as the United Nations and the World Council of Churches, are believed to be evil institutions that will be used by the Antichrist when he begins his attack on God's faithful. Theologically, it is presumed that John's Revelation does not change Jesus' teaching on this matter. God still honors peacemaking; it is the devil that makes war.

This battle begins with Michael on the offensive. He and his angels attack; and the beast and his angels respond in kind. The good news is that the beast **was not strong enough** to overcome the forces sent by God (12:8). The beast, regardless of his horror or might, is not able to compete with the heavenly hosts. He loses his place in heaven, being **hurled down** (12:9). As quickly as the battle ensued, it is over. The devil, the one **who leads the whole world astray**, has been put in his place. He, along with all of his angels, is brought low to the earth.

But if the book as a whole is seeking to depict this war,

LIFE CHANGE
BLESSED ARE THE PEACEKEEPERS

Can organizations promote and support peace? Is it likely that Satan will use peace organizations to launch his evil against God's faithful ones? How can God be honored by organizations and people who are seeking peace? Romans 12:18 says, "If it is possible, as far as it depends on you, live at peace with everyone." How can we live at peace with everyone if we're fighting in a war? Should Christians be pacifists at all times? How do you obey Jesus' call to love our enemies when your family or country is threatened? How are you keeping peace?

with its visible manifestation seen in the confrontation of Christians with Rome, as a horrible blood bath, it is important to notice the songs of victory that intersect the narrative at key points. At the conclusion of Satan's defeat such an antiphonal song erupts:

> **Now have come the salvation and**
> **the power and the kingdom of our God,**
> **and the authority of his Christ.**
> **For the accuser of our brothers,**
> **who accuses them before our God day and night,**
> **has been hurled down.**
> **They overcame him**
> **by the blood of the Lamb**
> **and by the word of their testimony;**
> **they did not love their lives so much**
> **as to shrink from death.**
> **Therefore rejoice, you heavens**
> **and you who dwell in them!**
> **But woe to the earth and the sea,**

> **because the devil has gone down to you!**
> **He is filled with fury,**
> **because he knows that his time is short** (12:10–12).

What a beautiful song to fill the universe! It is a song of praise to God, but more directly to those who have remained faithful in their witness to God. The song celebrates the vindication of **our brothers** (12:10) whose reputation in the world and before God had been maligned by this accuser. The atonement for their lives came about by the two cooperative works of **the blood of the Lamb** and **the word of their testimony** (12:11). Though they did not **shrink from death,** it was the Lamb's blood that validated their worth and it was the word that they proclaimed that gave witness to Christ's authority. Therefore the heavens (and all that dwell in them) are called to join in the praise; the earth and the sea must lament **because the devil has gone down** (12:12) to them. And now we understand the cosmic picture as it is. Because the Dragon has been cast down to the earth, his fury is felt on the earth—even if his days are numbered.

The descriptions of the dragon's activities and composure up to this point have been graphic. He was relentless in his pursuit of the woman and her child; he **pursued** (12:13) and **spewed** (12:15) a torrent of water trying to overtake her. He was filled with fury and **enraged** (12:17). It is painfully clear why the "offspring" of Jesus Christ are the whipping post of Satan's anger in the present. The primeval picture that John has painted shows every generation of the Church the motivation for Satan's relentless hatred of all that are righteous. Having lost the great cosmic battle, he has decided to vent all his anger on those **who obey God's commandments and hold to the testimony of Jesus** (12:17). The Christians are being told through this story what Jesus had taught His disciples: that the real persecutor was that of Satan—and not the imperial soldiers. "Father, forgive them; for they know not what they do" (Luke 23:34 KJV) can be heard in this text. The persecuted of Jesus' disciples should not be surprised that they are being treated in the same way their Rabbi was treated (John 15:21).

The woman, conversely, **was given the two wings of a great eagle, so that she might fly to the place prepared for her in the desert**

(12:14) where she would be taken care of for **a time, times and half a time, out of the serpent's reach.** The time frame here adds up to the usual period associated with a limited time of unleashed sin and unrighteous activity (see 11:2). The connection with Daniel's seventieth "seven" (Dan. 7:25; 9:27) is also noted, that John's vision understands this event as a season of persecution prior to an eventual vindication.

Given the cosmic features of this story, it is interesting to note that the serpent's attempt to **overtake** and **sweep away** (12:15) the woman by spewing a torrent of water from his mouth at her is foiled by the earth itself. **The earth helped the woman by opening its mouth and swallowing the river** (12:16). God's creation is not only being renewed; it is intricately involved in that renewal.

THE BEAST FROM THE SEA 13:2–10

Chapter 13 puts the "trinity" of evil together. As **the dragon stood on the shore of the sea** (13:1), we see his two henchmen crawl out to aid him in his tantrum of revenge. The woe of the earth and the sea has been consummated by the two beasts that come forth from them. If there ever were an anti-Trinity, here is the cohort! The visions found in the book of Daniel (Dan. 7:2–7) appear to be portrayed in the beasts that are now parading across the cosmic stage.

The beast coming out of the sea had **ten horns and seven heads, with ten crowns on his horns** (13:2). Given that the names on these heads were **blasphemous,** it would be good to discern whom they represent. As with other such symbols representing historic persons, there have been many options offered. The most common interpretation is to see this sea monster as the power of the Roman Empire, and particularly as it is depicted through its succession of emperors. After these connections, the interpretive questions multiply. In a variety of ways the visions of the two beasts are placed before us to test our loyalty. Because the battle between Michael and the dragon has now come to earth via these beasts of the earth and sea, the faithful of God will need to see clearly their demand for authority and control over the earth. Blasphemy is a political event. It offers allegiance to the powers of this world, when God alone is worthy of such homage. The power of the beast was enhanced by his appearance, resembling **a leopard, but had feet like those of a bear and a mouth like that of a lion** (13:2). The four beasts of Daniel (7:4–6) seem to be combined into this one creature, all images of ferocious danger and strength.

We are told that **the dragon gave the beast his power and his throne and great authority** (13:2). Satan is seen as the authoritative source behind the Roman Empire. Though it is true that God is ultimately the Sovereign that gives all kings and rulers their power (Rom. 13:1–7), those who would pour out such wrath and fury on God's innocent children have no other source than Satan. A theodicy that attempts to credit suffering with God eventually will fall apart. We can make the assumption that this beast was a counterfeit Messiah, mimicking the Christ's saving act on the cross, because one of the heads on the beast **seemed to have a fatal wound** (13:3). This is an obvious allusion to the Lamb, **looking as if it had been slain** (5:6). In the case of Jesus, He was in fact dead, but through resurrection He is victorious. This beast only appears to be dead; his **fatal wound had been healed** (13:3).

John understood now that that when one worshiped the Emperor (the beast) one was actually worshiping the Satan (the dragon) who gave the beast his power. The adoring public was enamored with power, and lusted after the Empire's war machine and impressionable might. They worshiped this power, asking: **"Who is like the beast? Who can make war against him?"** (13:4). The language of invincibility lies behind these questions. All through history powerful civilizations have had such questions asked of them. As each of these world powers have receded into the backdrop of time, others have taken their place with more assumed power and might.

The activity of this beast is blasphemous toward God. This evil came through the beast's words (opened his mouth), through making war, and through authority given him. We are aware that **all inhabitants of the earth will worship the beast** (13:8). This description of the first beast's power to bring the world under his almost hypnotic spell—and to even conquer the saints in war—may leave the Christian wondering, "What will be my response? Will I also succumb to the beast's power?" John is reminded that the beast's followers included some from every **tribe,**

people, language and nation (13:7), but not those who had their names **written in the book of life belonging to the Lamb that was slain from the creation of the world** (13:8). The power and protection of the Lamb predates any authority granted this new beastly system injected into the old world order.

Following the presentation of this second manifestation of power and evil, the revelation of John gives a warning: **He who has an ear, let him hear. If anyone is to go into captivity, into captivity he will go. If anyone is to be killed with the sword, with the sword he will be killed. This calls for patient endurance and faithfulness on the part of the saints** (13:9–10). The warning begins with a formula reminiscent of Jesus himself: "He who has an ear, let him hear." Another way of saying, pay attention! Then using a combination of texts taken from Jeremiah (15:2; 43:11), he reminds his hearers that worshiping the power of the beast will lead to an inevitable confrontation with that force and violence.

THE BEAST OUT OF THE EARTH 13:11–18

Then John **saw another beast, coming out of the earth** (13:11). Because **he had two horns like a lamb**, you might mistake him for being placid and safe—perhaps even appearing to be like Christ. But the beast **spoke like a dragon,** so we know him to be of the same ilk as Satan himself. Some have interpreted this beast to symbolize religious authority which has compromised to the state and its secular designs. Others see it as the false prophet (see 16:13), because, like that prophet, **he performed great and miraculous signs, even causing fire to come down from heaven to earth in full view of men** (13:13). What is interesting to note is that this evil trinity, consisting of Satan, the Antichrist, and false prophet, is destined for destruction in the Abyss (20:10) while the Trinity of God reigns forever.

We are told that the role of this beast was to support the "ministry" of the first beast by exercising **all the authority of the first beast on his behalf**, and make the earth and its inhabitants worship the first beast (13:12). The second beast's main task was to deceive **the inhabitants of the earth**. The people would acquiesce and **set up an image** (see Dan. 3

and 2 Thess. 2:4) in honor of the first beast (13:14). The beast would be **given power to give breath to the image, so that it could speak** (13:15). Some commentators have felt that this referred to a common practice in the Roman world to use a form of ventriloquism to amaze people gathering around the statues of famous Roman leaders. People were known to do whatever the voice told them because of this deception. Perhaps the word "breath" (*pneuma*—Gk. spirit) here is to remind us of this second beast's role as a type of evil spirit. It is the role of this beast, as the Holy Spirit is to Jesus Christ, to make contemporary in every generation that which began in the source. The second beast's purpose is to give immediate life to Satan's incarnation in the world. And so we see, even though the first beast is quasi-dead—**whose fatal wound had been healed**—the second beast continues to give animation to its cause of destruction. As Eugene Boring has said, "All who support and promote the cultural religion, in or out of the church, however Lamb-like they may appear, are agents of the beast. All propaganda that entices humanity to idolize human empire is an expression of this beastly power that wants to appear Lamb-like."[2]

The beast out of the earth **also forced everyone, small and great, rich and poor, free and slave, to receive a mark on his right hand or on his forehead, so that no one could buy or sell unless he had the mark** (13:16–17).

The "mark of the beast" has given many novelists great imaginative fodder. Early in the advent of computer technology, preachers enjoyed pointing out the insidious nature of bar code scanners at the supermarket, personal identifications imbedded in computer chips, and the plastic card replacement of cold hard cash. Perhaps we have found these technologies to have hidden dangers, but they also have made our lives more convenient.

In the ancient world, branding or tattooing was often used as a way of marking prisoners or criminals. There is some evidence that such markings were used as well in the religious practices of the imperial cult, as some who worshiped Dionysus expressed their loyalty with such a tattoo (3 Macc. 2:29–30).

It might be more important to note here that John has in mind the mark that Christians received in chapter 7, distinguishing them as sealed (7:3;

see also 14:1) from harm prior to the unleashing of the seventh seal. The seal on the foreheads is in contrast to the mark of the beast. Those Christians who would choose to participate and benefit from the system of power and domination will be marked with that beast's mark, but the faithful will have the seal of the Lamb.

Because the mark, we are told, is actually **the name of the beast** (13:17) via a number, many have attempted to **calculate** that name's number which is 666 (13:18). The long history of debate over the number of the beast must belie a lack of the prerequisite **wisdom** and **insight** that is required to decipher the identity of the second beast. Scholars go in two basic directions at the start of any attempt to handle this mystery: (1) understanding the number 666 to be a symbol in and of itself, or (2) finding a formula that when applied to a person or name derives the number 666.

The first approach usually rests upon the trinitarian nature of the numbers (three "sixes") and the symbol of incompleteness or imperfection that the number six describes. This approach argues, given the propensity for the Revelation's use of the number seven, this number makes all the attempts at being an equal to it, but only approximates and falls short. Therefore, the number represents a type of false God, or antichrist, with little inference past that concept.

The second approach to the number usually is related to the ancient practice of gematria, a type of riddle where words or names are hidden in numbers. The letters of the alphabet are assigned a number in order, and then all of the letters of the name are added together. In this case, the Greek letters in Caesar Nero add up to the number 666. If this was to be a mere coincidence, it should be noted that a dominant variant in the manuscript tradition has the number 616, the sum of all letters if Nero's name is written in the Latin alphabet. This lends great support to the beast of Revelation being thought of as Caesar Nero. No other name would have given rise to the variant tradition of 616.

Because we have been supporting the time for the writing of the revelation to be during that of Domitian's reign, why then would the name of a previous ruler Nero be assigned to this beast? To explain this discrepancy, scholars have argued for a theory known as the *Nero Redivivus* (or Nero Reborn). Nero, as the Church's first imperial persecutor, had an infamous reputation for horror and bloodshed. Though it may be that Nero's persecution was local to Rome, the stories of his atrocities had spread into the Diaspora and down through the second generation. John now knows that the entire Roman system has been led by this same Nero. This may be the meaning of the cryptic phrase in 17:11: "The beast who once was, and now is not, is an eighth king." In this case, John envisions all of the seven kings (Caesars) of Rome coming to end, and Nero coming back to culminate the reign of terror as the Antichrist himself. Nero becomes the prototype for all subsequent evil rulers.

In the end, we are told that the number of the beast is the number of a person (13:18), that is, it is a "human" number. The beast is discernable to human beings through human processes because the beast will never obtain the divine status that it seeks. The beast's power will always remain in the province of human activities and failures.

Chapter 14 begins a transition in the interlude that prepares us for the pouring out of bowls of God's wrath in the next chapter. The use of the interlude (as in 7:1–17 and 10:1–11:14) in the Revelation tends to offer a kind of psychological reprieve for the faithful and persecuted Christian to assure them before the scene of suffering that is to come that they will be safe and secure in the Lord. In this case a series of three vignettes, beginning with the Greek (*kai eidon*), loosely translated "then I saw." These visions are all sights of comfort to those about to see the horrible unleashing of God's wrath. The scenes in chapter 14 contrasts the blissful fate of those who worship the Lamb with horrible demise of all those who choose to worship "the beast and its image."

THE LAMB AND THE 144,000 14:1–5

Then I looked (14:1) begins the first of three such visions. And what a sight! **The Lamb,** and with Him all those who had been sealed with the name of the Lamb and His Father's name, are **standing on Mount Zion.** Mount Zion, being the first fortress city of Israel's eventual capital Jerusalem (2 Sam. 5:7), continues to offer hope to God's people as the final safe house and perfect abode.[3] The transition from those who took the mark of the beast is obvious. Our vantage has transposed us to a different place with a different kind of people. The Lamb is clearly the same Lamb that John has seen earlier in the Revelation (chapter 5), but now the Lamb is standing on Mount Zion, not merely standing on the center of the throne, and He is surrounded by those who longed for support through their trials, and not merely incense bowls, representing the prayers of the saints. This truly is a sight for sore eyes!

After this awesome spectacle, John's ears are filled with an equally beautiful experience—**a sound from heaven like the roar of rushing waters and like a loud peal of thunder.** John likens it to **harpists playing their harps** (14:2). Again, as in chapter 5 (5:9)**, a new song** of deliverance and overcoming is sung **before the throne and before the four living creatures and the elders** (14:3). The song was only able to be sung by those who had been proven through their faithful witness and lives, for **they kept themselves pure** (14:4).

This is signified by the metaphor of "defilement with women," perhaps attributed to temple prostitution or, as some commentators have suggested, to the Old Testament commands of a Holy War oath. But because, categorically, this would exclude women from the new reign of God, a more figurative meaning is probably warranted. By not "whoring" (a figure used for Babylon and her cohorts, see most immediately in 14:8) with the world system, these faithful **follow the Lamb wherever He goes** (14:4). This form of discipleship of Jesus Christ was taught as even to follow Him to the cross. Therefore, **they were purchased from among men and offered as firstfruits.**

The "firstfruits" of the Old Testament offering system became a picture of those faithful who pioneer the way, either in Christian conversion (Rom. 16:5) or in victory over death (1 Cor.15:20). In this case, those who have gone ahead in martyrdom are seen as a "firstfruits" offering to God, a choice offering representing the best the earth has to offer. No wonder the last depiction of this holy crowd was as **blameless** (14:5). In a world of deception, lies, and false claims, these have been proven to be the real thing.

THE THREE ANGELS 14:6–13

Then I saw begins the second vision; a vision that is still upward but which affects those on earth in a deeper way. **Another angel flying in midair** is seen carrying **the eternal gospel to proclaim to those who live on the earth—to every nation, tribe, language and people** (14:6). This list is the same list seen in 7:9, following the announcement to the 144,000. The good news that is delivered rings out: "**Fear God and give him glory, because the hour of his judgment has come. Worship him who made the heavens, the earth, the sea and the springs of water**" (14:7).

This is good news! The final judgment has finally come, and we are able to do what we have been destined to do: worship God. And just in case we did not understand this good news, a **second angel** followed this up with a report: Babylon the Great (14:8) has fallen. This announcement is what we have desired to hear, but we will not see the actual fulfillment of that fall until chapter 18. But for those on earth, this message of good news must be experienced now. The ancient city of Babylon, the center of Israel's memory of captivity, was a biblical synonym for moral decadence and luxurious hedonism. They know how she **made all the nations drink the maddening wine of her adulteries**, by enticing God's children into their culture of self-indulgence and debauchery (see Jer. 51:7).

But perhaps the worst judgment on the city was the blasphemous name that comes from Dan. 4:30, "the Great Babylon." God will not allow any power to stand that replaces His greatness. Some then would see Babylon as a symbol of the Roman Empire that currently persecuted the Church or others as a greater prism into viewing all systems of earthly political power.

A minority opinion would understand Babylon to be a real nation, needing to rise from the ashes of the old Babylonia often identified currently with modern Iraq and its rise to power. The importance here is that the Church would see that Babylon had indeed fallen, and it no longer held any power or sway on the faithful.

This truth would be punctuated by **a third angel** crying out: "**If anyone worships the beast and his image and receives his mark on the forehead or on the hand, he, too, will drink of the wine of God's**

fury, which has been poured full strength into the cup of his wrath!"
(14:9–10). We are reminded again of the need to resist being branded
with an allegiance to the ruler of this worldly system. Just as we see the
result of those that have been faithful, being sealed, and standing with the
Lamb on the mount of rest and victory, we understand the fate of those
who do not. They **will be tormented with burning sulfur** (14:10) and
there is **no rest day and night** (14:11). The depiction of God's wrath as
a cup of wine to be drunk is a common Old Testament image (Jer. 25:15).
By mixing the wine-cup image of Jer. 51:7 with that of 25:15, we are to
see another contrast:

Jeremiah 51:7	Jeremiah 25:15
Babylon was a golden cup in the Lord's hand,	Take from my hand this cup filled with the wine of my wrath and make all the nations to whom
she made the whole earth drunk.	
The nations drank her wine;	I send you drink it. When they drink
therefore they have now gone mad.	it, they will swagger and go mad. . . .

By combining these texts, the Revelation is able to reconcile God's
ultimate control over all nations, Babylon's role as a seducer of nations,
and the wrath that is soon to come. Those who have drunk from the cup
of Babylon will now taste **the wine of God's fury** (14:10). The fact that
the smoke of their torment rises for ever and ever (14:11) will argue
against most annihilation theories of damnation, but the real import is
that they will finally experience the type of anxiety that the persecuted on
earth are now experiencing. As those damned must endure a prolonged
experience of torment without any rest, those remaining **faithful to Jesus**
must have a **patient endurance** (14:12).

Finally, the second beatitude comes from **a voice from heaven**:
"Write: Blessed are the dead who die in the Lord from now on"
(14:13). This blessing is ratified by the Spirit with a concurring **"Yes."**
The issue of rest is again given support. Those who are able to endure

will rest from their labor, because the work that they have accomplished on earth will have its final reward in the last days.

THE HARVEST OF THE EARTH 14:14–20

The third vision begins with **I looked,** as the two before it. We again see, as in the first chapter, an anonymous person **"like a son of man"** (see 1:13). Where in the first vision, the head was adorned with white woolen hair; here the person has **a crown of gold on his head** (14:14). The crown here is the victory crown and not a mere headpiece for royalty. The placement of this crowned monarch on a cloud instead of a throne may have connections with the hope of the Son of Man coming on the clouds (Matt. 24:30). This connection with the apocalyptic Olivet Discourse in Matthew seems to continue with the image of the **sharp sickle in his hand** (14:14) as this entry will see God gathering up the elect from all over the earth.

In this vision, the gathering is accomplished through the angel's announcement that the **"time to reap has come, for the harvest of the earth is ripe"** (14:15). The harvest is done by this Son of Man with the simple phrase **and the earth was harvested** (14:16). Some would see this as a picture of what Matthew was referring to when God comes to gather in all of those who are followers of Jesus. Others see this as a representation of a general judgment coming to all the earth. The former makes sense in light of the next series of events.

But now **a second angel** (14:17) comes from the temple in heaven with his own sickle. And yet **another angel** (14:18) who was given the task of keeping the fire (a symbol of punishment) cries out from the altar, **"Take your sharp sickle and gather the clusters of grapes from the earth's vine, because its grapes are ripe."** This second harvest is now thrown **into the great winepress of God's wrath** (14:19), a common Old Testament image for the judgment of God on the wicked (Joel 3:13).

The image appears to move from a mere harvest to that of an all out war. The grapes representing the harvest of unrighteous for judgment are thrown into the winepress where the juice (now blood) flowed as high as the horses' bridles, extending to the entire breadth of the Holy Land (about 180 miles). The whole land is now flowing with the blood of the wicked, though its effect is only **outside the city** (14:20) so as not to defile God's holy place.

This illogical portrayal reminds us that John's image contains more theology than military instruction. The final vision is a reminder of how serious God's call to faithfulness and endurance is. In the harvest that is to come, we want to find ourselves "ripe" (ready) for His collection, not consumed by God's wrath.

Having come to understand the fundamental reasons for the extremities that the Church is facing on earth, John is able to move to the scene of God's wrath that is about to unfold.

ENDNOTES

1. Christopher Rowland has called the beginning of chapter 12 "one of the most abrupt transitions in Revelation," "The Book of Revelation: Introduction, Commentary, and Reflections," *The New Interpreter's Bible*, 12 vols. (Nashville: Abingdon, 1998), 12:648; see also, Jürgen Roloff, *The Revelation of John: A Continental Commentary*, Continental Commentaries, trans. John E. Alsup (Minneapolis: Fortress, 1993), p. 139; and Bruce M. Metzger, *Breaking the Code: Understanding the Book of Revelation* (Nashville: Abingdon, 1993), 11.

2. M. Eugene Boring, *Revelation. Interpretation: A Bible Commentary for Teaching and Preaching* (Louisville: John Knox, 1989), 157.

3. The book of Hebrews (12:22 ff.), as well as the book of Revelation (chapter 21), sees Zion as representing the New Jerusalem. Holiness songs, such as "We're Marching to Zion," often used this image as well. Perhaps the Old Jerusalem was no longer a fit metaphor for God's holy city, as it had wedded herself too closely to the powers of Babylon. A New Jerusalem was built on the foundation of Zion, a new creation, after the old has passed away.

POURING OUT THE SEVEN BOWLS OF JUDGMENT

Revelation 15:1–16:21

With the start of this new section, dealing with seven angels and their seven bowls of wrath, the series of seven resumes again. The conflict narrative (12:1–14:20), containing stories of battles between beasts, dragons, and the followers of Jesus Christ, was a brief hiatus in the mounting depiction of end-time woes by a seven-fold series of events. Avoid the temptation to see the unfolding of these events in a linear fashion; this new series of sevens serves as a recap of the same period of plagues and hardships that the consummation of this world order demands.

One could see the series of sevens as following along in a type of spiral fashion, each time building on the taxonomy behind it. The chapters 12–14 took us to the core of the vision to see into the primal origins of the events unfolding. Perhaps John needed to show and be reminded that the same conflicts are at work in every age. And yet, in every age, the culmination of Christ's victory over Satan and all things visible and invisible is still the determinative event of history.

SEVEN ANGELS AND SEVEN PLAGUES 15:1–8

Again John uses the phrase **I saw** to begin **another great and marvelous sign** (15:1). These words are used over forty times in the book of Revelation and serve to emphasize the visual nature of the revelation. John's eyes can barely keep up with the rapid progression of images that parade before him. Having been drawn along by the images and actions of the revelation, the **last** sign is about to be seen: **seven angels with the seven last plagues** (15:1). The bowls that carry these plagues will not be mentioned until chapter 16, and the dramatic literary approach used in the first two sets of seven is not followed in as great a detail. They come in rapid succession, without the artistic flair of the earlier sets. Perhaps even God is tiring of the pace of His creation's redemption and is speeding His wrath's end. Indeed, there is a hopeful overtone to 15:1, giving rationale for the word "last," **because with them God's wrath is completed**. God has in mind the perfection of the world's salvation. It has been incremental in nature, but it has been heading to the conclusion we are about to behold.

John then **saw what looked like a sea of glass mixed with fire** (15:2). The **sea of glass** that was seen in front of the throne of heaven as crystal (4:6) now appears to be **mixed with fire**. As this image begins the discussion of the seven bowl plagues—and as the book of Revelation mixes images from the plague narratives of the Exodus—this sea may represent the path to redemption that the Christians must take if they are to make it to the Promised Land. The **fire** (red) mixed with the waters may express the judgment that will fall upon evil, just as the sea covered Pharaoh's chariots. Furthermore, when we see who stands **beside the sea** (15:2), we may discover a better interpretation for the fire imagery. Reflected in the sea like fire is the blood of **those who had been victorious over the beast and his image and over the number of his name**.

The martyred saints **held harps given them by God and sang the song of Moses the servant of God and the song of the Lamb** (15:2–3). The passive **given** is used often in the book of Revelation to represent divine control over the action being done by others, often unnamed. Here we know it is God who gave them their harps. The new song that the martyrs sing has its source in God himself. The combination of **the song of Moses** and **the song of the Lamb**, as if mixed in a heavenly recording studio, places the musical celebration on the bank of the Red Sea sung by the children of the Lamb. These verses had their origin in Exodus 15 and Deuteronomy 32, which were a part of the evening synagogue celebration for all of Israel. Now the song of the Lamb depicted the same liberating act for these believing Christians.

> **Great and marvelous are your deeds, Lord God Almighty.**
> **Just and true are your ways, King of the ages.**
> **Who will not fear you, O Lord,**
> **and bring glory to your name?**
> **For you alone are holy.**
> **All nations will come and worship before you,**
> **for your righteous acts have been revealed** (15:3–4).

In comparing this "song of Moses" with its original in the Exodus story, we immediately notice that it is out of order with the plagues that follow. Moses' confrontation with Pharaoh eventually culminates with the horses and riders of Egypt being thrown into the sea. Moses and all his company sing of this triumph from their vantage on the other side. But here the declaration **Great and marvelous are your deeds** (15:3) is sung before the horrible plagues are unleashed in the subsequent chapter (16).

The song of the Lamb can be sung before we see our redemption because recounting the victory of Christ over death and Hades is a narrative that gives sense to the possibilities of our own death and suffering. If the people of God are to be involved in the plagues that follow, a song of praise to God, acknowledging God's righteous power and control over all things, must be on their lips from the start.

This song, pointing to the eventual and universal acceptance of Israel's God, a common Old Testament theme, has been the center of prophetic interest in international affairs. The need to have a historic moment when all the nations of the world come to Jerusalem to worship has motivated some interpreters toward a literal conclusion to this prophecy. Certainly other biblical texts remind us that "every knee should bow, in heaven and on earth" (Phil. 2:10), but may point to the ultimate rule of Christ over all things. Evangelical Christians have sometimes contributed to the fragile political climate of the Middle East by too closely identifying the center of apocalyptic activity to modern Israel. Perhaps it is enough to notice that this inference to the Exodus narrative is surpassed by the song of the Lamb, a far less militaristic model for world domination and power.

Following this song, John saw the opening of a **temple, that is, the tabernacle of the Testimony** (15:5). The name given to the dwelling place of God during the wilderness wanderings of Israel and the reference to the two tablets of the Testimony received on Mt. Sinai harkens the reader back to the same act of deliverance in the Exodus (Num. 17:7). Since the temple is opened, one would expect an invitation to enter and to meet with God. But this temple was not accessible because it was **filled with smoke from the glory of God and from his power** (15:8). **Seven angels with the seven plagues** (15:6) dressed in garb representing a royal priesthood (**clean, shining linen** and **golden sashes around their chests**, see Ezek. 9:2; and Dan. 10:5), come out from the temple. They receive from the four living creatures **seven golden bowls filled with the wrath of God** (15:7). We now know, just as in the Exodus event, we must go through a godly formation before we are able to know God in such fullness.

THE SEVEN BOWLS 16:1–21

The stage has been set. God has assured the safety of His Church by showing the saints as onlookers from the shore of the sea. We are about to see the last of the judgments of God, finishing God's ugly but necessary business. The seven angels have been readied to **pour out seven bowls of God's wrath on the earth** (16:1).

The first angel went and poured out his bowl on the land (16:2). We are immediately reminded of the first of the four trumpet plagues. After close inspection, one can see a direct parallel with the first four trumpets and the first four bowls (see 8:7–12), but not as ordered or direct. The same connection with the Egyptian plagues is found, but here the events are not as graphic or developed, almost suggesting that John is tiring in his report. He desires for it to be over, but he still must watch as **ugly and painful sores broke out on the people who had the mark of the beast and worshiped his image** (16:2). The mark of God's judgment is now more powerful than the mark of the beast.

When the **second angel poured out his bowl on the sea**, the effect was to kill **every living thing in the sea** (16:3). This was accomplished as in the first plague in Egypt when God turned the Nile to blood. Whereas the second trumpet blast turned the sea to blood and killed a third of its occupants, this plague finishes the job by killing all living things.

As if that first Egyptian plague could not do enough in one blow, the revelation shows the effect of this coagulated bloody water on all the creation. **The third angel poured out his bowl on the rivers and springs of water** (16:4). In the same manner, this completes the destruction of the trumpet plague (cf. 8:11). At which point **the angel in charge of the waters** said: **You are just in these judgments . . . because you have so judged; for they have shed the blood of your saints and prophets, and you have given them blood to drink as they deserve** (16:5–6).

In Jewish tradition, God gave angels authority over the various elements of creation. In Rev. 14:18 we see a similar angel having authority over fire. With this angel's approval, God, the Holy One, who goes by the name of Yahweh (**you who are and who were**) has given the correct punishment to match the evil deeds done. They shed blood; God gave them blood to drink. The **altar**, the space that makes all things holy, is animated and adds its own response: **"Yes, Lord God Almighty, true and just are your judgments"** (16:7). The possible voice of the altar is coming from the collective mouth of those martyrs whose lives were poured out as God's witnesses.

Now the **fourth angel** will **pour out his bowl on the sun** (16:8). This had the effect of intensifying the heat of the sun and causing people to be scorched and seared (16:9). Remarkably, the people **refused to repent and glorify** God. Instead they curse God, the very one having control over the plagues. John now sees that the acts of God's punishment have not served to turn these who have been intoxicated by the power of the beast. Unlike the terrifying effect on the survivors of the earthquake prior to the seventh trumpet blast (11:13), this group refuses to give glory God.

The fifth plague parallels the Egyptian plague of darkness; it is the opposite of the horrific fire that was just let loose on the earth's inhabitants. Actually, the **fifth angel** released his bowl's contents on **the throne of the beast** (16:10). It would make sense that the seat of the power of the world, when struck by God's wrath would leave the world in darkness. The world where the beast reigns needs to worship the power and authority which comes with this system. Some people would rather have Satan sitting on the throne of the world because they fear the chaos that might come without the control of such a world order. When one places faith in the economic and political systems of this world, the darkness that ensues without it is too much for such people to bear. The loss of the beast's throne only heightened the **agony** and cursings coming from the pains and sores of the last plague. But again **they refused to repent** (16:11).

A strange mixture of references to the plagues of Egypt makes up the **sixth angel**'s bowl. The great Euphrates River is **dried up to prepare the way for the kings of the East** (16:12). The description here of a plague striking the Euphrates, allowing a free entrance for a military invasion from the East, has a parallel with the sixth trumpet in chapter 9. Added to this is the strange advent of frogs hopping out of the mouths of the dragon, the beast, and the false prophet (16:13). They were actually three evil—or unclean—spirits of demons that had the ability to do miraculous signs (16:14). They become the recruiters, enlisting the kings of the whole world for the battle that is about to ensue. Some commentators have wondered why a more hideous animal might have been used to depict this agent. They have answered the question by showing how various ancient religions, such as Persian Zoroastrianism, saw a magic quality in the frog. However a more compelling explanation is that the revelation is merely carrying through the images of the Egyptian plague.

The backdrop behind these images of a marauding army marching across the Euphrates to overthrow Rome and all its citizens is tied to at least two traditions being overlapped in this sixth plague. Foremost is the common Old Testament idea that God would bring together all of the armies of the world to bring about His judgment, sometimes on Jerusalem (Israel) and sometimes on the all the wicked. John, in the Revelation, will use Ezekiel 38–39 in chapter 19 (vv. 11–21) to express the same thing; it appears to be in the mix in this image as well.

A second tradition that has been used by John as well comes from the *Nero Redivivus* myth that we looked at in 13:18. Many living with the benefits of the Empire feared that the peace they felt in the powerful military economy of Rome would someday all come falling down like a house of cards. They could almost feel the breath of the Parthian soldiers' horses coming from the east. Their worst fear was to see Caesar Nero riding at the front of the charge, come back to life to reap from his anger.

The difference here is that God is not bringing the armies together, but rather the anti-trinity of Satan, the Antichrist, and false prophet. God will allow this gathering only because God will use it to finish His purging of evil on earth. At this point, on the verge of this gory and horrible war, the third beatitude is interjected: **Blessed is he who stays awake and keeps his clothes with him, so that he may not go naked and be shamefully exposed** (16:15).

At first glance this saying comes out of nowhere. We recognize it at the same time as the voice of God and as the evangelical language of Jesus (Matt. 24:42–44). We can hear Jesus in His earthly ministry teaching His small group of disciples through the parable about proper wedding garments and the need to be ready when the reign of God comes. Now the words break on to the cosmic stage, and the risen Christ speaks again the same message. The connection of the ethical teaching of Jesus with the eschatological goal of preparedness is made.

LIFE CHANGE

BE DRESSED AND READY

It has been thousands of years since Jesus first spoke the parable about the virgins waiting the arrival of the bridegroom (Matt. 25:1–13). He concluded, "Therefore keep watch, because you do not know the day or the hour." There have been some who have said, "I've heard that Jesus was coming all my life. I'm not looking for Him any longer." There are others who have said, "I'll do the things I want since He's not come yet." Still others are watching, looking for His return, ready to welcome Him. Where are you? Are there times you've been ready and times you've been careless? How can you keep dressed and ready for a whole lifetime?

The blessing is necessary because the fear that arises from the next verse would send tremors through the unprepared, because the kings were amassing their armies together to **the place that in Hebrew is called Armageddon** (16:16).

Armageddon as a place is rarely seen in Scripture or other ancient sources as a place with any infamous connections. The word seems to be the combination of two Hebrew words, "Har" and "Mageddon," meaning the "Mountain of Megiddo." On the other hand, Megiddo as a city did fit into the historical memory of Israel. Because of its strategic location, it often had stories of militarism associated with it. Armageddon, as is the case with many such technical words in the Apocalypse, may be lost to our interpretive skills. The importance of the place is that it represents the final overthrow of Satan, the Antichrist, and all those desiring the power and authority known only to God. This is the place where God is victorious over all the military forces the world's kings could muster.

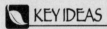 **KEY IDEAS**

NATIONS AGAINST GOD

Why do the nations conspire,
   and the peoples plot in vain?
The kings of the earth take their stand,
   and the rulers gather together
against the LORD
   and against his Anointed One.
           —Psalm 2:1–2

When **the seventh angel poured out his bowl into the air**, a loud voice came out of the temple, **"It is done!"** (16:17). Because it came **from the throne**, we presume it be God, who as Alpha and Omega, knows when things are finished. The similarities with the seventh trumpet blast are clear. In both of these endings of a seven series, the temple is open, the kingdom has been announced, and the voices announcing this event are accompanied with **flashes of lightning, rumblings, peals of thunder and a severe earthquake** (16:18). We are told that it is the most tremendous earthquake in human history. But this time, in contrast to the earthquake prior to the seventh trumpet (11:13), there are no repentant hearts to be found. Even though the **great city**, presumably Rome,[1] is **split into three parts** (16:19), and the rest of the cities of the world are destroyed. Even though the land masses of the world are completely torn asunder and hailstones (weighing about one hundred pounds each) fall upon the people of the earth, they merely **cursed God** (16:21).

All is in place now for the final judgment of God on the earth. Because God's memory is good, Babylon the Great will be given **the cup filled with the wine of the fury of his wrath** (16:19). We are about to see the great city Babylon (Rome) come to its demise and rightful end.

ENDNOTES

1. It is possible that this city is to mean Jerusalem, as the phrase "great city" appears to be speaking of Israel's Holy City in 11:8. But the movement of the text toward the demise of Babylon seems to point to Rome. Of course, this city now becomes representative of every human system that deifies its own power and prestige over that of God's rightful reign and worship.

BABYLON, THE GREAT PROSTITUTE, FALLS

Revelation 17:1–19:10

C hapter 17 is a continuation of the plagues of the seventh bowl. We are seeing a more detailed picture of the destruction of Babylon that was mentioned in the previous chapter (16:17–21). Literarily, the use of **one of the seven angels who had the seven bowls** (17:1) to inaugurate this depiction makes a direct connection with the seventh bowl plague and helps us see that the same messenger is giving a clearer meaning to those bowls.

BABYLON, THE PROSTITUTE 17:1–18:24

With the vocative "**Come!**" John is invited to look closer at Babylon's demise. Being given an unflattering feminine personification, she is called **the great prostitute, who sits on many waters** (17:1).

Feminist scholar Catherine Keller sees this personification as an instance of a pervasive anti-female theology in the Apocalypse. As John's "revealing gaze is male," she says, the ultimate demise of evil in the world comes through the destruction of a woman.[1] Though her interpretation of the Prostitute's significance for all women may be a bit overstated, she underscores the Bible teacher's sensitivity to the role images play in our interpretations. The book of Revelation's depiction of women should not to be used to deride a future role for women in God's redemptive plan but rather to create new images offering restorative powers to all readers of the Revelation. In fact, identifying the great prostitute with the rise of modern women's liberation, as some preachers have done, is a much greater stretch for this image.

The obvious moral implication of identifying Babylon with a prostitute is that she was not alone in her debauchery. **With her the kings of the earth committed adultery** (17:2). We are aware that the drunken thirst for power is a lust often more addictive than sexual desire. Her ability to influence the kings of the earth shows us the intoxicating nature of Babylon, trickling down to all the **inhabitants of the earth**. The Prostitute is not a harlot because she is a woman, but although she is a woman, her nature is to prostitute herself.

We might, with Keller, ask what a truly feminized world might look like if the woman is able to offer equal and prophetic insight to the powers and personalities that men have embodied throughout most of world history. Certainly the heavenly woman of chapter 12 participates in the conflict with the satanic dragon with great success, providing a much more positive image.

Giving some attention to the metaphor of the woman in this section, mostly because of modern concerns for the role she plays in the church and society, is an important exegetical sidebar. But more important is the question as to what this prostitute represents in the larger revelation. The most obvious Old Testament reference to this image is found in Jeremiah 51. There the prophet speaks of the sins of the city of Babylon, as also is the reference to its location **on many waters** referring to the Euphrates and the various canal systems that surrounded the

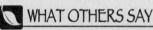

WHAT OTHERS SAY

THE PROSTITUTE OF BABYLON

Possible Identities of the Prostitute of Babylon

- The Roman Empire
- The Holy Roman Catholic Church
- Some new European renaissance of the Roman Imperial system
- Modern Iraq
- Interestingly, most European and now former Soviet church scholars see the description of the woman, centering mostly on the themes of economic prosperity and international dependency, fitting better with the contemporary United States
- Christians must be willing to see the evils of Babylon wherever they may arise.

ancient city (17:1; Jer. 51:13). We later discover that these **many waters** are representative of the **peoples, multitudes, nations and languages** (17:15) that have followed after the Harlot. The nations are said to be drunk on Babylon's wine (17:2; Jer. 51:7). The image of the peoples of the earth finding their source for sustenance and addiction is likened to the waters that flow out from a commerce-driven city.

Throughout the years of interpretation, many suggestions have been made: the Roman Empire, the Holy Roman Catholic Church, some new European renaissance of the Roman Imperial system, and, most recently, because of the ancient connections with Babylon and the Euphrates basin, modern Iraq. It would not be surprising to find that many American interpretations of the Prostitute of Babylon have been tied to its enemies, both ideologically and politically. Interestingly, most European and now former Soviet church scholars see the description of the woman, centering mostly on the themes of economic prosperity and international dependency, fitting better with the contemporary United States. America must be willing to see the evils of Babylon wherever they may arise.[2] In the end, we are aware of the name given by the angel—**the great prostitute** (17:1)—showing up on her forehead along with BABYLON THE GREAT (17:5). The image of prostitute carries the seductive quality of the power of the nations, people putting their faith in it rather than in God Almighty. Using a common Old Testament image of God as a jealous spouse, watching the lover go to others for fulfillment, this image can be applied to national allegiance during any age of human history.

Then the angel carried John **away in the Spirit into a desert** (17:3). Being **in the Spirit** is the operative experience for John at the onset of receiving a divine epiphany (see 1:10; 4:2; 17:3; and 21:10). In this case, John needs such spiritual insight to tear off the curtain that shrouds the mystery of the Roman Empire. The Christian who has given allegiance to Christ is confused by the controlling oppression that comes from Rome. If God is sovereign, then why is something else controlling the world? One wonders if the place of the desert to which John refers is similar to Jesus being led by the Spirit into the desert for His own time of trial and temptation. As Christians are being asked to come out from the world's powerful, tempting, even addicting clutches, they must depend on the Word and God for their strength and purpose.

We now know this great prostitute to be the power of Rome, because she is sitting **on a scarlet beast that was covered with blasphemous names** and **seven heads and ten horns** (17:3). We have seen this beast before in chapter 13 as the beast that came out of the sea. The **scarlet** color probably points to the meaning throughout the Revelation having to do with the murderous and bloody nature of this beast. As with the dragon of chapter 12, the color probably also alerts us that this is an agent of Satan. The beast is one of the dragon's henchmen, generally in charge of political and economic authority.

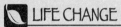 LIFE CHANGE

OVERCOMING TEMPTATION

Christians must depend on the Word and God for strength to come out from the world's powerful, tempting, even addicting clutches. Even though the powers of temptation are great, the grace of God is greater. "No temptation has seized you except what is common to man. And God is faithful; he will not let you be tempted beyond what you can bear. But when you are tempted, he will also provide a way out so that you can stand up under it" (1 Cor. 10:13). We will face temptation, but we can overcome it with God's help. In what areas of your life are you most often tempted? How has God given you victory? Where do you need forgiveness for past failures and boldness for the future?

The **blasphemous names** (17:3) would be the very names of the Roman emperors who loved to attach divine status and roles to their imperial titles. The seven heads and ten horns cryptically point to the Roman system, but we must wait just a few more verses to discover the true meaning of this vision.

At this point, John notices that she is dressed with **purple and scarlet, and was glittering with gold, precious stones and pearls** (17:4). This clothing would be comparable to the clothes of a wealthy prostitute.[3] The opulence and decadence of these trappings is highlighted by the **golden cup in her hand** (17:4). This cup is probably a direct connection with Jer. 51:7: "Babylon was a gold cup in the LORD's hand, she made the whole earth drunk." John depicts the cup held firmly in Babylon's hand, now filled **with abominable things and the filth of her adulteries** (17:4). The wine has been replaced with unclean things.

As in the Old Testament, these words usually conjure up pictures of idolatrous and blasphemous worship. We are reminded of the desolation of the temple (Dan. 9:27) accomplished by Antiochus IV Epiphanes when he turned God's Temple into a center for the worship of Zeus. (Refer also to Mark 13:14, "the abomination that causes desolation.") In all we see here, the ultimate depiction of all the seductive power of the world order, drunkenly careening with sadistic glee over the death of God's faithful and offering toasts to the power it has idolized and adorned.

John reads the title written across the woman's forehead:

MYSTERY

BABYLON THE GREAT

THE MOTHER OF PROSTITUTES

AND OF THE ABOMINATIONS OF THE EARTH (17:5).

The woman is Babylon. Or better, the woman is the source of all Babylon-like **prostitutes** and **abominations**. This **mystery** is an interpretive key to help us understand how John is to see all of the epiphanies of God in the Revelation. Are we to see this woman as representing Babylon, a city that existed hundreds of years before the first century reader? Is this to be a New Babylon as is discovered in the Roman Empire? During the Gulf Wars, the direct connection between modern Iraq and ancient Babylon was used to add apocalyptic furor to the political rhetoric.

But is Mother Babylon to be found residing in all her offspring through history, both Rome and the West, even America? As we read the descriptions of the power residing in this woman, we wonder what nation could control the economic futures, the political destiny of all small nations of the world. At any given time since the Apocalypse was written, we have seen such powerful nations come and go, but we recognize in them all the image of "Babylon the Great." Whatever we come to believe about this, John saw that the woman of this mystery is alive and well and not lost in Israel's history books. We should notice the same.

He saw that the woman **was drunk with the blood of the saints, the blood of those who bore testimony to Jesus** (17:6). **Blood** runs through the apocalypse like life through the body's veins. Sometimes the word is used metaphorically (6:12; 8:7, 8; 11:6; 16:3, 4). Many times, as here, it is the blood of the saints themselves (6:10; 16:6; 17:6; 18:24; 19:2). Rarely does it refer to the blood of the Christian's enemies (14:20). The most powerful usage is to depict the atoning work of Jesus Christ (1:5; 5:9; 7:14; 12:11; 19:13).

As well, the word **testimony** is generally connected with death and martyrdom in the book of Revelation (6:9; 11:7; 12:11; and 20:4). It is the reason John gives for writing and being on Patmos (1:2; 9). Testimony is why the dragon is angry and bent on killing the heavenly woman's off-spring (12:17). At the conclusion of the Revelation, Jesus describes the book itself as "this testimony" (22:16). An interesting relationship between blood and testimony is found in the hymn of chapter 12. "They [the saints] overcame him [the great dragon accuser] by the blood of the Lamb and by the word of their testimony" (12:11). Christ's blood and the Church's testimony are commingled and undiscernibly equal. It is no wonder that the Greek word for testimony, "martyr," became the ultimate definition of those who died giving faithful witness to Christ. We now know the contents of the gold cup in Babylon's hand. This cup is not merely the embodiment of idolatrous worship. The ultimate blasphemy against God is not ritualistic in nature; it is to defile the very people of God. Spilling the blood of the Christians, the temple of God, is akin to the earlier desecrations of the Temple of Jerusalem.

John **was astonished** (17:6) at the awesome sight of this woman. He, like the rest of the world, was at first mesmerized by the siren call of the prostitute's ability to be worshiped and treated as an object of erotic power. But the angel snapped him to consciousness: **"Why are you astonished? I will explain to you the mystery of the woman and of the beast she rides . . ."** (17:7). God's antidote for the possessive qualities of nationalism, idolatry, and materialism is to **explain . . . the mystery**.

Exposing the powers for what they are leaves them impotent to exert any influence on God's faithful. All those who have been impressed and astonished at the power of this imperial goddess and who have drank from her toxic and intoxicating goblet are given freedom by the clarity of this revelation. The angel is soon to expose to John the real nature of the Great Prostitute, Babylon. When this demystification comes, freedom and insight will surely be the result. Rather than seeing an alluring beauty adorned with luxury and seductive power, we see a drunken harlot, bibbing on the very blood of God's holy saints.

Who has not been astonished at the sights and experiences of living in a secular society with its abilities to accomplish virtually any stated goal that it imagines? Like a country boy looking dizzily into the towering skyscrapers of the modern city, many are in awe of human technological capability. The "shock and awe" of modern warfare has caused the victim below to wonder at the power of the unseen enemy. Furthermore, because the mechanisms for accomplishing those goals are always beyond the individual's grasp, our culture is always tempted to deify those mechanisms. The codependence between the corporation and its many addicted disciples keeps smaller and poorer nations and persons coming back to the economic and political trough for more. The social forces that elevate the kings and nations of the world do so by blinding the eyes of those who must lay down their lives for its continued growth and existence.

The mystery of the prostitute and the beast on which she sits is now made clear. The beast who **once was, now is not, and yet will come** (17:8) has often been thought to refer to Caesar Nero. As mentioned earlier, Nero's reputation as an enemy of Christians had traveled far and wide throughout the Roman Empire. The rumors of his murderous, bloodthirsty rampages on the saints of God may have surpassed the actual facts of history, but they endured long past his death and fueled speculation about a resurrected return to do even more. Again, this theory has been called *Nero redivivus*, "Nero come back to life." We should also note the close connection that this description has with the description of God himself: the one "who is and who was and who is to come" (1:4, 8; 4:8).

The beast is an anti-God. God fills the cosmos from beginning to end; He has been constant and faithful in history. The evil one depicted through the image of the beast had an end and will have a final end as well. We know this because even though he **once was** and **now is not**, the beast **will come up out of the Abyss and go to his destruction** (17:8). It is a resurrection to be feared, but one that is doomed from the start.

Whether John believed that Nero would literally come back to life is debatable. But certainly he understood this enemy of Christians to be always on the horizon of history, being embodied in butchers and dema-gogues at the head of powerful nation states.

At the close of this description of the woman and her beast, we are left with the realization that people who are not of God's protected (**whose names have not been written in the book of life from the creation of the world**) will be taken in by this spectacular power, particularly, because **he once was, now is not, and yet will come** (17:8). Perhaps we are also to see in this repeated formula an allusion to the same rhythmic cadence of the one "who is, and who was, and who is to come" (1:4), the God who spans the cosmos and history. This pseudo-authority commands astonishment, but he will never be worshiped as having all authority.

In 17:9–14 we find a more detailed interpretation of the heads of the beast calling **for a mind with wisdom** (17:9). The **seven heads** of the beast were a clue to the beast's identity. Being the **seven hills on which the woman sits** (17:9), we know this to be the seven hills of Rome. But they are also **seven kings** (17:10), which we should read as Caesars. The order is enumerated as: **Five have fallen, one is, the other has not yet come; but when he does come, he must remain for a little while. The beast . . . is an eighth king. He belongs to the seven and is going to his destruction.** (17:10–11). The actual order and chronology of the imperial line that each head represents is difficult to decipher. They depend on which emperor one would start with, whether some emperors should be left out due to short reigns or assessed as unimportant, and the contem-porary ruler. The best we might say is that the five that have fallen might represent emperors from the past who have died. While the one that is and the one to come represent the players on the stage of the Apocalypse at present. We offer Domitian as the contemporary Caesar, and the reve-lation tells us that the end of the succession is coming to a close.

Some have offered up other substitute suggestions for this description of the seven-headed beast. Some have seen the kings representing five periods of rulers over God's people: i.e. Egypt, Nineveh, Babylon, Persia, and Greece. Rome-at-large would be the present reigning king, and a sub-sequent reign by an antichrist government to come.[4] Mounce seems to have the more balanced interpretation that "the number seven is symbolic and stands for the power of the Roman Empire as a historic whole."[5] In

178

this succession of kings, we note that there is no more to follow. The Lord God Almighty, who was, and is, will reign for eternity. Kings take note!

As for the ten horns, they **are ten kings who have not yet received a kingdom, but who for one hour will receive authority as kings along with the beast** (17:12). Some would argue, given the future sense of these kings' authority that they would be in a historical line with the present seven. But the idea that this authority would go along with the beast may imply that they are provincial rulers of Rome or lesser kings of vassal states. This group could hearken back to the "kings of the whole world" gathered together at Armageddon to battle God (16:14). Again, the more important thing to note is that they will only rule for **one hour**, a conspicuously short time to rule anything. As in chapter 16, they will battle **against the Lamb, but the Lamb will overcome them because he is Lord of lords and King of kings** (17:14).

One cannot help but notice how much rancor and energy is spent in banding together beasts, demons, kings, and armies in these last scenes in the unfolding apocalypse, only to have such brief and innocuous statements like "the Lamb overcame them" summarize the whole blood-soaked war. The irony is that the Lamb has already conquered all of earth's enemies at the start of the book in chapter 4, and all of the saints merely show up to see the victory march since **with him will be his called, chosen and faithful followers** (17:14). This group—**called, chosen and faithful**—is, after all, *His* followers.

Our attention is drawn next to the seat of the prostitute. Under her are many waters, representing **peoples, multitudes, nations and languages** (17:15) that flow out from her. But then there is a surprising turn in the narrative: **The beast** and the lesser kings **will hate the prostitute** (17:16). When **God's words are fulfilled** (17:17), they will turn on the prostitute, Babylon (Rome), and **will bring her to ruin and leave her naked; they will eat her flesh and burn her with fire** (17:16). Now we have come to know that this whole scenario of prostitute, beast, and authority ultimately was in the hands of God Almighty. The powerful network that fed on the power of the great prostitute implodes and the kings of the earth awaken from their drunken orgy only to find themselves cannibalizing the source of their hunger.

BABYLON DESTROYED 18:1-24

Chapter 18 is an interlude of discourse. Another angel with **great authority** (18:1) and a **mighty voice** (18:2) comes down from heaven to deliver the prophetic message of Babylon's demise. This may be the same angel that had enough authority to address the cosmos in 5:2, because this messenger illuminated the whole earth with his **splendor** (18:1). The splendor of heaven now replaces the splendor that is lost on earth (18:14).

In the concluding picture of the New Jerusalem (chapter 21), the kings bring their splendor into God's new temple space and, synonymously, the nations bring their glory and honor. Eventually all splendor is heavenly splendor, and the splendor of the earth—its wealth, power, and might—is extinguished and replaced.

TAUNTING BABYLON

The shout, **"Fallen! Fallen is Babylon the Great!"** (18:2), begins a descant of conquest. David Aune calls this gleeful song an angelic "taunt song."[6] Jeremiah 50–51 and Ezekiel 26–27 are examples of songs glorying in the defeat of Israel's enemies, mocking past national accomplishments in light of their being brought low by God. The phrase "Fallen! Fallen is Babylon!" finds its predecessor in Isa. 21:9.

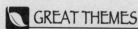

GREAT THEMES
THE REVELATION AND JEREMIAH

"Babylon will suddenly fall and be broken. . . . I am against you, O destroying mountain, you who destroy the whole earth . . . I will stretch out my hand against you, roll you off the cliffs, and make you a burned-out mountain. . . . The sea will rise over Babylon; its roaring waves will cover her."
—Jeremiah 51:8, 25, 42

The eerie portrait of the once great Babylon is found echoed in many prophetic references to Israel's conquered foes (cf. Isaiah and Jeremiah). Their once prosperous lands now have **become a home for demons and a haunt for every evil [or unclean] spirit, a haunt for every unclean and detestable bird** (18:2). None of the signs of vitality and power are left, only the now exposed sources of that power (**demons**) and the vulture-like predators of the life that once thrived there. In ancient times, desolate places were thought to be the residence of demons and unclean things. Later in the song, the kings, merchants, and sea captains will lament the glory of Babylon's once thriving economy and the vanishing signs of wealth and prosperity. Rome, being the epitome of a bustling city of commerce filled with lively chatter and life, transforms into a vacuum containing only a haunting echo of its former glory.

The reason for this flight becomes painfully clear as the angel recounts the laments of those who have benefited from the power and wealth of Babylon the Great. **The kings of the earth who committed adultery with her and shared her luxury** (18:9) are seen wailing and crying over her destruction. Alliances all over the globe were made with this economic power, sharing in the illicit and unjust practices that allow for such luxury while victimizing God's people.

The parallels that are being made between the city of Babylon and Rome can hardly be missed. But the comparisons with first-world countries like America and the European Union hold even greater prophetic application for Christians today. Ron Sider's classic *Rich Christians in an Age of Hunger* teaches evangelicals the harsh inequities that exist in our modern world. But more importantly, he has shown that biblical faith does not allow the Christian a clear conscience when these inequalities are uncovered.

Much like the kings, merchants, mariners of chapter 18, we too participate in this complex of economic structures and benefit from them. While the industrial world represents just a little over 20 percent of the population on the planet, it controls and consumes over 80 percent of its natural resources. By so doing, this consumption machine also spews hazardous wastes into the atmosphere and waters of our world, polluting those who have received little if any benefit from its production.

The easy reading of these chapters that deal with the judgment and destruction of Babylon (Rome) would be to equate this symbol of prostitution with medieval Roman Catholicism or some personified evil of a political enemy. The obvious connections with Western opulence can hardly be bypassed and must grip modern readers to do something about their responsibilities with the drunken power and wealth as depicted by the Great Prostitute.

THE JUDGMENT OF BABYLON

After taunting the fallen Babylon, the faithful are encouraged to flee the city. As the destruction of Babylon is imminent, another angel calls out to God's people (as if to keep the messages distinct): **"Come out of her, my people!"** (18:4). The separation of God's people from the people of Babylon is for a dual purpose: (1) so that they **will not share in** Babylon's **sins** and (2) experience **any of her plagues**. The call to refrain from assimilation into the prevailing world is similar to the warnings to the seven churches at the beginning of the book. The clear message is that God's wrath is meant to destroy evil forces in the world and it should not be viewed as directed at those who keep the testimony of Jesus Christ.

God, on the other hand, has remembered the crimes of Babylon. God will **give back to her as she has given;** actually **a double portion** to be mixed in her own cup (18:6). The cup that she was drinking from (17:4), filled with abominable things, will now be twice as horrible and with her own suffering. The proportion of **torture and grief** will be equal to **the glory and luxury she gave herself** (18:7). She will keep thinking that she is **a queen**, in control of all her subjects, and have no reason to **mourn** her loss of power. So, even though it took her a history to build her legacy, she will lose it all in **one day** (18:8). **Plagues, death, mourning and famine** will be lumped together with the punishment **by fire**. This cringing carcass will understand the mighty **Lord God who judges her**.

Now come those who have benefited from the great prostitute's excesses. First we see **the kings of the earth who committed adultery with her and shared her luxury** (18:9). From their **far off** vantage they **see the smoke of her burning**, and weep and mourn over her. The kings are afraid for what they see, because they were enamored with her power. No wonder they cry out: **"Woe! Woe, O great city, O Babylon, city of power! In one hour your doom has come!"** (18:10). That's all it took to bring that powerful empire down—one hour.

In turn, **the merchants of the earth** will do their own mourning **because no one buys their cargoes any more** (18:11). The list of their **cargoes of gold, silver, precious stones and pearls; fine linen, purple, silk and scarlet cloth; every sort of citron wood, and articles of every** kind made of ivory, costly wood, bronze, iron and marble; cargoes of cinnamon and spice, of incense, myrrh and frankincense, of wine and olive oil, of fine flour and wheat; cattle and sheep; horses and carriages ends with the true commodity of their market—the **bodies and souls of men** (18:13). As they stand far off, they will say, **"The fruit you longed for is gone from you. All your riches and splendor have vanished, never to be recovered"** (18:14). It will be hard for merchants to watch her demise because they too worshiped what they were. So they must lament: **"Woe! Woe, O great city, dressed in fine linen, purple and scarlet, and glittering with gold, precious stones and pearls!"** (18:16).

Again, it took just **one hour** of judgment to fall and all to be lost. The reader is struck by the reading of long lists of material wealth in this vision of the merchants. The wealth of the city Babylon was impressive as well. But with rapid destruction, all is lost, and the merchant is tormented by the smoke billowing up. The pillar of smoke as a funeral pyre was a reminder of God's judgment, even as representative people viewed it from afar.

Now **every sea captain**, and all who are associated with **living from the sea** (18:17), will watch the **smoke of her burning** from **far off**, and they will cry out, **"Was there ever a city like this great city?"** (18:18). They have made their living from this port and have gained great wealth from its commerce. Throwing **dust on their heads**, a sign of mourning and dismay, they also lament: **"Woe! Woe, O great city, where all who had ships on the sea became rich through her wealth!"** (18:19). But the same fate of total destruction comes in but one hour. But is it the sea farers that turn their attention to God? As they continue their sailor's song: **Rejoice over her, O heaven! Rejoice, saints and apostles and prophets! God has judged her for the way she treated you** (18:19–20).

Finally someone acknowledges the reason for this ruin. Even though the financial ruin is felt, the cry to heaven, to the saints, apostles, and prophets is a call to rejoice. The destruction of this diabolical city, so well-connected and loved by the haughty, has come about because of God's judgment and, in particular, for the treatment of God's saints. So if Babylon has killed God's prophets and saints, she will now be destroyed.

THE DEATH OF BABYLON

Then, as if those who were far off needed an even more graphic object lesson, **a mighty angel picked up a boulder the size of a large millstone and threw it into the sea** (18:21), saying:

> **With such violence**
> > **the great city of Babylon will be thrown down,**
> > **never to be found again.**
> **The music of harpists and musicians, flute players and trumpeters,**
> > **will never be heard in you again.**
> **No workman of any trade**
> > **will ever be found in you again.**
> **The sound of a millstone**
> > **will never be heard in you again.**
> **The light of a lamp**
> > **will never shine in you again.**
> **The voice of bridegroom and bride**
> > **will never be heard in you again.**
> **Your merchants were the world's great men.**
> > **By your magic spell all the nations were led astray.**
> **In her was found the blood of prophets and of the saints,**
> > **and of all who have been killed on the earth** (18:21–24).

The activity of Babylon, as a great city, is remembered. The city itself will not be found, nor will any of its tradesmen; music, millwork, voices from marriages will never be heard; no light will shine. But what was found in the city? **The blood of prophets and of the saints, and all who have been killed on earth** (18:24) was found, so Babylon will never be found again. This is the fate of all nations and peoples who seek to make something of themselves while displacing the rule of God.

BABYLON'S FALL PRAISED—HALLELUJAH! 19:1–10

A LAST SONG

After this (19:1), meaning after the series of funeral dirges for the fall of the great city, Babylon, John heard the shout: **"Hallelujah!"** Hallelujah, a word much like that of Armageddon, was a contraction of Hebrew words meaning something like "Praise the Lord!" For as popular a phrase as this is, all of the uses of the term in the New Testament is confined to these four instances in verses 1–6.

The antiphony that comes on the heels of the taunt song is no longer interested in the fate of Rome, but it directs a proper worship to God. Christians, even when persecuted, do not gloat in the destruction of their enemies, but they find vindication in the restoration of God's rightful place of honor. **"Salvation and glory and power belong to our God, for true and just are his judgments"** (19:1–2). The judgment of the great prostitute Babylon (Rome) is understood to be **true and just** because God alone possesses the glory that was presumed by the nations.

In the end, all of the virtues that are thought to belong to kings and nations—the wealth, power, honor, and glory—are

> ### WHAT OTHERS SAY
> #### LO! HE COMES WITH CLOUDS DESCENDING
>
> Lo! He comes with clouds descending,
> Once for favored sinners slain;
> Thousand thousand saints attending
> Swell the triumph of his train:
> Alleluya!
> God appears, on earth to reign.
>
> Every eye shall now behold Him
> Robed in dreadful majesty;
> Those who set at nought and sold him,
> Pierced and nailed him to the tree,
> Deeply wailing
> Shall the true Messiah see.
>
> Those dear tokens of his passion
> Still his dazzling body bears
> Cause of endless exultation
> To his ransomed worshipers:
> With what rapture
> Gaze we on his those glorious scars!
>
> Yea, Amen! Let all adore Thee,
> High on Thine eternal throne;
> Savior, take the power and glory:
> Claim the kingdom for Thine own:
> O come quickly!
> Alleluya! Come, Lord, come!
> —*Charles Wesley*

185

seen to be in the sole possession of God. Though the people of this earth scrape, scratch, and claw to acquire these things, He will not share His place with anyone or anything.

The connection with the original glaring issue of the revelation is now made. Our God **has avenged on her the blood of his servants** (19:2). The prayer of the saints from under the altar who had called out, "How long?" wanted to know how long it would be until their blood was avenged (6:10). At that time, God had told them to wait just a little longer. That wait is now over. The **great multitude** of 7:9 was now shouting like a roar the Hallelujah chorus.

And again they shouted: "Hallelujah! (19:3). The song goes on, as the smoke of Babylon goes up **for ever and ever**. We are back worshiping in the throne room, as in the first vision (chapters 4 and 5). The same participants are there as **the twenty-four elders and the four living creatures fell down and worshiped God, who was seated on the throne** (19:4).

But now the smoke that was the incense representing the prayers of the saints (5:8; 8:4) is the billowing residue of the fallen Babylon. The damned will find their place in the orchestration of God's praise even if by the remains of their annihilation (14:11; 18:9, 18). The concept of eternal damnation has often been developed alongside these texts; the book of Revelation itself does not answer all of the questions related to whether the wicked will be tormented forever or destroyed in the final fire. The many later Christian concepts about the fate of those dying without salvation were derived from Dante's *Inferno* and the Greek philosophical tradition.

Today, even among conservative Christians, there is a renewed discussion on the biblical idea of eternity when it relates to punishment. Are the damned to suffer in eternal torment or are they, in the end, completely annihilated so as to "clear the slate" of all evil in God's renewed creation? The Revelation has many symbols relating to punishment (such as the lake of fire or being thrown into the sea) but does not always give conceptual completion to these ideas. At least we can see that here the idea of the fallen Babylon's smoke rising **for ever and ever** (19:3) was more importantly a statement about God than about Babylon. Even if God's enemies are gone, the justice of God is seen forever in the New City. The eternal column of smoke is more a remembrance of God's power and holiness than a continued memory of Babylon's demise and suffering.

The twenty-four elders and the four living creatures continue their activity of falling down and worshiping **God, who was seated on the throne** (19:4). And they called out: **"Amen, Hallelujah!"** The voice from the throne follows, saying:

> **Praise our God,**
>> **all you his servants,**
> **you who fear him,**
>> **both small and great!** (19:5).

THE BETTER ENDING

At this transition many commentators want to begin a new point in the outline. Some will connect verse 6 with the coming reign of Christ in chapter 20. The usual suspects of thunder signal another epiphanal event. The **great multitude**, accompanied by **loud peals of thunder** (19:6), began shouting:

> **Hallelujah!**
>> **For our Lord God Almighty reigns.**
> **Let us rejoice and be glad**
>> **and give him glory!**
> **For the wedding of the Lamb has come,**
>> **and his bride has made herself ready.**
> **Fine linen, bright and clean,**
>> **was given her to wear** (19:7–8).

Our attention has completely turned now. The praise of God for the destruction of Babylon—even praise for avenging the blood of the servants who did God's earthly bidding—has now turned to a shout announcing the Feast of the Lamb. This seems to be the opening opportunity for all those who have experienced the horror and devastation to begin a life of joy. The fourth beatitude is offered when the angel said, **"Write: 'Blessed are those who are invited to the wedding supper of the Lamb!'"** (19:9). To people who have been accustomed to deception and lies, and who have known only suffering and death for their testimony, it is if it is too good to be true. The angel must add a notation, **"These are the true words of God"** (19:9). As if rubbing our eyes, we turn our attention away from the billowing smoke of the damned Babylon, and we turn to see the bride, as if at the start of a wedding ceremony.

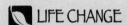

LIFE CHANGE

PREPARING FOR THE WEDDING

The bride of Christ is dressed in finest linen and is ready for the marriage supper of the Lamb. The toils and temptations of earth are past; the celebration is ready to begin. We Christians are that bride of Christ, saints adorned with our righteous actions. Our efforts to serve others are an evidence of our faith and help us weave fine linen for the wedding supper. While it's not our good works that get us to heaven, our righteous, good actions do dress us. We need to stay alert for opportunities to serve those in need. Who can you help? How will you do it? When will you help them?

The obvious connection of the wedding and feast motif with Old Testament images of God and Israel (Isa. 25:6–9; 54:5–8) and the teachings of Jesus about the reign of God (Matt. 8:11; 22:2–14) is made with the wedding of the Lamb announcement. The bride (the Church) has **made herself ready** with the **fine linen . . . given her** (19:7–8). This interesting synergism displays the active part the faithful play in their own participation in the wedding. Too, the revelator, at the point, seems to tire at the strain of interpretation. The parenthetical clue is clarifying: Fine linen equals **righteous acts of the saints**. The saints are adorned with their own righteous actions.

There is no longer a false dichotomy between faith and works, between evangelism and social action. We are reminded of the words of those entering the Kingdom offered to the Lord: "When did we . . . ?" (Matt. 25:37, 44). When we are ushered into the wedding of the Lamb, we are what we are—and perhaps for the first time in our lives.

After this epiphany John felt the need to fall at the angel's **feet to worship him** (19:10). The angel quickly sets John straight as to who is worthy of such worship. This same phenomenon will repeat itself near verbatim in the last chapter (22:9). Perhaps this caution is important enough to discourage any false worship at a time when the deification of human power had swayed so many to give honor and glory to it. Even when there is no longer any evil to worship (for it has all been destroyed in Babylon), there is still the temptation for John to worship the bearer of the good news. God alone is worthy of our worship. The reason for this worship seems to be tied to the final cryptic phrase: **For the testimony of Jesus is the spirit of prophecy** (19:10). Though there have been many suggestions as to what this verse means and how it fits with the preceding admonition to worship only God, the best sense seems to be tied to an acknowledgment that all prophecy has its source in the Spirit of God, which attests to the work of Jesus. The angel is only an agent of that prophecy and should not be worshiped.

ENDNOTES

1. Catherine Keller, *Apocalypse Now and Then* (Boston: Beacon Press, 1996), 1.

2. Undoubtedly one of the best political expositions on the book of Revelation was written by William Stringfellow entitled *An Ethic for Christians and Other Aliens in a Strange Land* (Waco: Word Books, 1973.)

3. David E. Aune. Revelation 17–22, *Word Commentaries* (Dallas: Word Books, 1998), 935.

4. It would not be surprising to find commentators of the dispensationalist bent enjoying this interpretation. See John F. Walvoord, *The Revelation of Jesus Christ* (Chicago: Moody, 1966), 297. Few would see any biblical parallel of using the word "king" for "kingdom" interchangeably.

5. Mounce, 317.

6. David E. Aune. Revelation 17–22, *Word Commentaries* (Dallas: Word Books, 1998), 976.

THE VICTORIOUS CHRIST AND THE MILLENNIAL REIGN

Revelation 19:11–20:15

A t this point we are moving quickly to the end.

THE RIDER ON THE WHITE HORSE 19:11–21

John **saw heaven standing open** (19:11). Being **open** is at the root meaning of the Greek word "apocalypse" (a revealing). The Revelation is a book of open doors (3:7–8, 20; 4:1), opened scrolls (5:2–5 and 10:2, 8), opened seals (6:1–12), open books (20:12), an open temple (11:19 and 15:5), as well as an open Abyss (9:2). It discloses that which beforehand was obscure.

God is now opening himself to His faithful, keeping back no secrets that would aid and support them in their hour of need. **Heaven**, the place of ultimate mystery, now stands open for the viewer to ponder and examine. The source of

KEY IDEAS	
	OPENED IN REVELATION
Open doors	3:7–8, 20; 4:1
Opened scrolls	5:2–5; 10:2, 8
Opened seals	6:1–12
Open books	20:12
An open temple	11:19; 15:5
An open Abyss	9:2

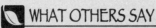

our salvation is not be to be found on earth, among earthly projects and ventures, but in heaven, the abode of God.

With the destruction of Babylon and the final judgment of the damned immanent, the heavenly leader is in view. The **white horse** (19:11) is acknowledged first, probably in juxtaposition to the earlier four horses in chapter 6. Though there was a white horse leading that charge of tribulation and persecution, this horse is known by a different **rider**. He is **called Faithful and True**, so we know it is Jesus Christ (see 3:14). Bringing to mind the connection with the *logos* of the prelude to the gospel of John, He is also named the **Word of God** (19:13).

Some have suggested that this scene must have a non-Christian source, as they find it difficult to identify the "gentle Jesus" with the following description. One might think that the Jesus who came to save and to serve does not make war. But this war, unlike any war before it, comes **with justice** (19:11). Despairing of any consensus on what makes for a just war, the world must know that this true judge will do so with impunity. **His eyes are like blazing fire** (19:12), so He is able to discern the enemy's heart. His head is adorned with the **many crowns** of victory; He is not accustomed to losing. Interestingly, we are told **He has a name written on him that no one knows but he himself**, only to discover many names given to Him in this description (19:11, 13, 16). Even if Christians come to know this warrior in the specific ways of their salvation, Christ will always retain for himself some mystery, for this is the nature of God, and so it is the nature of Jesus Christ. As with the Hebraic concern for reverence for the name of God, this name cannot be used to manipulate or to control the workings of the Savior. He is Yahweh, He "will be who He will be," and this warrior remains true to himself.

GREAT THEMES • CHRIST'S REDEMPTIVE WORK

This picture of the atonement shows that Jesus has taken the martyrs' blood on himself and has given them pure lives.

Christ	His Followers
Riding a white horse	Riding white horses
Dressed in a robe dipped in blood (19:13)	Dressed in fine linen, white and clean (19:14)

Some theologians have disparaged at the lack of a systematic treatment of the atonement in the book of Revelation. Actually, a fairly developed understanding of Christ's redemptive work is found throughout. Here is a beautiful example of the intuitive theological method that John uses. Christ is **dressed in a robe dipped in blood** (19:13), and His followers, also **riding on white horses**, are **dressed in fine linen, white and clean** (19:14). The substitution of Jesus' death for others is obvious; He has taken the blood of the martyrs for His own and has replaced their own soiled lives with pure ones. Some have suggested that the blood on Jesus' robes may have some connection with the Old Testament image of Isa. 63:1–6, where God's robe is splattered with the blood of Israel's enemies. Here, the battle has not yet been fought, so probably it is Jesus' own or the blood of Jesus' witnesses that is symbolized.

Many of the same descriptions of the Son of Man in chapter 1 are incorporated into this picture of the warrior God. He is **dressed in a robe**

(19:13; 1:13). His **eyes are like blazing fire** (19:12; 1:14) and a **sword** comes **out of his mouth** (19:15; 1:16). But here the significance of these symbols is given a specific political connection. He is to be the victor over all the nations and rule with sovereign power. The messianic Psalm 2:9 **"[He] will rule them with an iron scepter"** (19:15) is used for the third and last time in the Revelation. There is to be no doubt in the Second Advent as to the reign of Christ. His sector is iron, and the nations will know Him. Despite what was said in the preceding section, His name now is in full view—**KING OF KINGS AND LORD OF LORDS** (19:16).

KEY IDEAS • SON OF MAN AND WARRIOR OF GOD

He is **dressed in a robe**	19:13	1:13
His **eyes are like blazing fire**	19:12	1:14
A **sword** comes **out of his mouth**	19:15	1:16
He is to be the victor over all the nations and **rule them with an iron scepter**	19:15	2:27; 12:5

A blood bath is to ensue. The angel calls out to the vultures to prepare for **the great supper of God** (19:17). The vision is preparing us for a battle that never comes. Because the rider on the white horse **treads the winepress of the fury of the wrath of God Almighty** (19:15), he is on the offensive from beginning to end. **The beast and the kings of the earth and their armies gathered together** (19:19), but the beast and the false prophet are **captured** and **thrown alive into the fiery lake of burning sulfur** (19:20). Following a sweeping destruction by **the sword that came out of the mouth of the rider** (19:21), the **birds gorged themselves** on the flesh of this wonderfully spread meal of the diverse flesh of wicked humanity. The weapon of God is solely related to what He says He will do, the sword of His tongue, the Word of God. There is no attempt to argue that the messianic armies are better equipped or strategically led. The picture of the last battle is rather like the Exodus account of chariots and soldiers going belly up in the Red Sea. The people of God merely stand on the shore and watch.

THE THOUSAND YEARS 20:1–6

An angel finally deals out the fate of the evil that has pursued the righteous throughout history. All of the names given to the personified evil in this book are enumerated—the **dragon, that ancient serpent, who is the devil, or Satan** (20:2). The **key** and the **great chain** (20:2) that the descending angel holds are symbols of the ultimate control of all that would seek to control God's universe. He uses them to bind up the devil **for a thousand years** (20:2). The angel **seizes**, **binds**, **throws**, **locks**, and **seals**, in a series of decisive actions against Satan. Despite the perceived power of the evil one to destroy and kill, God alone is seen as the controlling force of that power. Much as with the binding of the four angels in chapters 7 and 9, God binds the dragon with a great chain until the appointed time of one thousand years is over. Keeping back this force makes it easier to understand why Christians believe Jesus Christ reigns though the final culmination of that reign has yet to be experienced. We live in an age when Satan's powers are decimated, but he is still alive and well.

The millennium—or the one-thousand-year reign of Christ on earth—is one of the more controversial interpretive issues of the Apocalypse. When one reads the book in its wide sweep of images and drama, one should not give such pause to this problem as to miss the more impressionable and unifying features of the whole book. Some would feel that this particular issue dominates the purpose of John's vision so that all the other chapters must be understood through it. Given this obsession by so many with so-called "millennialism," it is interesting to note that Wesleyans have given so little doctrinal significance to it. Within the diversity of worship communities in the Wesleyan traditions, all of the varieties of positions can be found.

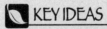 **KEY IDEAS**

PRE- AND POSTMILLENIUMISM

Premillennialism is the belief that Christ returns bodily pre- or before the thousand years of peace and righteousness over which He rules. Postmillennialists believe that the world will eventually become Christianized and that the millennium is a long period of righteousness and peace on earth before the bodily return of Christ.

The number "one thousand" as the duration of the kingdom is a unique invention of John's apocalypse. The Old Testament has many messianic texts with implicit or explicit reference to the Day of the Lord and a coming reign of God, but there is no mention of a millennial period. In other references found in apocryphal books pointing to the coming kingdom of God, this time frame has been designated as forty, four thousand, or even 365 thousand years. As with most numbers in Revelation, the symbolism is of more importance than the literal amount. The one thousand years probably refers to a long period of time, but having a beginning and an end. The questions relating to the advent and duration of the thousand years have given rise to a number of positions and viewpoints.

HISTORIC PREMILLENNIALISM

Probably the oldest millennial view was that of premillennialism. But to differentiate the use of the term from the later dispensational premillennialists, those holding this view today often call themselves historic premillennialists. It is "historic" because much of their position was the view that was held by many of the church fathers during the first several centuries of the Church.

Generally the early Christians held to a literal reading of the millennial reign of Christ, some being associated with early millenarianism or "chiliasm" (the Greek word for a "thousand"). This chiliasm colored early sectarian movements that looked so intently for the soon return of Christ that they disengaged themselves from this-worldly affairs. This has carried over today in discussions over the psychological nature of words like "immanent," "immediate," or "soon." Believing in Christ's return to earth in a Second Advent does not mean that we must jettison ourselves from earthy concerns or future preparation. We must be careful of keeping the delicate balance contained in Jesus' desire that His disciples be in the world but not of it.

The foundation of historic premillennialism is built on Christ's advent into history occurring before He establishes His thousand-year reign and that the Old Testament prophecies associated with promises to Israel are to be identified with the Church as the spiritual Israel.

George Eldon Ladd, a leading proponent of the historic premillennial view, writes, "I do not see how it is possible to avoid the conclusion that the New Testament applies Old Testament prophecies to the New Testament church and in doing so identifies the church as spiritual Israel."[1] Though they have some things in common with the dispensational variety (i.e., they also believe that Christ will return prior to the thousand-year reign), there are significant differences along the scriptural interpretation of the Church and Israel.

Dispensationalists feel that even if the church *participates* in the blessings of the New Covenant, the eternal and unconditional nature of the New Covenant demands a *fulfillment* with literal Israel. John Feinberg writes, "The crucial point is *how we know* whether something in the Old Testament (especially prophecy about Israel's future) is still binding in the New Testament. . . . If an Old Testament prophecy or promise is made unconditionally to a given people and is still unfulfilled to them even in the New Testament era, then the prophecy must still be fulfilled to them. While a prophecy given unconditionally to Israel has a fulfillment [application] for the church if the New Testament *applies* it to the church, it must also be fulfilled to Israel. Progress of revelation cannot cancel unconditional promises."[2]

This obvious use of a literal reading of the text causes dispensationalists to see no other option than all of Israel's prophecies must be fulfilled in

 WHAT OTHERS SAY

ISRAEL'S RELATION TO THE MILLENNIUM

All premillennialists also anticipate that Israel will have a special place in the millennium. They disagree, however, as to the nature of that special place. Dispensationalists hold to a continuing unconditional covenant of God with national Israel, so that when God has completed his dealings with the church, he will return to his relations with national Israel. Jesus will literally sit upon David's throne and rule the world from Israel. All of the prophecies and promises regarding Israel will be fulfilled within the millennium, which will therefore have a markedly Jewish character. *Nondispensationalists put much less emphasis upon national Israel*, holding instead that Israel's special place, being spiritual in nature, will be found within the church. Israel will be converted in large numbers during the millennium.

—*Millard Erickson (emphasis mine)*

a real nation of Israel, including events that surround the temple sacrifice and national politics.

The historic dispensationalist believes that there is a priority given to the New Testament over the Old Testament: "Here is the basic watershed between a dispensational and a nondispensational theology. Dispensationalism forms its eschatology by a literal interpretation of the Old Testament and then fits the New Testament into it. A nondispensational eschatology forms its theology from the explicit teaching of the New Testament. It confesses that it cannot be sure how the Old Testament prophecies of the end are to be fulfilled. . . ."[3]

When it comes to the millennium itself, Ladd continues, "A millennial doctrine cannot be based on Old Testament prophecies but should be based on the New Testament alone. The only place in the Bible that speaks of an actual millennium is the passage in Revelation 20:1–6. Any millennial doctrine must be based upon the most natural exegesis of this passage."[4]

Those who would refute this clear sounding would argue that the concept of a reign of God on earth is well-grounded in the Old Testament (Gen. 13:15; Isa. 2:1–4; Dan. 2:44; Zech. 14:9). It does not rest on Rev. 20:1–6 alone. Herman Hoyt wrote, "It is unfortunate that he [Ladd] cannot see that the Old Testament supplies the vast portion of material for putting the picture in full perspective."[5] Ladd would describe this as the New Testament reinterpreting the Old Testament. The Christ event becomes the key to unlock most of the covenantal language of the Hebrew Scriptures.

For instance, Ladd would argue that Matt. 2:15 reinterprets Hos. 11:1 and that Rom. 9:25–26 reinterprets Hos. 1:10; 2:23. In *Evaluation of Historic Premillennialism*, John Feinberg argues:

> In passage after passage Ladd insists that the New Testament is interpreting the Old when the New Testament is simply applying a principle found in the Old Testament. Rushing to the conclusion that these references identify the church and Israel as the same body of the saved is wholly gratuitous. Even though "the New Testament applies Old Testament prophecies to the New Testament

church," it does not do so in the sense of identifying the church as spiritual Israel. It makes such application merely for the purpose of explaining something that is true of both.[6]

Feinberg offers a second rebuttal:

New Testament (NT) application of the Old Testament (OT) passage does not necessarily eliminate the passage's original meaning. No NT writer claims his new understanding of the OT passage cancels the meaning of the OT passage in its own context or that the new application is the only meaning of the OT passage. The NT writer merely offers a different application of an OT passage than the OT might have foreseen; he is not claiming the OT understanding is now irrelevant.[7]

Historic premillennialism has three main weaknesses. Paul Benware argues that a nonliteral approach "spiritualizes the prophecies of the Old Testament, applying them to the church, which is viewed as spiritual Israel."[8]

Second, it does not do justice to God's eternal covenants with Israel. Benware continues, "It fails to give the nation of Israel its proper place in the program of God. The unconditional, eternal biblical covenants ratified by God require that Israel as a nation be the recipient of certain blessings."[9]

Third, Benware argues it is a faulty view of progressive revelation:

There is some inaccuracy in its view of progressive revelation. It is true, of course, that God has revealed more and more truth progressively over the years. And it is true that the New Testament reveals new truth and develops truth previously given in the Old Testament. However, it fails to recognize that many of the Old Testament prophecies should be understood on their own merit because they are clear in their meaning. The idea of progressive revelation does not mean that the Old Testament cannot be understood apart from the New Testament. It does not mean that clear Old Testament prophecies must be reinterpreted, changed or altered.[10]

DISPENSATIONAL PREMILLENNIALISM

Dispensational premillennialism understands the plan for God's reign as coming in periods of time. Like historic premillennialism, the dispensationalist believes the coming of Christ will precede the thousand-year reign of God. But unlike the earlier premillennial view, a great distinction is made between the prophecies meant for Israel and those meant for the Church of Jesus Christ.

Some scholars in this category have attempted to incorporate the great strides made in understanding the nature of apocalyptic writing and its role in the historical setting of the early Christian Church into a more nuanced understanding of the two eras of God's work in Israel and the Church.[11] But, in general, premillennialists believe in two separate and unequal salvation histories: a national or racial (*rather than individual*) salvation for the race of the Jews, and another one for everyone else (*any non-Jew or Gentile*). They hold that a future redeemed Israel will be the center of government and the spreading of the gospel to the nations of the world.

Though there are many different schemes worked out by these interpreters of the millennium, they hold to many common tenets. For one, dispensationalists hold to a literal reading of the Apocalypse, and they discourage the natural symbolic nature of the Apocalypse as a liberal plot to deceive the faithful. They have a generally negative view of the flow of the human history, and that the tribulation mentioned in the book of Revelation will be the ultimate slide into a catastrophic end time destruction. However most believe that the Christians will be "raptured" from the earth before that terrible time comes (pre-tribulation dispensationalists).

Depending on how one sets out the weeks of Daniel in the dispensational model, one might argue for a pre-, post-, or even a mid-tribulation rapture for the faithful.

Modern dispensational premillennialism has its roots in the teachings of Plymouth Brethren preacher J.N. Darby (the founder of the sectarian group known as the "Darbyites"). Some modern proponents of this view are C. I. Scofield, Charles Ryrie, Louis Sperry Chafer, J. Dwight Pentecost, Norman Geisler, and John Walvoord.[12] Walvoord describes dispensational premillennialism in this summary paragraph:

Dispensational premillennialism tends to emphasize the governmental and political character of the millennium itself. Christ will reign on the throne of David on earth over restored Israel as well as the Gentile world. Spiritual qualities such as righteousness and peace, spiritual power, and the visible glory of God will be evident. It will fulfill literally the glowing expectation of Old Testament prophets for a kingdom of God on earth embracing all nations. Satan will be bound and inactive. The curse upon the earth will be lifted and the desert will blossom. All will know the Lord from the least to the greatest. This final dispensation before the creation of the new heavens and new earth will in many respects be climactic in blessing and a demonstration of divine sovereignty and glory. Christ's reign on earth will gloriously fulfill Old Testament prophecy.[13]

Many of the preachers who advocate this view of the millennium often use the argument that theirs is the most obvious (viz. literal) and natural reading of the Apocalypse, but in reality it requires a complex set of hermeneutics with intricate analysis of the Old Testament referents in Daniel (the seventy weeks) and Ezekiel. Too, the eschatology of the New Testament found in Jesus' Olivet Discourse (Matthew 24–26) and Paul's Thessalonians correspondence is modified to suit the needs of their derived schemes.

Despite the most reliable and developed biblical studies on the nature of the Apocalypse of John, the popular writings of Hal Lindsey (*The Late Great Planet Earth*) and Jerry Jenkins and Tim LaHaye (the *Left Behind* series) as well as the electronic media blitz of various Bible teachers hold sway over most conservative evangelicals today. Like countless futurologists before them, they appear to tap into humanity's need to make sense of its place in history. They offer a rational, structured view of the modern world, often experienced as confusing and meaningless. In one sense, astrology and new age insights into extra-dimensional realities are just as attractive to those needing such surety to their intellectual curiosity.

The most attractive feature of the pre-millennial view of the end of history is that it short-circuits the long held Christian belief in glory coming at the end of a redemptive suffering and purge. The rapture, a relatively recent interpretation of the Bible's images of the end, provides a type of collective cheap grace. Prior to the work of a few Enlightenment exegetes, the historic Christian community had understood the "rapture" language of 1 Thessalonians to refer to the means by which Christ would order the homecoming when He returned. The dead in Christ would rise first, while those left behind (the Christians who were still alive at His return) would be "caught up" with them in the air. This was meant to be an encouragement to those Christians lamenting the loss of their brothers and sisters in the Lord. Only later, when schemas of the end of history were developed to identify a series of events associated with the final coming of Christ, did interpreters of Revelation introduce "rapture" as a historic event.

AMILLENNIALISM

As the practical implications of historic premillennialism became problematic, a non-millenarian approach to Revelation 20 arose some time after the fourth century. The amillennialism (or sometimes inaugurated millennialism) became dominant in the Roman Catholic Church through the teaching of St. Augustine in his theology of history called *The City of God*. Augustine identified the reign of God with the Church on earth. The thousand-year period, therefore, was not to be taken literally, but rather to be understood as the time between the first and second advent of Christ. This understanding helped to give rise to the Roman Catholic Church's preeminence in the secular life of the medieval world.

Amillennialists believe there will be no (the negative prefix "a-") literal thousand-year reign of Christ with the saints on earth. The return of Christ is followed by the general resurrection of the righteous and the wicked, the last judgment, and the passage into the eternal state. When it comes to specific interpretive approaches to the book, generally, the amillennialist sees the order of events in the Revelation coming in a cyclical fashion. Revelation 20 must be understood historically in relation to the rest of the book, and the two resurrections in verses 4–5 are interpreted whereby the first is spiritual and the second, physical. There is no expectation of revealed prophecy to be fulfilled in the future except for the general beliefs about the Lord's return. Basically this viewpoint holds that all has been fulfilled in Christ or will be fulfilled in the new earth.

Like premillennialism, and contrary to postmillennialism, there is a general feeling that things will get worse before Christ's triumph in the end times. The Christian's participation in suffering is a prominent part of this view. The Christian will receive the same treatment that Christ received. The hope of the Church is to be discovered in her longing for release from this earth and its trials, and the advent of the time when what has been experienced through faith in Christ will then be seen within its fullness.[14]

POSTMILLENNIALISM

The view known as postmillennialism has been around Christian history since Augustine, but it was very popular in America at the beginning of the twentieth century. Following the perceived triumph of the Civil War, a great deal of optimism filled the ecclesial horizon. Christianity, having wiped out the evil institution of slavery, was now turning its attention to other social evils—alcoholism, frivolity, and dance to name a few. Others put renewed vigor into education, hospitals, and political cooperation as a way of bringing peace and justice to the world. Many preachers were heralding the eventual kingdom of God on earth. None was more famous than that of New York City's Riverside pastor Harry Emerson Fosdick, as he wrote in his now famous hymn *God of Grace and God of Glory*:

> God of grace and God of glory,
> On Thy people pour Thy power.
> Crown Thine ancient church's story,
> Bring her bud to glorious flower.
> Grant us wisdom, grant us courage,
> For the facing of this hour,
> For the facing of this hour.

Cure Thy children's warring madness,
Bend our pride to Thy control.
Shame our wanton selfish gladness,
Rich in things and poor in soul.
Grant us wisdom, grant us courage,
Lest we miss Thy kingdom's goal,
Lest we miss Thy kingdom's goal.

Postmillennialists believe that the Kingdom was founded on earth during the earthly ministry of Christ in fulfillment of Old Testament prophecy, making the New Testament church the transformed Israel. During the thousand-year period, Christ's spiritual reign is felt on earth by a gradual, yet pervasive, transformation of society and culture by an unprecedented Christian expansion. The nations are evangelized, while political and religious institutions become saturated with Kingdom values and purpose. Most postmillennialists have some form of belief in a second coming of Christ, but the event is barely noticed as the kingdom of heaven merges with the kingdom of earth. At this point, a general judgment occurs, and sinful humanity is punished and the righteous become partners in an eternal form of the Kingdom.

Through the promise given to Abraham that "all peoples on earth will be blessed" (Gen. 12:2–3), postmillennialists are optimistic about the eventual world conversion through a winsome gospel, eventually making all nations coming to worship God.

Though elements of postmillennialism are surely discovered in the teaching of Jesus and the scope of the biblical story, such a positive evaluation of world affairs has virtually vanished from the Church's thinking today. The succession of wars in the twentieth century squashed the almost utopian optimism found at its beginning. Even the most ruby-red of rose-colored glasses would find it impossible to see a triumph over evil in the horrors associated with human pride and sin. No sooner does society rid itself of one demon than many more take its place. As an inoculation for one bacteria is discovered, new drug-resistant diseases replace it. Racism erupts from people groups that have once been the victims of prejudice; sexism tips the scales of injustice from one angered gender to another. The general assumption that things in the world are getting better and better is not a common experience in our world, even though there have been quantum leaps in helpful technology and the quality of life.

At this point there are two types of postmillennialists. Pietistic postmillennialists deny that the postmillennial advance of the Kingdom involves the total transformation of culture through the application of biblical law. They would argue that a more spiritual permeation of the people who live and work in the society will eventually provide a moral light to the institutions of this world. These Christians see great reason to be engaged in the social matrix of the world, and they seek to be the salt and light necessary for its transformation.

Another more militant-like form of postmillennialism is called theonomic postmillennialism.[15] Sometimes identified with dominion eschatology, writers like David Chilton and Gary North consider the Old Testament political and economic law to be a necessary ingredient in creating a new Kingdom order. They advocate replacing present political institutions with the essential biblical counterparts of courts and councils in secular and religious leadership. Many of these ideas provided the philosophical framework for some quarters of the Christian School Movement, and continue to be advanced by the Calvinistic heirs of the lively experiment at Geneva. There John Calvin sought to create a society built upon the principles of Christian politic and society. Generally, the belief is that in this millennium the Church will exercise Christ's power and authority in this world whereby the wicked rulers are hindered in their wickedness and the influence of Christianity will excel until some future time when most of the world will be in obedience to God's laws. They expect that after they have created a just, God-fearing society, Christ will then return and the judgment and resurrection occur.

Though these particular views of the millennial reign of Christ have been associated with concurrent movements within theology, most biblical scholars rarely feel that any of these positions fully describe the symbolism and dynamics of John's revelation. Most Christians have been discipled by Church traditions that aid them in a view of history and human destiny. These worldviews tend to be supported by one of these understandings of Revelation 20.

WHAT OTHERS SAY

THE MILLENNIUM: THREE MAJOR VIEWS

	Premillennialial	Amillennial	Postmillennial
Bible interpretation of OT prophecies	Tendency toward literal interpretation	Mostly figurative, based on NT use of OT prophecies such as Luke 3:3–6; Acts 2:16–21; 15:15–18	
Return of Christ	Before the millennium	After the millennium	
Israel	Church and Israel are to be understood separately and must be fulfilled separately.	Israel has no literal future; Church has taken over the fulfilled promises of God's chosen people.	Israel and Church are symbolic of the whole people of God.
Rev. 20	Follows Rev. 19	Takes us back in time	
Rev. 20:1–3	Satan will be bound after Christ returns, sealed away completely	Satan was bound at Christ's first coming, is now unable to stop the gospel. We are already in the millennium.	Satan will be bound 1,000 years or a long time before Christ's return; he may already be considered bound
Rev. 20:4–6	Saints will be immortal, reigning with Christ over mortals on earth	The saints "live again" in heaven — the first resurrection is not like the second, just as the first death is not like the second. Some see "live again" as a reference to regeneration in this age.	
Advocates	Justin, Irenaeus, J.N. Darby, Ladd, Dispensationalists	Augustine, Luther, Calvin, many mainline churches	A.H. Strong, G. Bahnsen, K. Gentry, some Calvinists, Wesley(?)
Scriptures emphasized	OT prophecies; Rom. 11:26; 1 Cor. 15; Rev. 2:26–27; 20:1–10	Matt. 12:28–29; 19:28; John 5:28–29; 2 Th. 1:6–10; 2 Pet. 3:10–14; Jude 6	Isaiah 55:11; Matt. 13:31–33; 28:18–20; John 12:31–32

For example, those churches that tend to see history in a pessimistic perspective attach themselves to those views of the millennium that see Christ's return as the end of this negative flow of history and the beginning of a newly injected reign of God. Perhaps it would be good if we could emphasize the main features of the millennium language in this section and attempt to find a common ground regarding these diverse interpretations.

THE REIGN OF GOD

For one, the reign of God is both present and future (already and not yet). Even though Christ is presently reigning in heaven, we anticipate a future earthly aspect to His reign.

Second, the question as to whether a rapture of God's people precedes or concludes the great tribulation poured out on the earth can be reduced to the fact of God's ultimate protection over those for whom God cares.

A resurrection of believers takes place at the beginning of the millennium. One would think that it would be enough to believe that God will judge fairly those who are righteous and those who are wicked.

The various interpretations of how the millennium fits in the plan of God have raised more questions about chronology than purpose. At the least, dispensationalists have tended to argue that the thousand-year period allowed God to technically offer to Israel the vindication and reign on earth that He promised her. Once it is over, then He will continue on with His universal promises to the rest of humanity. In this interpretation the kingdom of God is a requirement to protect God's integrity. The release of Satan after the millennium may offer further insight into the two-phased feature of the end.

SATAN'S DOOM 20:7–10

When the thousand years are over, Satan will be released from his prison (20:7). In the beginning of chapter 20, Satan was incarcerated in the Abyss, preventing him **from deceiving the nations anymore until the thousand years were ended** (20:3). His complete incapacitation was described in detail, but he has yet to be judged and, therefore, Satan's demise remains unfinished. The thousand-year period provides a dramatic and yet uneasy experience for the seer. He is enjoying the repose, but he always knows the evil one is still there.

Two distinct ideas about the end of history were handed down through Jewish theology to combine in this vision: (1) that Israel would experience an earthly reign where their martyred people would be vindicated and the righteous ones rewarded, and (2) the idea that the end of the world would wipe the slate clean and a new creation would take its place. The millennium provides the framework for holding both of these views together and in tension.

The reason for Satan being let go for this period of time is not made explicit, other than it **must** take place (20:3). "Must" (1:1; 4:1; 11:5; 17:10; 22:6) has been used to describe a divine control over all things, including the will of the evil powers in the world. God binds Satan; God releases him. As was foreshadowed and expected of Satan, he immediately goes **out to deceive the nations in the four corners of the earth** (20:8). The specific nations—**Gog and Magog**—have been interpreted as various historic and modern countries, but their use here appears to represent all the evil nations of the earth taken from Ezekiel 38–39. There people from the north, led by a leader Gog from the land of Magog, attack a secure Israel to show forth God's holiness. Rather than meaning one (or two) nations, the vision shows nations coming from all **four corners of the earth**, and numbering **like the sand on the seashore** (20:8). This is the final battle, and all nations of the earth seek to retain their own interests until the end. This is the nature of nations, kings, and powers. Eventually all the old nations are under the control of the deceptive power of Satan; only the New Jerusalem is allowed to remain.

As these armies fell upon **God's people, the city** that God loves, **fire came down from heaven and devoured them** (20:9). Again, as before the thousand-year reign, there is no great battle even though Satan had gathered them for that purpose. The clamoring of swords, the amassing of troupes and weaponry was all for naught. All of the bravado of Satan's warriors and their claims of glory were never accomplished in this postmillennial event. Whatever was to be made of the millennial period and what was to follow is finished with a whimper. The culmination comes when **the**

devil, who deceived them, was thrown into the lake of burning sulfur, where the beast and the false prophet had been thrown (20:10). The devil's finish comes swiftly. He has the same fate as his evil partners before him (cf. 19:20), the lake of burning sulfur, with its putrid flames, providing a torment for its inhabitants **day and night for ever and ever.**

THE DEAD ARE JUDGED 20:11–15

All that is left to do is mop up the mess. The powers that were behind all of the evil on the earth are not only impotent and unable to effect human history anymore; they have come to their final end. **Then I saw** begins the final reckoning with John's new vision of **a great white throne and him who was seated on it** (20:11). Being **white**, the **throne** represents the just, holy and divine character of the judgment that would be carried out there. The seat has no significance other than that given to it by the One seated upon it. All space is humbled by this place; even the elements of the creation—**earth and sky**—cannot exist here. Eventually they too must be recreated to prepare a proper environment for the new people of God. The earth and sky had been the domain of the two beasts, and their tainted smell is still present on them. God will not allow a place for these to hide from His presence.

The vision continues with a vision of **the dead, standing before the throne** (20:12). John sees two sets of opened books. One provided an account to judge the dead **according to what they had done** (20:12), another, **the book of life**, was checked to find the names of those who

 WHAT OTHERS SAY

The new creation, which is absolutely new, comes only through judgment and destruction. . . . There then is no continuity. The city of God is not at the end of human progress, at the end of history by a sort of accumulation of the works of man; at this end there is found only Babylon.

—Jacques Ellul

would be saved from **the lake of fire, the second death** (20:14). The judgment is inclusive of the **great and small** (20:12), having come from the **sea, death**, and **Hades** (20:13). No person can avoid standing in front of this throne, no matter who you are or where you are.

Since the Protestant Reformation there has been the constant need to comment on the supposed "works righteousness" reflected in a judgment based upon "what we have done." This same polemic appears when reading the gospel of Jesus, who unashamedly taught that humanity would be judged in some way by our works. Rather than place upon these texts the debates of the sixteenth century, the reader should be open to the specific meaning that is behind the opened books of a person's life. In the context of witness and faithfulness, the idea of "what we have done" has more to do with the Christian's discipleship and spiritual formation than with winning salvation through a specific amount of good deeds. In this case, the Revelation appears to have a similar theology of that found in the Epistle of James, a "faith-works" which fully describes the believer's true credo because a person's deeds match up with who the person is.

ENDNOTES

1. George Eldon Ladd, *The Meaning of the Millennium: Four Views*, ed. Robert Clouse (Downers Grove: InterVarsity Press), 23.

2. John Feinberg, *Continuity and Discontinuity: Perspectives on the Relationship Between the Old and New Testaments* (Westchester: Crossway, 1988), 76.

3. Ladd, 27.

4. Ladd, 32.

5. Herman Hoyt, "Dispensational Premillennialism" in *The Meaning of the Millennium*, Robert G. Clouse, ed., (Downers Grove: InterVarsity Press, 1977), 44.

6. Feinberg, 77.

7. Feinberg, 77.

8. Paul N. Benware, *Understanding End Times Prophecy* (Chicago: Moody Press, 1995, 94.

9. Ibid.

10. Ibid.

11. For a history of the problem of defining dispensationalism and the call for a new breed of dispensational schemes, see Craig A. Blaising and D. Bock, eds., *Dispensationalism, Israel and the Church: The Search for Definition* (Grand Rapids: Zondervan, 1992), 13–34, 377–79.

12. Some commentators representing this model are John F. Walvoord, *The Revelation of Jesus Christ: A Commentary* (Chicago: Moody Press, 1966); J. Dwight Pentecost, *Things to Come* (Grand Rapids: Zondervan, 1978); and Charles Ryrie, *The Basis for Premillennial Faith* (New York: The Loizeaux

Brothers, 1953).

13. Proponents of this approach, among others, are Gregory K. Beale. *The Book of Revelation: A Commentary on the Greek Text. New International Greek Testament Commentary.* (Grand Rapids: William B. Eerdmans Publishing Company, 1998); and William Hendriksen, *More Than Conquerors: An Interpretation of the Book of Revelation* (6th ed.; Grand Rapids: Baker Book House, 1952).

14. John F. Walvoord, "Dispensational Premillennialism," *Christianity Today* (September 15, 1958), 13.

15. Kenneth L. Gentry, "Postmillennialism," *Three Views of the Millennium and Beyond*, ed. Darrell L. Bock (Grand Rapids: Zondervan, 1999).

THE NEW CREATION

Revelation 21:1–22:5

The year A.D. 70 must have been a devastating year for Christians and Jews alike. The Roman military had destroyed the holy Temple of the God of Israel, leaving Jerusalem in ruins. If ever there had been reason to hold to a negative view of history, it would have been now. But the revelation of John, rather than sliding into a more dreadful picture of the doom of the world, reaches its climax with a picture of the New Jerusalem and her place in a new world environment.

The visions of woes, destruction, and judgment are behind us now, and we walk over the threshold of our new eternal home. We are shown three images that aid our imaginations in seeing the hope before us, The images of creation (the Garden of Eden), the city of Jerusalem, and the temple itself are intertwined to give us a splendid understanding—if not description—of the new city that we are to occupy at the end of all things.

After we have watched the demise of the "great city," we behold the rising of a New City, where the people of God no longer have to call out to a distant and hidden throne room for help. For **the dwelling of God is with men, and he will live with them** (21:3). We remember Wesley's deathbed words—"The best of all, God is with us!" Given the many wonderful attributes that the heavenly city offers us, this is the most compelling and delicious.

THE NEW HEAVEN AND NEW EARTH 21:1–8

For the tenth and last time, John introduces his visionary report with the technical words: **Then I saw** (21:1). John's eyes land upon **a new heaven and a new earth**, a view that must have had an enduring impact.

With the collapse of the powers and principalities in the preceding chapters, John summarizes the catastrophic end with a simple phrase: **for the first heaven and the first earth had passed away**. The redemption of all creation is complete. The first creation, the one that was broken and plagued by the pervasive effects of evil, was now gone and replaced with a new one.

We are inclined to think of this new heaven and new earth as a purged and sanctified world, much like the first but without its violent and destructive qualities. The new heaven and new earth replaces the old one, but John notes that **there was no longer any sea** (21:1). The sea throughout the revelation has been both a symbol of separation from God (4:6; 15:2) and the place from which evil actors percolate (13:1). In 20:13 the sea is a parallel place of the dead along with Hades. Even though most of the uses of the sea in the book were to describe the natural order as such (along with the land and the sky), the fact that there will be no sea in the new creation undoubtedly is symbolic of the chaotic and destructive use it has served in the visionary drama. Without the sea, the center of all chaotic political forces, there is no danger that the demise of God's creation will repeat itself.

Theologians of history generally think of the relation of the first cosmos to the new one in two main ways: (1) as a radical discontinuity between them with an abrupt ending and a new beginning or (2) as a gradual, even indiscernible, move from one to the other.

Those who see the first heaven and earth as coming to a catastrophic end often discern the times in ways that almost hasten that destruction. In 1983, President Ronald Reagan intimated to an Israeli official, "I wonder if we aren't the generation which will see the fulfillment of the portents of Armageddon?"[1] An American president, having the power to bring about the final destruction of humanity, shows a very dangerous use of the language of the Apocalypse. Such a view of the destiny of the old cosmos often leads to a lack of ecological concern as well. If the world is going to end in such a catastrophic way, then why bother investing in the long-term security of its resources? Generally, the call to discipleship does not come with a concern for the present age and a redemptive engagement with it. In fact, this model often will display contempt for this present world and could even encourage people to engage in activities that contribute to its demise.

The second way of understanding this transition recognizes the worth of God's creation—the first and the last—as redeemable. But the problem with the language of continuity is that it fails to capture Jesus' proclamation of the reign of God and the radical character of the end of the world. Perhaps the language of "passing away" is necessarily ambiguous, expressing both ideas. God declares the old order of existence as null and void. There is no danger that the horrors of evil will someday erupt again and disrupt His creation. At the same time, God's creation has from the beginning been declared "good" and has provided the basis for what is new in the coming creation.

The Revelation has a sounding of completion at this point; there is no chance that the New Creation could occur without the knowledge that old has passed away. At the same time, there are elements of the old order that now find their way into the New City, but they are holy and redeemed. We do not mean by this that God has some how remodeled the old Jerusalem and has moved in with new furniture and wallpaper. The New City has come from **heaven** (21:12), showing its origin from God and not from any earthly builder. Still, it has come to earth. We know then that this is to be built into the fabric of the redeemed world where God has placed us.

The new world order is made up of **his people** (21:3). There will be no longer a robotic, listless populace taking their script from the Harlot and the beast. God's people will be in a place where God's energy is no longer taken up with pouring out wrath on the faithless, because He will be able to devote himself to His beloved community. **They will be his people, and God himself will be with them and be**

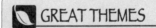

GREAT THEMES

ISAIAH AND THE REVELATION

For I am about to create new heavens and a new earth;
   the former things shall not be remembered or come to mind.
But be glad and rejoice forever in what I am creating;
   for I am about to create Jerusalem as a joy,
and its people as a delight
                    —*Isaiah 65:17–18, NRSV*

their God (21:3). For those presently suffering on earth, the vision of God wiping **every tear from their eyes,** with all **death or mourning or crying or pain** (21:4) vanished, describes the most valuable commodity in the city. The older order no longer has any effect on this new creation.

The newness of the creation is the most striking characteristic of the vision. In describing the death of the old, the new situation is amplified by the voice of the one on the throne, **"I am making everything new!"** (21:5). We see Paul affirming this same hope to the disruptive Corinthian Church (2 Cor. 5:17). This text seems to have its antecedent in Isaiah 65:17–19. "Behold, I will create new heavens and a new earth . . . But be glad and rejoice forever in what I will create . . . I will rejoice over Jerusalem and take delight in my people."

With wording having the same feel as the Genesis account, the Creator beholds His own work with almost gleeful abandon. God, in Christ, is like a child in a sandbox, calling out to anyone who might hear, "Look what I am doing!" The preparation of the new bride, the new city, and the new order of things is not a condemnation of the old but rather seen as a fulfillment of that order. God is the one that is handing over this new situation to John. In no way can this grand design be seen as the end product of human endeavor or progress. The new creation is a gift, just as the first. When God declares the creation finished ("**It is done**"), He calls himself, **"the Alpha and the Omega, the Beginning and the End"** (21:6). He dispels any potential confusion that the first creation was a mistake of a lesser god. God the Creator has been at work from beginning to end to bring about this newness.

This same one that was sitting on the throne is recognized as the Lamb Jesus. Because the new creation has in it all that the first garden had, He offers to **give without cost from the spring of the water of life** (21:6) to any one that thirsts. As in John 4, the symbol of living water represents the abundant, eternal life. For those wishing to rely only on this world's offer, they will forfeit their privilege of drinking from this spring. John continues the same theme of "overcoming" (conquering) that was found in the letters to the seven churches: **All who are victorious will inherit all these blessings, and I will be their God, and they will be my chil-**

dren (21:7, NLT). The character of the new people of God is on display in this new city.

For this reason, the description of those unfit to inherit this new home—**the cowardly, the unbelieving, the vile, the murderers, the sexually immoral, those who practice magic arts, the idolaters and all liars** (21:8)—is not merely a traditional vice list (as in Rom. 1:29–31; Gal. 5:19–21; or 1 Tim.1:9–10). Rather than a Stoic-style concern for the personal morality of temperance and self-control, this list has specific vices for the world of John's prophecy. In the present age, cowards lead the pack, bending their wills to their oppressors. In the face of the powers that persecute and coerce, only the courageous will overcome. Unbelief is not so much a lack of doctrinal orthodoxy as it is a falling away in the face of confrontation and testing. Even **the vile, the murderers, the sexual immoral** have more to do with the hostile and debased socio-religious climate of the first century Roman Empire than with moral and criminal behavior. All of the actions being done against the witnesses of Christ are vile in God's sight, even if they are accepted practices of the prevailing society. **All liars**, at the summary of the list of villains, is a fitting description for false witnesses of God (see 2:2 and 3:9). Earlier, in describing the sealed 144,000, "no lie was found in their mouths" (14:5) was synonymous with being "blameless." A similar list of the non-invited, found at the conclusion of John's book, is ended with a synonymous phrase: "and everyone who loves and practices falsehood" (22:15). No ambiguity will exist between the true and the false in the new creation. The old order allowed for such a mixture of people.

But the New Jerusalem will have a pure population, one that looks like the faithful heroes of the present age. Those who reject God and His commandments will have a place, but it will be **in the fiery lake of burning sulfur** (21:8). Such a punishment by fire was spoken of by the Old Testament (see Lam. 1:13; Jer. 7:31), and probably refers to "gehenna," a site of ancient human sacrifice to the god Molech. Later it became a refuse pile that was always burning with rotting decay of human garbage, and a synonym for the place of eternal punishment. We are told: **This is the second death** (21:8).

THE HOLY CITY 21:9–27

The next vision **the bride, the wife of the Lamb** (21:9) is set up as a contrast with the earlier depiction of the Great Prostitute Babylon (chapters 17–18). Both of these feminizations are, in fact, representations of cities. From his high mountain perspective, John is able to see **the Holy City, Jerusalem, coming down out of heaven from God** (21:10). The city is a **holy** city, what the original Jerusalem was meant to be from the beginning. Because it comes **down out of heaven**, John knows that the city has its source **from God**. If the dating of the Apocalypse during the reign of Domitian (late 90s) is correct, we are made aware that the old Jerusalem, which was destroyed in A.D. 70, is now being replaced.

The splendor of the city is metaphorically like a **very precious jewel**, but is actually the **glory of God** (21:11). God on the throne of chapter 4 appeared with this same luster (4:3) and so the city would reflect the same appearance as its chief resident. Whatever this jewel is, it is **clear as crystal**, emphasizing the uncorrupted and holy character of both God and the New City. Any description that follows will be a mere attempt to get at the indescribable wonder of such a perfectly divine city.

The dimensions of the city are a bit odd as far as architecture goes. The wall and its gates are first noticed. The number twelve, representing completeness and wholeness, dominates the symmetrical features of the four-sided wall. Each side—east, west, north, and south—has three gates, each having an angel on guard. **The names of the twelve tribes of Israel** (21:12) are found written on the gates; **the names of the twelve apostles of the Lamb** (21:14) are written on the twelve foundations that hold up **the great, high wall** (21:12). The difficulty of understanding how twelve foundations could hold up a four-sided wall highlights the symbolic character of this description. This new city will find its security in the traditions of the Old and New Testaments, the people of Israel, and the community of the apostolic faith.

The angel of verse 9 now begins to take the measurements of **the city, its gates and its walls** with a **measuring rod of gold** (21:15), an accurate and wonderful design. Our first observation was correct: the city is a perfect square. In fact, as the angel uses the rod to measure height, width, and length, John discovers that the city is a 12,000 (12 x 1,000) stadia (about 1,400 miles) cube. The 144 (12 x 12) cubit-thick walls would be a bit flimsy, being 1,400 miles high but only 200 feet thick. Obviously the measurements are depicting the perfection of the design using the number twelve as the derivative of all the building dimensions. We are also mindful, that as a perfect cube, it matches the interior room of the Holy of Holies in the Temple and tent of meeting. The city itself is large and great (the meaning of the 1,000), and it has been prepared for the complete chosen people of God (the meaning of the number 12). The perfect city has been built for a new and holy people. We are told that the angel was using human measurements to show us something of the divine architecture. The importance may lie in the image of this new creation as a new people and not so much as a city. For the first time in history, a city fits the shape of the people rather attempting to cram and press its people into its own form.

Given the data of the city's shape, John's attention is now directed at the color and texture of its brilliance. The wall is **jasper** (God's brilliance of 4:3 and the city itself in 21:11) and the city itself being **pure gold** (21:18). Both of these precious elements are said to be **pure as glass** (21:21), putting the precious character of the elements together with its uncorrupted state. One could debate if gold or jasper in their pure state is actually clear but would miss the value of this language for the vision of the New City. Each of the twelve foundations are decorated **with every kind of precious stone**—in order, **jasper, sapphire, chalcedony, emerald, sardonyx, carnelian, chrysolite, beryl, topaz, chrysoprase, jacinth,** and **amethyst** (21:19–20). Scholars have various opinions about the actual stones that these Greek words represent. One would doubt if the color and property of each has any significance other than the amazing worth and endurance of the materials used to create such an awesome living place.

But what of the temple? The Jewish Christian of this age would have first looked for the beloved centerpiece to any Holy City, especially the New Jerusalem. Ezekiel's prophecy of the New Jerusalem included the temple as the center of that city's life. In John's vision the *shekinah* presence of God fills the entire city and not just the temple area. Furthermore, he **did not**

see a temple in the city (21:22). The void does not bother John (or the Revelation's readers) anymore because he knows immediately the reason: **because the Lord God Almighty and the Lamb are its temple**.

This is a far better city than the first. The buildings no longer hold its occupants; the occupants make up the city. Anyone who would be impressed with the gold of the city's main street, fearing that a thief might want to chip it up and hoard it in their banks, would be unfit to live here. Likewise, anyone who would be disappointed to see that Solomon's temple had not been rebuilt, or would be amazed to see standing what their Roman oppressors had destroyed, would miss the most spectacular of all religious events. Emmanuel! God with us! Both the transcendent and immanent aspects of God—**the Lord God Almighty and the Lamb**—are combined in this new form of temple. God remains the mystery and powerful divine, yet He becomes radically close and intimate.

Now that the most basic religious need of the Holy City is met—the worship center—John turns his attention to human needs. Earthly cities exist mostly for the communal occupations of security and commerce. A mass of people huddle together within a city wall, lighting its homes and closing its gates against the dark surroundings. But this **city does not need the sun or the moon to shine on it, for the glory of God gives it light, and the Lamb is its lamp** (21:23). This seems to be a direct adaptation of Isaiah's text: "The sun will no more be your light by day, nor will the brightness of the moon shine on you, for the LORD will be your everlasting light, and your God will be your glory" (Isa. 60:19).

Also, whatever was good about the human occupation of the old order of being is now brought into this one place, as **the kings of the earth will bring their splendor into it** (21:24). The reason that God made the human in the first place was not to stifle creativity but to share it. For that reason, **the glory and honor of the nations will be brought into** the New City (21:26). In this new world, God takes delight in the offerings of His people, for now proper worship is accomplished. Human work is not perceived as an idolatrous threat bent on achievement and luxurious wealth. Rather the saints of God are encouraged to participate in the life of the city by bringing into it the best of what humanity has to offer.

This is a strange city indeed. We see a walled, well-fortified city, with angels guarding powerfully constructed gates, but **on no day will its gates ever be shut** (21:25). The enemies of God and His children no longer exist; fear is not felt in this city.

Twice in this section, John tells us that **there will be no more night** (21:25; see also 22:5). Night is synonymous with fear. Because of the presence of the Light itself, the inhabitants can open themselves to anything. The biblical use of light often signifies a moral value. As in the Genesis cre-

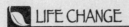

LIFE CHANGE
THY WILL BE DONE ON EARTH

In the New City, God takes delight in the offerings of His people.

- Proper worship is accomplished.

- Human work is not bent on achievement and luxurious wealth.

- The saints of God bring the best of what humanity has to offer.

This is not only for a future city, but right now as we attempt to do His will on earth as it is done in heaven. How can you better do His will on earth? In what ways are you offering pleasing gifts to God though your life?

ation, God creates light first, allowing all the rest of His creation to be bathed in the illuminating glow. God is able to behold His work as "good." In Ephesians, Paul uses light as a means of separating the deeds that are done by sinners and saints (Eph. 5:8–14). The light of God exposes all of these deeds done in the darkness for what they are. James tells us that the moral character of God, the Father of the heavenly lights "does not change like shifting shadows" (James 1:17). Similarly, in the holy City, God's light is a constant and **nothing impure will ever enter it, nor will anyone who does what is shameful or deceitful, but only those whose names are written in the Lamb's book of life** (21:27).

THE RIVER OF LIFE 22:1–5

Then comes a third and further nuanced metaphor for the new creation. Though there is to be no sea in the new city, **the river of the water of life** (22:1) dominates the terrain. John sees that it is clear and pure as **crystal**; no murky waters from which evil might erupt. Blending pastoral and urban components, the heavenly vision resorts to images from the Garden of Eden to give further meaning to this new city home. **Flowing**

from the throne of God and of the Lamb (22:1), the river splits Main Street in two.

To further complicate the image, **the tree of life** stands on **each** bank of the river. There is no "wrong side of the tracks" in the heavenly city. The tree that God had placed out of the reach of humankind following the Genesis rebellion is now easily accessible, **bearing twelve crops of fruit, yielding its fruit every month** (22:2). Again, the number twelve shows this to be a sufficient supply, offering sustenance to the residents forever and ever. Further, even the leaves have an enduring function, for in this city, eating is not our only need for existence. The leaves provide a medicine that will heal the nations. Strong people, fed on the tree of life, make up a strong society, healed of its volatile throws for self-destruction and violent affliction.

The obvious use of the Genesis image is to show the reversal of the effects of creation's fall. **No longer will there be any curse. The throne of God and of the Lamb will be in the city, and his servants will serve him** (22:3). Not only will life be better, without the pain and brokenness of the curse, it will have purpose. Sometimes (perhaps jocularly) people suggest that heaven, as a place of perpetual worship and singing, will be a dull place to live. When they compare the images of heaven (probably taken from the Greek ideas of Paradise) with the entertainment and fun of modern life, thrill-seeking people find heaven to be a lot of idle sitting and harp playing. In fact, humanity will find its purpose in serving God to be a far more liberating experience than the captive nature of earthly pleasures.

This is not meant to negate the goodness of this present offering of enjoyment in God's good creation. Certainly a world-denying theology is not the foundation of the Christian understanding of life in this present age. But when one enjoys the new creation and partakes in the bounty of experience, while at the same time placing God at the proper center of that creation, life will have its ultimate and unconfused meaning. We will not seek fulfillment in our jobs, our relationships, or our status. But one understands that we will all have appropriate vocation. All of these things will make sense when we live out our lives in the presence of the **throne of God** and discover our place as His **servants**.

They will see his face (22:4) carries with it a powerful thought. Through the biblical story we realize the struggle of seeing the face of

God, a metaphor for knowing God and experiencing the holy, transcendent power of God. But to those who have suffered so greatly in the service of this King, the ability to see the Lord's face carries even greater meaning. In the ancient world, when criminals were banished "from the face of the king," it was understood that such people were no longer worthy citizens and were not permitted the privilege of being in the presence of the sovereign. In the horrid picture of Isaiah 53, where the Suffering Servant is described as "a man of sorrows," despised, rejected, even smitten, afflicted, pierced and crushed, one of the striking features of this Savior is that He is "like one from whom men hide their faces" (53:3). The scandal of the Christ's death is too great for us to look upon Him. We understand this shame; we recognize that we have caused His suffering and pain. But, here in this place, we behold His face. We can look upon it and find God's healing presence of eternal forgiveness.

Again we are told that the city will have no more night. This time the direct contrast with the description of the demise of Babylon in chapter 14 is made: "And the smoke of their torment rises for ever and ever. There is no rest day or night for those who worship the beast and his image, or for anyone who receives the mark of his name" (14:11). The victorious Christians will have **his name** [the name of God] **. . . on their foreheads**. (22:4). The final rest longed for in the Book of Hebrews is finally achieved. A world without need for a night is a very different experience than the constant torment belonging to those of the beast. This is reason enough to long for heaven. For many, the cares and stresses of this world provide for many restless nights. But in the new city we are reminded again that **the Lord God will give them light. And they will reign for ever and ever** (22:5). It is a new day, without the fear of night, that will begin a new age where God will share His reign with all His creation.

With this final vision of the new city we are made aware of the choice we have before us. Do we wish to take up residency in the old city, the Prostitute's City of Babylon and with all her progeny, or are we to enter a city with no gates, with comfort and reward, and with life everlasting?

The prerequisite is simple: holiness. This city contains no evil and will be sustained, not by the power of political and economic systems, but by God alone. The obvious comparison of this city **as a bride beautifully**

dressed for her husband (21:2) causes our memory to reflect, if just for a moment, on the contrast with Babylon the Prostitute. George Beasley-Murray called the apocalypse "a tale of two cities" saying, "The harlot city reposes on the beast from hell—she partakes of the character of the devil, and the bride-city descends from heaven—she is the creation of God. But one thing they have in common, they stand alike on earth, and invite humanity to come to them."[2]

ENDNOTES

1. Chicago Sun-Times, 29 October 1983.

2. George R. Beasley-Murray, The *Book of Revelation. New Century Bible Commentary* (Grand Rapids, Michigan: William B. Eerdmans Publishing Company, 1978), 315.

EPILOGUE

Revelation 22:6–21

The last paragraphs of the Revelation of John at first glance appear to be a hodgepodge of phrases, admonitions, and benedictions, but on closer inspection, we can see how they serve a number of purposes.

First, the epilogue serves to tie the beginning of the apocalypse with its end, like tying a knot around the whole. By serving as a type of bookend for the opening chapter, it repeats some of the same form and content of that material.

A second use of the final chapter is to highlight the message of the book by way of emphasis and exhortation. Therefore, the exhortations found in this epilogue serve to highlight the themes of the book as a whole. If the vision of the world depicted in the Revelation makes sense, then the final invitation to enter and engage it comes just in time. The hearer or reader responds to the finish with expectation and response.

A third literary purpose of the epilogue is related to the trappings that the apocalyptic material was first enveloped. At the conclusion of the work, we are reminded anew that this prophecy is set in an epistolary form. The salutatory words are now recounted and extended into the conclusion. John gives blessings—and admonitions—to the letter's readers. The apocalypse is meant to be handed on as an encouraging missive to the Church-at-large.

As a finish to the book, the angel who spoke to John in the preceding vision validates the prophetic words as **trustworthy and true** (22:6), the same couplet used to name the rider of the white horse (Greek, "pistos kai alethinos"). Because the one who gave the message to the angel to deliver to John is trustworthy, then it follows that the message is as well. We are being reminded of the origin of the revelation as coming from Jesus. At times we may be confused if the message was from God (22:6) or Jesus (22:16) or an angel on their behalf. The message is not novel either. The same **God of the spirits of the prophets** has delivered an oracle **to show his servants the things that must soon take place** (22:6). For the first of three times we hear the promise of Jesus: **"Behold, I am coming soon!"** (22:7). Like the end of John's gospel where Peter's three denials are addressed by Jesus' three inquiries of love, the conclusion to the apocalypse salves our concerns of being left lonely with a tri-fold assurance.

Blessed is he who keeps the words of the prophecy in this book (21:7). This is the sixth of the beatitudes in the book of Revelation. To receive this blessing, the reader must do more than just understand and figure out the many complicated symbolisms in the book of prophecy. The revelation that John recounts **for the churches** (21:16) is not merely informative; it is doctrinal and demands discipleship. To **keep the words** does not imply holding them close or even memorizing them; it demands a way of life, a consistent pattern of faithfulness to God's Word.

Next in the format is a reminder that the author **John** was the same one that saw and heard the vision which was reported. He experienced it deeply, and now describes himself by this revelation and by his position before the revealed Lord. He says that he is the one who **fell down to worship** what appeared to be **the angel** (22:8) that had shown him the vision. This format harkens back to the start of his revelation (1:17) when John had fallen down as if dead before Jesus Christ himself. It would almost appear that John has been in such a state of worship that he cannot distinguish anymore between the experience of the vision and the source of the revealed Lord. The angel tells him to get up, and **worship God** (21:9; see also 19:10). Because of this strange interaction, some commentators have suggested that this angel is, in fact, Jesus. He now is identifying so closely with John, and His fellow martyrs, that the filial relation has superseded His divine status. This seems to be a spurious interpretation of "the angel" as John has never referred to Jesus in this way before. Too, the need to redirect John's worship away from himself to God confuses the role of Jesus in the Godhead and makes little sense in this situation. Even if this angel is the angel of Jesus, it is not to be confused with Jesus.

Worship of God has with it so many dangerous side roads and pitfalls. The use of technological aesthetics has enhanced the entire worship experience today so that many are tempted to fall down and worship the means of the revelation rather than God himself. In the West, there has always been the danger of worshiping the technology of doing Church: a program of evangelism that works in the suburbs being forced on the rural or urban setting, a leadership model that has proven results in the corporate world now being heralded as the most dynamic model for church growth and development. But a more seductive temptation presently is the danger of "technologizing" worship. Many attendees leave our sanctuaries, having had their senses bombarded from beginning to end with multimedia impulses, to report a powerful experience of awe and power. The problem comes when they try to discern whether this experience was induced by the Holy Spirit or manipulated through human psychology. If we have discovered new means by which the religious experience of God can be prodded and excited, we are not far behind the development of drug-induced worship. Even at the conclusion of this great vision—where John too was highly stimulated via his sensory organs—John is still not permitted to reduce God to His own experience. The angel reminds John that worship is reserved for God and must be directed away from the mediation of that worship.

Worship has been a major theme throughout the book of Revelation. It should not be surprising that the angel's command to John to "worship God" is representative of "keeping the words of this book." As Jürgen Roloff has said, "Worship is the place where the church experiences

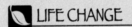

LIFE CHANGE

"WORSHIP GOD!"

Worship has been a major theme throughout the book of Revelation. It should be a major theme of each Christian's life. When we consider all that God has done to bring us to himself, we fall in worship of Him. When we think about the death and victory of Jesus Christ, we are overwhelmed to enter His presence. When we hear the invitation to "come . . . take the free gift of the water of life" (Rev. 22:17), we have to praise Him. In this study of Revelation, what has encouraged you to worship God? How has your worship changed? What will you do to encourage others to worship God?

the presence of the One who is coming, where again and again it subordinates itself to His dominion; at the same time it is also the place of departure for a refusal of obedience to the cult of humanity, who celebrates one's own power over the world. Revelation is both an eminently political book and an eminently liturgical book."[1]

In contrast to Daniel's instruction to "close up and seal" the scroll given him "until the time of the end" (Dan. 12:4), John is told **[not to] seal up the words of the prophecy of this book** (22:10). Reflecting back to the beginning of the epistle, John is instructed to make the vision accessible to all those who need to hear it. Given that the Lamb has broken the seals and opened the book of prophecy, it is expected that it not be resealed or hidden from the Church.

What is strange about the words that follow is the reason given for liberating those words of prophecy. By way of a parallel construction, John is told that people who do wrong will continue in this way; just as those who do right. The vile will stay vile while the holy **continue to be holy** (22:11).

Some commentators have given a deterministic reading to this text, explaining that the reason God opens prophecy to people in the end times is so that they will not be able to say they did not know the truth. They just won't be able to do anything about changing their position before that truth. This seems to be unfair for the unrepentant. Certainly it is out of keeping with the implied purpose of the letters delivered to the seven churches: that they repent, overcome, or persevere.

It might be better to see this as a result of the phrase **the time is near** (22:10), as if it is *almost* too late to change. This obviously gives great hope to those who read the Revelation who have cried out, "How long?" Their persecutors are on the verge of receiving the consequences of their deeds. There is no last minute reprieve for any of the evil doers, but there will an imminent relief for those who have waited for the Lord's coming. The emphasis on stability is more for the benefit of those who continue in righteous living. God is coming back to judge and the judgment will be meted out to those who are set in their ways.

This form of predestination looks very much like the teaching of Jesus found in His parables. When attempting to defend why He taught so frequently in parables, Jesus quotes from the prophetic message (the same message given to each of the seven churches): Having ears they do not hear, eyes they do not understand. It was not so much that Jesus spoke in parables *in order that* the people would not understand the gospel of the Kingdom. Rather, He spoke in parables *with the result that* the people who didn't understand were now identified. The parables were a type of litmus test for belief and unbelief. The telling of the story provided an opportunity for faith to be created. When Jesus spoke a parable, it resulted in a stark division between those who accepted the teaching and those who did not. John wants us see the prophecy of this book in a similar way. The drama that has been rehearsed in this prophecy will pull people into it along this parallel track. They will either continue in the way of evil or they will be encouraged to stay on the path of holiness.

For the second time Jesus says, "**Behold, I am coming soon!**" At this point, the one who is to come gives description to what He brings with Him, namely His **reward** (22:12). What is that reward? For one it will be fair. To those who have been treated with injustice, Christ **will give to everyone according to what he has done** (22:12). Because He is **the Alpha and the Omega, the First and the Last, the Beginning and the End** (22:13), He will provide sovereign control over all and will finish the task that was started in God's redemption of the world. The greatest reward that Jesus gives is **the right to the tree of life** (22:14) by having access to the city. This is the last of the seven beatitudes of Revelation. **Blessed are those who wash their robes** (22:14). The washed robes will be the ticket through the gates, acknowledging Scripture's claim that "without holiness, no one will see the Lord" (Heb. 12:14).

KEY IDEAS

SEVEN BEATITUDES OF THE APOCALYPSE

1. Blessed are those who hear it and take to heart the things which are written in it (1:3).
2. Blessed are the dead who die in the Lord from now on (14:13).
3. Blessed is he who stays awake and keeps his clothes with him (16:15).
4. Blessed are those who are invited to the wedding supper of the Lamb (19:9).
5. Blessed and holy are those who have part in the first resurrection (20:6).
6. Blessed is he who keeps the words of the prophecy in this book (22:7).
7. Blessed are those who wash their robes (22:14).

In contrast to the holy saints of God marching into the golden city is the hideous crowd that is amassing outside the city gates. Generally, they are **the dogs,** a metaphor of derision in the Bible (and now); specifically, they are **those who practice magic arts, the sexually immoral, the murderers, the idolaters and everyone who loves and practices falsehood** (22:15). This list matches well the anti-type of the saints, describing those whose idolatrous worship of Babylon (Rome) and her power have caused such pain and suffering for God's children. The emphatic "**I, Jesus**" reminds the hearers that He himself sent **[His] angel** to give this testimony **for the churches** (22:16). Jesus has a direct interest in this message of hope. He is tied to all messianic hope through His titles: **the Root and the Offspring of David, and the bright Morning Star** (22:16). Both of these titles come out of the Old Testament arsenal of messianic texts that looked for the perfect King of Israel in the line of David (Isa. 11:1, 10) and a rising "star" ruler that would defeat Judah's enemies (Num. 24:17).

The somewhat cryptic comments concerning the inability for people to change on the eve of the end of time that were made before Jesus' soliloquy in verses 12–16 are now juxtaposed with an invitation to receive refreshment. **The Spirit and the bride say, "Come!" And let him who hears say, "Come!" Whoever is thirsty, let him come; and whoever wishes, let him take the free gift of the water of life** (22:17).

These words are reminiscent of the gospel of John: "If anyone is thirsty, let him come to me and drink . . . streams of living water will flow from within him" (7:37–38). The invitation to those listening to the words of the Revelation to "come" is interjected into an image of the coming Christ. **Whoever is thirsty** and **whoever wishes** appear to have a universal casting for salvation. We are certainly aware that some, even in the face of this invitation, will not thirst for nor wish to come to the water of life. But even as the end is near, Jesus Christ stands ready to offer His reward to any that would desire it.

The two verses that follow this evangelistic invitation are warnings — whether from John or Jesus himself is unclear — to any future editors not to alter the **prophecy of this book** (22:18). This was a common addition to books in antiquity and served to add an ominous warning to anyone who would attempt to change the words as the writer intended them to be heard. Other books in the Bible carry similar statements (e.g. Deut. 4:2; 12:32). Some have felt these verses should be applied to the entire canon of Scripture, but it is more important to note how John intended this to apply to the book of Revelation. The entirety of the prophetic word was to be taken seriously by the hearers.

This meant that the hearer did not have the right to decide what they would accept and what they would reject. The whole of the revelation of Jesus Christ must be followed. Literarily, the synonymous parallelism provides power to the couplet. If anyone **adds anything to** the words of prophecy, God will add to him the plagues (22:18), and **if anyone takes words away**, God **will take away** the rewards awaiting them in the coming holy city (22:19). It would be best to accept the book as it has been given. In the end, however, it is Christ who officially authenticates the book. **He who testifies to these things, says, "Yes, I am coming soon"** (22:20). The revelation, as John has recorded it, needs no greater attestation than that Christ, at the end of history, will show it to be true.

Amen. Come, Lord Jesus (22:20). The transliteration of the Aramaic words into Greek renders this phrase: *maran atha*. This same formula appears in 1 Cor. 16:22 and the *Didache* (10.6), belying its technical use in the early Church's worship and life. But here John uses it as a fervent prayer. Three times in this final chapter, Jesus has promised that He would return with some form of "I am coming soon!" (22:7, 12, 20). With this building desire to see the Lord's advent, John cries out, *"Maran atha! Come!"* In many ways, these words have been building from the beginning of the Revelation. From the opening vision of Christ and His desired presence in the seven churches to the climactic vision of the New Jerusalem and the fulfillment of all history in Christ, the reader of the visionary story has been drawn into John's plea. For the modern reader, the time and distance from the first reading of the words of the book have not diminished, but have heightened the maranatha cry even more.

We are reminded that the final words of the Church's credo in the Nicene Creed say, "We look for the resurrection of the dead, and the life of the world to come." This affirmation comes from the contemporary experience of the Holy Spirit in the believer's life. Jürgen Moltmann sees the work of the Spirit (see 22:17) giving the impetus for the maranatha

231

prayer. He writes, "It is the experience of the Spirit that makes Christians in every society restless and homeless, and on the search for the kingdom of God, for it is this experience of the God which makes them controvert and contravene a godless world of violence and death. . . . In praying for the coming of the Spirit, men and women open themselves for His coming."[2] It is no wonder that a tradition that supports and encourages the role of the empowering Spirit in the sanctified life would wish to see the eschatological hope that this brings to the Christian living in the world.

Just as in many of the Apostle Paul's letters, the last words on the hearer's ears are that of a benediction. The Revelation ends with such a blessing: **The grace of the Lord Jesus be with God's people. Amen** (22:21). The bestowing of grace on the hearer or reader is found in 1:4 where John offers **grace and peace to you from him who is, and who was, and who is to come**. These are the only two instances of the word "grace" in the Revelation. As is often the case in Paul, grace could be merely a conventional greeting or benediction in these instances—or it could point to a deeper, more theological meaning. Grace, as an enclosure in these epistolary placements, represents the context for the entire revelation. Having received a glimpse of what it means to be **God's people**, the hearers and readers are now able to experience the grace that was offered to them in the earlier blessing. Surely now the saints who have endured so much suffering understand the grace that God has given them.

The next to the last words to this blessing, the prayer of invitation for Christ's advent at the end of history, are often remembered and thought of as the last words to John's revelation. This blessing subtly changes the urgency of that plea to an attitude of resolve. Rather than a view to escapism, the final resounding of the text is one of engagement. Wherever the people of God are, grace is **with** them. Amen.

ENDNOTES

1. Jürgen Roloff, *The Revelation of John*, trans. J.E. Alsup (Minneapolis: Fortress, 1993), 254.

2. Jürgen Moltmann, *The Sprit of Life: A Universal Affirmation*, trans. Margaret Kohl (Minneapolis: Fortress, 1993), 73, 74.

SELECT BIBLIOGRAPHY

Aune, David E. *Revelation* Vol. 1, 2, 3, *Word Commentaries*. Dallas: Word Books, 1997–1999.

Barclay, William. *Revelation* Vols. 1, 2, *Daily Study Bible*. Philadelphia: Westminster, 1976.

Barker, M. *The Revelation of Jesus Christ: Which God Gave to Him to Show to His Servants What Must Soon Take Place Revelation 1.1*. Edinburgh: T. & T. Clark, 2000.

Barr, David L. *Tales of the End: A Narrative Commentary on the Book of Revelation*. Santa Rosa: Polebridge Press, 1998.

Beale, Gregory K. *The Book of Revelation: A Commentary on the Greek Text* of *New International Greek Testament Commentary*. Grand Rapids: William B. Eerdmans Publishing Company, 1998.

Beasley-Murray, G. R. *The Book of Revelation* of *New Century Bible Commentary*, 2d ed. Grand Rapids: William B. Eerdmans Publishing Company, 1978.

Boring, M. Eugene. *Revelation* of *Interpretation: A Bible Commentary for Teaching and Preaching*. Louisville: John Knox, 1989.

Buchanan, G. W. *The Book of Revelation: Its Introduction and Prophecy*, vol. 22 of *The Mellen Biblical Commentary*. Lewston/Queenston/Lampeter: Mellen Biblical Press, 1993.

Bullinger, E. W. *Commentary on Revelation*. Grand Rapids: Kregel Publications, 1984.

Caird, G. B. *The Revelation of St. John the Divine* of *Black's New Testament Commentaries*, 2d ed. London: Adam & Charles Black, 1984.

Charles, R. H. *A Critical and Exegetical Commentary on the Revelation of St. John*, 2 vols. of *The International Critical Commentary*. Edinburgh: T. & T. Clark, 1920.

Cohen, G. G. *Understanding Revelation*. Chicago: Moody Press, 1978.

Collins, A. Y. *The Apocalypse*, vol. 22 of *New Testament Message: A Biblical-Theological Commentary*. Wilmington: Michael Glazier, Inc., 1979.

Corsini, E. *The Apocalypse: The Perennial Revelation of Jesus Christ*, vol. 5 of *Good News Studies*. Translated & edited by F. J. Moloney, S.D.B. Wilmington: Michael Glazier, Inc., 1983.

Court, J. M. *Revelation* of *New Testament Guides*. Sheffield: Sheffield Academic Press, 1994.

Ellul, Jacques. *Apocalypse: The Book of Revelation* New York: Seabury Press, 1977.

Fiorenza, Elizabeth Schüssler. *The Apocalypse* of *Herald Biblical Booklets*. Chicago: Franciscan Herald Press, 1976.

————. *Invitation to the Book of Revelation: A Commentary on the Apocalypse with Complete Text from the Jerusalem Bible*. Garden City: Image Books, 1981.

————. *The Book of Revelation: Justice and Judgment*. Philadelphia: Fortress, 1985.

————. *Revelation: Vision of a Just World* of *Proclamation Commentaries*. Minneapolis: Fortress, 1991.

Ford, J. M. *Revelation*, vol. 38 of *The Anchor Bible*. Garden City: Doubleday & Company, 1975.

Franzmann, M. H. *The Revelation to John: A Commentary*. St. Louis: Concordia Publishing House, 1976.

Garrow, A. J. P. *Revelation* of *New Testament Readings*. London and New York: Routledge, 1997.

Giblin, C. H. *The Book of Revelation: The Open Book of Prophecy,* vol. 34 of *Good News Studies*. Collegeville: The Liturgical Press, 1991.

Gilmour, S. M. *The Revelation to John* of *The Interpreter's Bible Commentary*. New York: Abingdon Press, 1957.

Glasson, T. F. *The Revelation of John* of *Cambridge Bible Commentary*. Cambridge: Cambridge University Press, 1965.

González, C. G. and J. L. González. *Revelation*. Louisville: Westminster John Knox Press, 1997.

Harrington, W. J. *Revelation,* vol. 16 of *Sacra Pagina.* Wilmington: Michael Glazier, 1993.

Hendriksen, W. *More Than Conquerors: An Interpretation of the Book of Revelation,* 6th ed. Grand Rapids: Baker Book House, 1952.

Howard-Brook, W. and A. Gwyther. *Unveiling Empire: Reading Revelation Then and Now* of *The Bible and Liberation Series.* Maryknoll: Orbis Books, 1999.

Hughes, P. E. *The Book of the Revelation: A Commentary* Grand Rapids: William B. Eerdmans Publishing Company, 1990.

Hunt, G. *Revelation: The Lamb Who Is the Lion* of *A Fisherman Bible Studyguide,* 2d ed. Wheaton: Harold Shaw Publishers, 1994.

Keller, Catherine. *Apocalypse Now and Then.* Boston: Beacon Press, 1996.

Jeske, Richard L. *Revelation for Today: Images of Hope.* Philadelphia: Fortress, 1983.

Johnson, A. F. *Revelation Bible Study Commentary.* Grand Rapids: Zondervan, 1983.

Kealy, S. P. *The Apocalypse of John,* vol. 15 of *Message of Biblical Spirituality.* Wilmington: M. Glazier, 1987.

Kiddle, M. and M. K. Ross. *The Revelation of St. John* of *The Moffatt New Testament Commentary.* New York: Harper & Brothers, 1940.

Knight, J. *Revelation.* Sheffield: Sheffield Academic Press, 1999.

Krodel, G. A. *Revelation* of *Augsburg Commentary on the New Testament.* Minneapolis: Augsburg Publishing House, 1989.

Ladd, George Eldon. *A Commentary on the Revelation of John.* Grand Rapids: William B. Eerdmans Publishing Company, 1972.

Lange, J. P. *Revelation,* vol. 24 of *Lange's Commentary on the Holy Scriptures: Critical, Doctrinal and Homiletical.* Edited by E. R. Craven. General editor P. Schaff. Translation by E. Moore. Collaborator J. H. Woods. Grand Rapids: Zondervan, 1950.

Metzger, Bruce M. *Breaking the Code: Understanding the Book of Revelation.* Nashville: Abingdon Press, 1993.

Morris, Leon. *The Revelation of St. John: An Introduction and Commentary*, vol. 20 of T*yndale New Testament Commentaries*, 2d ed. Grand Rapids: William B. Eerdmans Publishing Company, 1987.

Mounce, Robert H. *The Book of Revelation* of *New International Commentary on the New Testament*, rev. ed. Grand Rapids: William B. Eerdmans Publishing Company, 1977.

———. *The Book of Revelation*. Grand Rapids: William B. Eerdmans Publishing Company, 1998.

Mulholland, M. Robert. *Revelation: Holy Living in an Unholy World*. Grand Rapids: Francis Asbury Press, 1990.

Palmer, E. F. *Mastering the New Testament: 1, 2, 3 John & Revelation* of *The Communicator's Commentary Series*. General editor L. J. Ogilvie. Waco: Word, 1982.

Prévost, Jean-Pierre. *How to Read the Apocalypse*. New York: Crossroad, 1993.

Reddish, Mitchell G. *Revelation* of *Smyth & Helwys Bible Commentary*. Macon: Smyth & Helwys, 2001.

Richardson, D. W. *The Revelation of Jesus Christ*. Richmond: John Knox Press, 1939.

Robbins, R. F. *The Revelation of Jesus Christ*. Nashville: Broadman Press, 1975.

Roloff, J. *The Revelation of John: A Continental Commentary*. Translated by J. E. Alsup. Minneapolis: Fortress Press, 1993.

Rowland, Christopher C. The *Book of Revelation: Introduction, Commentary, and Reflections*, vol. 12 of *New Interpreter's Bible*. Nashville: Abingdon, 1998.

———. *Revelation* of *Epworth Commentaries*. London: Epworth Press, 1993.

Russell, D. S. *Apocalyptic: Ancient and Modern*. London: SCM Press, 1978.

Smith, R. H. *Apocalypse: A Commentary on Revelation in Words and Images*. Collegeville: Liturgical Press, 2000.

Swete, Henry Barclay. *The Apocalypse of St. John: The Greek Text with Introduction, Notes, and Indices* 3d ed. London: Macmillan and Co., 1909.

Tenney, Merrill C. *Interpreting Revelation*. Grand Rapids: William B. Eerdmans Publishing Company, 1957.

————. *Interpreting Revelation: A Reasonable Guide to Understanding the Last Book in the Bible*. Peabody: Hendrickson, 2001.

Thompson, Leonard L. *The Book of Revelation: Apocalypse and Empire*. New York & Oxford: Oxford University Press, 1990.

Walhout, E. *Revelation Down to Earth: Making Sense of the Apocalypse of John*. Grand Rapids: William B. Eerdmans Publishing Company, 2000.

Wall, Robert W. *Revelation,* vol. 18 of *New International Bible Commentary*. Peabody: Hendrickson Publishers, 1991.

Walvoord, John F. *The Revelation of Jesus Christ: A Commentary*. Chicago: Moody Press, 1966.

Wesley, John. *Explanatory Notes upon the New Testament*. London: Epworth Press, 1976.

Witherington III, Ben. *Revelation* of *New Cambridge Bible Commentary*. Cambridge: Cambridge University Press, 2003.